MORE WORDS
MORE ARROWS

Shirley Kumove

MORE WORDS
MORE ARROWS

A Further Collection of **Yiddish Folk Sayings**

Wayne State University Press Detroit

LIBRARY OF CONGRESS CATALOGING—IN—PUBLICATION DATA

More words, more arrows : a further collection of Yiddish folk sayings
   / [edited by] Shirley Kumove.
      p.   cm.
   Sayings presented in Yiddish characters, in transliteration, and in
English translation.
   "This volume is a continuation of the work begun in Words like
arrows"—Pref.
   Includes bibliographical references.
ISBN 0-8143-2740-0 (alk. paper)
   1. Proverbs, Yiddish. 2. Proverbs, Yiddish—Translations into English.
I. Kumove, Shirley, 1931-   . II. Words like arrows.
PN6519.J5M67   1999
398.9'391—dc21   98-10851
                                                                      HE

WITH LOVE AND APPRECIATION TO MY HUSBAND

ARYEH KUMOVE

Contents

List of Subjects

9

Preface

This volume is a continuation of the work begun in *Words Like Arrows*. The enthusiastic response to that volume has encouraged me to proceed with a second volume on the subject of Yiddish folk sayings, culled from a collection which now stands at more than seven thousand sayings.

The task of collecting, classifying, editing, and translating began many years ago and has expanded in scope and complexity far beyond my initial expectations. It continues to grow as new oral and written sources become available to me. Among these sources are the readers themselves, who do not hesitate to share with me comments, recollections, and suggestions, as well as numerous sayings. A writer about Yiddish enjoys a special relationship with her readers; together we form a partnership. From the very beginning of my involvement with this material, people have come forward with sayings, ditties, rhymes, and wordplays. The first volume, *Words Like Arrows*, elicited both praise and suggestions for improvement. There are those who differed with some of the translations and interpretations offered. To all of you, I am grateful for your scrupulous attention and useful comments.

My motivation for continuing this ambitious project is similar to that which motivates many other writers on Jewish history, folklore, and literature, in this waning decade of the twentieth century. It is the concept embodied in the term *sharis hapleyta* (the rescuing of the remnant). The Holocaust wiped out an organic Yiddish culture in Eastern Europe which had existed and flowered for a millennium. In one devastating blow, this vibrant world was shattered and destroyed forever. To imagine that world, to appreciate its richness and texture, is the aim of this work. It is my hope that these collections will stand as a testament to the dynamism and variety of Jewish life in this setting, and later in immigrant North America.

As the work progressed, I gained new insight and understanding into the background and context of Yiddish folk sayings through the study of the Yehoash-Spivak *Dictionary of Hebrew and Aramaic Words in Yiddish*, published in 1926. This volume, acquired through the good offices of the National Yiddish Book Centre in Amherst, Massachusetts, was most helpful in establishing correct pronunciation, and was a source of some additional sayings. The body of work by the late Max Weinreich—in particular, that which has been made available in English translation as *History of the Yiddish Language*, published by the University of Chicago Press, 1980—gave me a broader and deeper understanding of both the Yiddish language and the way of life in Jewish Eastern Europe. I highly recommend the work to those who wish to delve further into this subject.

In the course of my work, a number of questions had to be addressed. I have chosen to keep explanation to a bare minimum, allowing the sayings to speak for themselves. The system of headings was devised to clarify the meaning of the sayings. There were specific instances, however, where I provided further explanation. These appear in square brackets following the translation.

A number of sayings are quite coarse and vulgar; others are disrespectful of people and institutions. Some have suggested that such sayings should be deleted but I have chosen to desist from censorship on the grounds they are all legitimate expressions in use by Yiddish-speaking Jews and as such, they belong in a complete collection that reflects the beliefs and sentiments, as well as prejudices, of a particular time and place.

Translation itself presents many choices. Oftentimes the translations are quite literal; in other instances, the need to convey essential meaning, to retain the playfulness of the language, or to maintain the integrity of the rhyme has dictated a more liberal interpretation. In some cases, both the literal and the interpretative translations are given. Corresponding sayings in English are included where applicable.

I am pleased to offer this volume as a continuation in the ongoing exploration of the world of Yiddish folk sayings. I hope that you, my readers, will continue to scrutinize this material. I welcome your participation and the sharing of the precious heritage which I hope is of interest to all people. In presenting this volume, I am reminded of the hope expressed upon the conclusion of the Yiddish stories of my childhood.

וואָס איז ווײַטער געווען וועט מען אַ צווייטן מאָל זען

Vos iz vayter geven vet men a tsveytn mol zen

What later occurred, will another time be heard

TORONTO, ONTARIO

Acknowledgments

This volume, *More Words, More Arrows*, like the previous volume, *Words Like Arrows*, was a family affair. Both my parents, Tsvi Meyer Recht and Rivka Lessman Recht, were consultants and editors and liberally shared their knowledge of historical, literary, religious, and sociological customs and practices. I held many discussions with my sons, Aaron and Joel. They were especially helpful in shaping the translations into an English that is clear, concise, and faithful to the intent of the original. In addition to his unflagging interest, my husband, Aryeh, acted as research advisor on this project. It is unlikely that this undertaking would have advanced beyond the embryonic stages without his encouragement and advice.

I thank the following: Ben Kayfetz for his always thoughtful comments and suggestions; the late distinguished Yiddish poet Peretz Miransky for his contributions and his valued counsel; Brina Menachovsky Rose, whose expert knowledge of Yiddish grammar and syntax helped clarify and correct the text; Dr. Leo and Bayla Chaikof for access to their library; Rabbi Bernard Baskin, Leon Goldgrab, Dr. Aaron Nussbaum, and the late Dr. Aaron Posen for making useful research material available to me; the late Ted Goldberg, Ph.D., for suggesting the title; and the members of Friends of Yiddish and the Yiddish Speaking Luncheon Club for providing a lively setting for Yiddish discourse.

Explanatory Notes

For the purposes of this work, the method of transcription used is the one established by the YIVO Institute for Jewish Research. This is the standard for Yiddish speech and is consistently used in academic circles today. The only deviations from this standard are those dictated by the necessity of adhering to the rhyme which is sometimes related to regional speech.

Sound	Example in text	English equivalent
Vowels:		
a	h*a*rts	p*a*rt
e	k*e*n	p*e*n
i	d*i*	m*e*
i	v*i*sn	p*i*n
i	v*a*yt	f*i*re
o	h*o*t	b*o*re
u	*u*nter	h*oo*d
oy	h*oy*z	b*oy*
ey	m*ey*dl	w*ay*
Consonants:		
g	*g*ib	*g*ive
kh	no*kh*	Ba*ch*
ts	tan*ts*	gu*ts*
tsh	men*tsh*	*ch*air
dz	un*dz*er	boun*ds*
zh	gri*zh*en	sei*z*ure

In order to avoid confusion for the English-speaking reader, I have made slight modifications. Where two vowels occur together in the middle of a word and both are to be articulated, an apostrophe is inserted between them to so indicate. Where a 'ph' or 'sh' appear together in the middle of a word and both letters are to be separately pronounced, an apostrophe is inserted to so indicate.

Words and phrases of Hebrew-Aramaic origin are transcribed according to their pronunciation in Standard Yiddish.

( ) Words occuring with parentheses in both transcription and translation denote variations in the same saying.

[ ] Words occuring within square brackets in translation only, offer clarification of the text.

" " Double quotation marks signify biblical or Talmudic quotations.

KEY TO SOURCES

Capitalized letters in the left hand margin denote the source of the saying and are explained according to the following:

A C	Those sayings gathered from among the author's circle of family, friends and acquaintances
I B	Ignaz Bernstein
I F	Israel Furman
L M F	Lillian Mermin Feinsilver
S K	Sholem Katz
S M	Sholem Miller
P	Popular sayings in frequent usage
M S	Maurice Samuel
N S	Nokhem Stutshkof
N W	Max Weinreich
W Z	Weltman & Zukerman

Authors cited here are listed in the Bibliography.

Many sayings listed under 'AC' and 'P' are also found in *Yidishe shprickverter un redensarten* by Ignaz Bernstein and in *Der oytser fun der yidisher shprakh* by Nokhem Stutshkof. Their citing under these headings indicates that they are still in use or remembered by my informants, who include European Jews as well as those from North America, Great Britain, Israel, South Africa and South America.

In dealing with written material, I found occasional archaisms of language as well as the inevitable typographical errors. In these cases, adjustments and corrections were made.

Translating Yiddish Folk Sayings
into English

This volume continues the work begun in *Words Like Arrows: A Collection of Yiddish Folk Sayings*. Since that time I have received many comments from readers expressing approval or disagreement. Their reactions indicate the complexities involved in translation and suggest that there are different approaches to rendering this material into English. No two fingerprints are alike, no two interpretations of a piece of music are alike, and in the same way, no two translations of the same work are alike. It is the very nature of translations to differ from each other, and good translators are aware of the variety of possibilities that are available. The process of refinement fuses the mechanical aspect of translation with the striving for interpretation. Even if the syntax is awkward and the colloquialisms unwieldy, the translator must caress the translation, knead it, and massage it until some degree of fluidity and sparkle is achieved. This seems an appropriate opportunity, therefore, to consider the joys and frustrations, as well as the issues and the problems, involved in translating Yiddish folk sayings into English.

A good illustration of the pitfalls awaiting the translator is the story about the Yiddish-speaking Jew who was put on trial, accused of stealing a chicken. The interpreter, whose knowledge of Yiddish is literal and who does not understand the effect of intonation, asks: *ir hot geganvet der hon?* (Did you steal the chicken?). The accused answers this question with one of his own: *ikh hob geganvet der hon?* (I stole the chicken?), implying that such an idea is clearly preposterous. The interpreter then turns to the judge and states: "He says he stole the chicken." The judge asks: *tsu vos hot ir badarft hobn der hon?*

(Why did you need the chicken?). The accused again replies with a question: *Ikh hob es badarft?* (I needed it?) The interpreter states: "He says he needed the chicken, your Honor." The interpreter asks again: "What did you need the chicken for?" With ironic laughter, the accused replies: *Ikh hob es gedarft oyf kapores!* The very literal-minded interpreter translates the response: "Your Honor, he says he needed it for a sacrifice." The word *kapore* refer to the ancient days of the Temple when animal sacrifices were performed. Using a popular idiom, the Jew in our story meant that he had no need for the chicken, and that it was useless to him, but this was lost on the interpreter. This example illustrates the dangers a translator of Yiddish folk sayings faces when failing to take into account context, idiom, and intonation. Every language has its own cadence or melody and it has been suggested that the Yiddish lilt be submitted to musical notation in order to convey its true melody to readers not familiar with the language.

The Yiddish language is one of the remarkable flowerings of Ashkenaz Jewry. Ashkenaz was one of two major divisions of the medieval Jewish world. During the Middle Ages, Sephardim lived first in Spain, and later spread out over the Mediterranean basin, while Ashkenazim lived first in western Europe, migrating to central and eastern Europe. These Ashkenaz settlements evolved a unique cultural, economic, religious, and social identification which distinguishes them as Ashkenazim. *Gants ashkenaz iz eyn shtot* (All Ashkenaz is one town) articulates this reality. What happened *oyf der yidisher gas* (on the Jewish street, that is, in Jewish society), was of interest throughout this world. On the eve of World War II, Yiddish was spoken by some eleven million people. Mass migration beginning in the 1880s spread Yiddish to all five continents.

Yiddish began in the Rhineland almost one thousand years ago when Jews began speaking a German vernacular which incorporated elements of biblical Hebrew, old French, and old Italian. This new language was written phonetically, using the letters of the Hebrew alphabet. When Jews moved into Poland, Slavicisms were introduced and modified, and in recent decades Anglicisms have been incorporated. Yiddish is considered a "fusion language" because its origins lie in more than one family of languages, much like English, which draws from both Germanic and Romance sources. Because the Yiddish language was born of such disparate elements, it often has been compared to a *tsholent*, that national culinary dish prepared for the Sabbath which is composed of many ingredients. Despite both the influence exerted by other European languages and the regional variations in pronunciation, vocabulary, and style, Yiddish was a language understood by all its speakers wherever they lived. Never merely a variant or watered-down version of one of its lingual components, Yiddish became a unique language born out of the experiences it was called upon to communicate. Jews borrowed vocabulary from several languages and absorbed them into Yiddish where the meanings were sometimes considerably altered. For instance, the Hebrew word *metsiye* means discovery, but in Yiddish it came to mean a bargain, a good deal, and it has reentered modern Hebrew with this altered meaning. *Yente*, from old Italian *gentile*, means genteel, refined. In Yiddish it has become a disparaging term for a woman, a vulgar busybody. Yet another example is the word *taytsh*, which comes from the word *deutsch*, meaning German. In Yiddish it means translation, and it also means to explain or to simplify, as in *Vos iz der taytsh?* (What is the explanation? or How do you explain that?).

This process of fusion is both continuous and cumulative and is best illustrated in the following expression: *Er hot gepravet a sude oyf yontef* (He celebrated the holiday with a feast). This sentence has a basic German structure, *sude* and *yontef* are Hebrew, and *gepravet* has a Slavic root with a Germanic prefix and suffix. These words form a sentence suited to the sensibility of the Yiddish-speaking Jew, so that the German which developed into Yiddish became Jewish. In spite of its Germanic and Slavic components, the above quoted expression would probably not make sense to a Slavic or German speaker. A similar saying, which incorporates French, is the following: *Moyshele hot aruntergetombet fun eskalye un hot zikh tseklapt zayn tetele* (Moses fell down the stairs and banged his little head). *Tombe*, *eskalye*, and *tete* are French, and the connectives, prefixes, and suffixes are Germanic.

Hebrew is a strong component of Yiddish, and the two form an indissoluble partnership. Whereas Hebrew is *loshn-koydesh*, the language of the sacred, Yiddish is the language of the everyday, affectionately referred to as *mameloshn*, or mother tongue. Most Jews had a degree of familiarity with the sacred texts, and their speech is laced with references to these sources. Words, phrases, and proverbs from the most diverse areas of life streamed into Yiddish speech from the Bible, the Talmud, and other sacred texts. This partnership furnishes Yiddish with a massive weight of cultural assumptions, historical references, and religious symbols: alliterations, puns, allusions, hints, and stylistic ironies related to Hebrew and Aramaic sources which may not be accessible to contemporary readers, especially those not raised in the Jewish tradition. These characteristics are natural to Yiddish and provide it with a rich texture, but one that is quite foreign in English. These references yield such frequently heard expressions as *yedn montik un donershtik* (every Monday and Thursday), meaning frequently, very often. This saying alludes to the fact that a portion of the Torah is read in the synagogue on these days. The Hebrew writer S. Y. Agnon, making reference to his constant battle with hunger, wryly commented: "If I did not fast every Monday and Thursday, I would die of hunger." Similarly, *Biz hundert un tsvontsik* (Until a hundred and twenty), said on wishing someone a long life, is a reference to the lifespan of the biblical Moses.

There is a wealth of allusions to and saying about *Moyshe rabeynu* (Moses our Teacher, the biblical Moses). This is probably because Jews of every generation, right up to and including the present time, felt they had an intimate relationship with Moses, held lengthy debates, and complained of every trifle to him. When something is considered lost or hopeless, a standard response is *Moyshe, zukh mikh!* (Search me, Moses!). A big shot would be referred to ironically as *Moyshe groys* (Moses the Great). Someone who could not get anything straight or who insisted on being contrary would be referred to as *Moyshe kapoyr* or *Moyshe farkert*, (Moses the Opposite). The story is told that during the first World War, Jewish prisoners would evade the scrutiny of the censors by sending letters home describing the glorious treatment they were receiving at the hands of their captors. These letters would invariably be signed *Moyshe kapoyr* or *Moyshe farkert*, alerting their families that their situation was the exact opposite of what they were describing. *Er hot gemakht a gesheft vi feter eysev* (He made a deal like Uncle Esau) immediately recalls the biblical Esau, who sold his birthright for a mess of pottage. A pithy rejoinder is the sardonic *Megst dernokh kadesh zogn!* (May as well recite the Memorial Prayer after it! or, in the vernacular, May as well kiss it good-bye!). *Vu shteyt es geshribn?* (Where is it written?), meaning, what is the biblical or Talmudic authority, is a classic embodiment of the concept of referring to and updating traditional sources, but today this expression is more often used in a strictly secular sense. *Es iz targum loshn!* (It's Aramaic to me! that is, it's pure gibberish) recognizes the frustration often inherent in coping with the Hebrew-Aramaic component of Yiddish.

The saying *er iz a guter b'tsedek* is one example of word play based on the partnership of Yiddish and Hebrew. At first glance, this saying seems to mean "he is a charitable man" because the Hebrew word *tzedek* means charity. However, *b'tsedek* is here used as an anagram for *biz tsu der keshene*, an ironic statement about a miser, meaning "he is only charitable until he touches his pocket." In another example, what kind of an ignoramus do we have in mind when we say: *Er shraybt noyekh mit zibn grayzn* (He spells the name Noah with seven errors)? In Hebrew, Noah is spelled with only two letters, *nun* and *khes*, so it requires a remarkable degree of incompetence to make seven spelling mistakes in this one word. Such expressions simply cannot be translated literally or economically, and so must be rendered into an English that will carry a similar impact rather than an identical meaning. Transposing this interwoven texture so that the double layer of Hebrew and Yiddish does not disappear is a considerable challenge. Even when the text is fairly straightforward, there still remain ponderous transpositions. One such example: *Az men lebt, derlebt men* (If you live long enough, you experience everything), said upon finally seeing a satisfactory conclusion to a difficult situation. The original is terse and its meaning immediately recognized; the translation, while accurate, is somewhat awkward.

At this point, it is worth reminding ourselves that a folk saying is an expression transmitted orally from one person to another, containing a summation of spiritual, cultural, and ethical values. It usually suggests a course of action, conveys guidance for behavior, or passes judgment on people or events. It is a rich artistic expression of everyday life. According to the medieval writer Moses Ibn Ezra, a proverb has three characteristics: few words, good sense, and a fine image.

Yiddish folk sayings are embedded in the oral character of Jewish life. Jews are called "People of the Book" but they are also people of the word, and Yiddish culture is oriented toward speech. Ruth Wisse of Harvard University points out that "this device [of two people talking] recurs so often it might be considered the natural form of the literature." Yiddish folk sayings range from commentary on the homeliest aspects of daily life to the loftiest aspirations of the Jewish people, but usually they reflect the daily struggle for survival: the exigencies of earning a living, bearing and raising children, educating the young, arranging marriages, growing old, and dying.

While most of the folk sayings are immediately understandable and need no further explanation, some are laden with cultural connotations that are not always immediately evident, requiring a context or frame of reference in order to be understood. Once the context is known, the folk saying is usually direct, terse, and to the point. One such example is *Vil nor vestu zayn a vilner.* Literally, it means "will it and you can become a Vilna-ite," that is, a resident of Vilna, Lithuania, often referred to as the Jerusalem of the north. Actually, however, it means "Will it and you also can become a great sage." The saying is predicated on the listener's knowing that *vilner* refers to the eighteenth-century rabbi the Gaon of Vilna. Another example is the following: *Eyder azoy tsu forn iz shoyn beser tsu fus tsu geyn* (Rather than ride like this, it is better to walk). On the face of it, this statement makes no sense, until we understand the conditions under which a person would prefer to walk when transportation is available. The saying becomes clear when the context is understood: Rather than ride like this (in a hearse), it's better to walk! Yet another example: *Purim iz nit keyn yontef un kadokhes iz nit keyn krenk* (Purim is no holiday and convulsions is no disease). What does this mean? Again, the explanation comes out of experience. Purim did not have the official status of the major festivals such as Succoth, Passover, and Shevuoth. Nevertheless, the mass of Jews in Eastern Europe, immigrant North America, and dispersed throughout the world loved and celebrated this holiday with lighthearted festivity, and this expression is understood in the context that *if* Purim is no holiday *then* convulsions is no disease.

The frequent use of the word *khazer*, pig, as a disparaging term points up cultural differences in attitude. Swine and anything related to swine is considered an abomination to Jews. Pigs are viewed with disgust and revulsion. They are considered unclean, not kosher, and are prohibited for consumption. There was a time when the pig was not even called by its rightful name but was referred to as *dover akher*, the other thing. In spite of this, Yiddish is peppered with references to this animal. Pig flesh is *boser kvitch* (meat that squeals). Of a hypocrite, it would be said: *Er iz azoy kosher vi a khazer's fisl!* (He's as kosher as a pig's foot!). Advice on how to become a millionaire (attributed to Yiddish writer Sholem Aleichem) is contained in the saying *Az men vil zayn a gvir muz men zikh farshraybn oyf tsvantsik yor a khazer* (If you wish to become rich, you must apprentice yourself for twenty years as a swine). Another useful piece of advice: *Es iz a mitsve a khazer a hor aroystsuraysn* (It's a good deed to pull a hair out of a pig, that is, to separate a miser from some of his money).

Lernen is a problematic term. *Der yid ken lernen* means "He is a man of learning; he continues to study and can expound on his learning," but *lernen* is a difficult concept to render into English because it has two meanings in Yiddish: to study and to teach. Further, *lernen* did not apply to practical or secular subjects, which were learned from actual experience or were delved into on one's own. The only subjects fit for study were the sacred texts; one pored over the Talmud and read into it all contemporary problems—problems of dietary laws, of family relations, of business practises—in general, how to be a Jew in the present day.

An issue of a different kind arises with the word *goy*. In Hebrew it means nation, but in Yiddish, it means a non-Jew, a Gentile, specifically a Christian. A second meaning arises out of the conditions under which Jews were forced to live. For centuries, limitations were placed on where Jews could live and what occupations they could hold. They were granted "privileges," not rights, and these privileges could be withdrawn arbitrarily. Violence was a periodic visitation. Jews were forced to defend themselves against accusations that they caused death and disease. From time to time blood libels were leveled against them. For Jews, it was all too often a hostile and uneasy world. *Es iz gut far yidn?* (Is it good for Jews?) was a question that reverberated throughout Ashkenaz. In this setting, where Jews were usually segregated and governed by special, often harsh laws, and in which periodic, violent pogroms against Jews took place, the word *goy* took on a negative meaning. It referred to a person who was to be treated with caution because he could quite unexpectedly, and without provocation, turn upon Jews. While the term *goy* continued to have the neutral meaning of non-Jew in some contexts, in other settings it meant an ignorant, hostile, and dangerous person. Many folk sayings bear out the fear and distrust with which the Gentile was viewed. *Her vos der goy zogt* (Pay attention to what the Gentile says) was a frequent admonition in Jewish quarters. *A goy blaybt a goy* (A Gentile remains a Gentile) and *Fang nisht on mit a goy* (Don't start up with a Gentile) were statements advising caution. Sometimes the word *goy* was also used to refer to a Jew. Calling a Jew a *goy* labeled the person as ignorant, uncouth, even sacrilegious as in the following: *A melamed—a yid vos handlt mit goyim* (A teacher is a Jew who deals in Gentiles [that is, the ignorant]).

Derogatory sayings were not confined to Gentiles only. Jews themselves were not spared the caustic comment, and we are reminded today that *Moyshe rabeynu hot mit di yidn oykh nit gekent oyskumen* (Not even Moses our Teacher could get along with Jews). *Oyf der matseyve zaynen ale yidn sheyn* (According to the gravestones all Jews were honorable) is a cynical comment. The dangers of living in a more open society with its attendant temptations are noted in the following: *Tsu vos darf a yid hobn fis? az in kheyder muz men im traybn, tsu der khupe firt men im, tsu kvure brengt men im, in shul arayn geyt er nit un tsu shikses krikht er. Iz tsu vos darf er hobn fis?* (Why does a Jew need legs? To school he must be forced, to marriage he must be led, to burial he is brought, to the synagogue he won't go, and after Gentile girls he crawls. So why does he need legs?).

Judged by today's standards, the attitude toward women evident in Yiddish folk sayings is, at best, ambivalent. Many sayings attest to negative, even hostile, feelings towards women. Aside from traditional functions of wife and mother, women played important economic and social roles—they were dealers at the markets and fairs, and many became healers and practitioners of folk medicine. In many ways, they were the backbone of the educational system, supporting husbands and sons through long periods of study. With some exceptions, scholarship and study were male prerogatives, as reflected in the saying *A hun vos kreyt, a goy vos ret yidish un a yidene vos lernt toyre iz nit keyn gute skhoyre* (A hen that crows, a Gentile who speaks Yiddish, and a woman who studies Torah are not good pieces of merchandise). The relationship between the sexes often elicited caustic comment, as in *Di tsung bay di vayber iz azoy vi a shverd un zey gibn akhtung az es zol nit farzhavert vern* (Women's tongues are like swords, and they're careful not to let them rust). Or this: *A froy iz vi an iberzetsung—nisht sheyn ven getray un nisht getray ven sheyn.* (A woman is like a translation—not beautiful when faithful and not faithful when beautiful). Women countered with sayings which expressed their own reality. One example is a comment on marriage: *Afile az der shukh drikt, muz men im fort trogn* (Even if the shoe pinches, one is nevertheless forced to wear it). Since few options were available to women outside the married state, even a bad marriage was preferable to remaining single.

Translation of poetry and rhyme presents a particular difficulty because Yiddish lends itself to versification more readily than does English. In Yiddish there is a wealth of similar word endings, for example, *brokh, dokh, vokh, tokh, lokh, kokh, nokh,* or *glaykh, taykh, raykh,* and so on. Consider the following Yiddish folk saying: *Toyre iz di beste skhoyre* (Torah-wise is the best merchandise, or, more literally, Torah is the best of wares). While the translation is perfectly accurate, it fails to capture both the rhyme and the intimacy with which the subject matter was understood by the Yiddish-speaking audience to whom it was directed. At one time, such a statement was universally accepted, but the secularization of modern times has somewhat eroded this concept. A translator trying to achieve the same effect in English would be hard-pressed to find an equivalent rhyme and is often better advised to use a free form of translation than try to reproduce the Yiddish rhyme. On the other hand, an expression such as *Az a zokher hot lib a nekeyve iz es b'derekh hateyve* (When a he falls in love with a she, it's as it should be) illustrates how a saying may be translated quite effortlessly into English without sacrificing the rhyme. In this case, even the complicating Hebrew does not pose excessive difficulty. Another example: *Der mentsh zol nit zorgn vos vet zayn morgn, zol er beser farrikhtn vos er hot kalye gemakht nekhtn* (A person should not sorrow for what will be tomorrow; rather, let him redress yesterday's mess). And again *der vos halt dem hak git dem k'nak* (The one with the axe delivers the whacks). These expressions retain the rhyme quite easily in translation into English. Sometimes a saying, quite unexpectedly, makes a better rhyme in English than in the original Yiddish, but this is not very often the case.

A translator of folk material faces yet another difficulty. When translating works of Yiddish literature, one deals with what is called standard Yiddish, that is, the type that is taught in schools. Folk sayings, on the other hand, come out of an oral tradition rich in colorful idioms, implicit assumptions, local traditions, and regional variations. In such virtually untranslatable words or phrases, the gap can be observed between one culture and another. For instance, *a nekhtiker tog* (literally, a yesterday's day, but as novelist Henry Roth points out, actually meaning "as irretrievable as a bygone day") defies easy transposition from Yiddish into English. It is an idiomatic expression whose sense depends not only on the tone and gesture with which it is spoken, but also on an atmosphere recalling conversations in dusky cafes or behind the stove. It is a vernacular eccentricity which a literal translation does nothing to bridge. "A yesterday's day" is incomprehensible in English. An equivalent is probably "fiddlesticks" or "poppycock" but these words strike us as precious, while *a nekhtiker tog* is common usage in Yiddish. "A likely story!" probably comes closest to the intent of the original.

The ironic nature of much of the material presents another complication. A saying expounding one concept may, in the next breath, propose a completely opposite point of view. A case in point is the familiar exhortation: *Zay a mentsh!* (Be a decent human being! in other words, behave yourself!). This expression was familiar to generations of Jewish children, but the retort is quite novel: *Zay a mentsh vestu zitsn purim in suke* (Be a decent human being and you'll sit in the *Succah* on *Purim*). The saying becomes absurd, since sitting in a *succah* (booth) is a feature of the holiday of *Succoth* and not of *Purim*, and it is also quite cynical, suggesting there is no value in being a decent human being.

Good Yiddish literary and oral style permits and encourages repetition for the sake of emphasis and intensity of meaning. English, on the other hand, does not tolerate this very readily. In Yiddish one often hears *a shande un a kharpe*, and *a kharpe un a bushe*. Both mean the same, a shame and a disgrace. Other alliterative repetitions are common, such as *pust un pas* (coarse and common), *mi'es umo'es* (ugly and disgusting), *umzist un umnisht* (for no reason), and *azoyns un azelkhes* (literally, such and such, but really meaning something quite exceptional). These and similar expressions are the rule rather than the exception in Yiddish.

Yiddish also allows for double negatives, which if translated literally produce poor English: *Tu mir nisht keyn toyves* (Don't do me no favors), *Freg mir nisht keyn shayles* (Don't ask me no questions), *Er veyst nisht fun gornisht* (He doesn't know from nothing), and, *Shtarbn a toyter* (Die dead).

In addition, there are the obvious flaws, the inconsistencies, or the so-called untranslatable words, phrases, and idioms that may be time or culture-bound, or may have no real equivalent in contemporary language. An example is the following curse: *Krign zol er der lemberger brokh!* (May the Lemberg disaster befall him!). One can readily imagine a variety of disasters likely to befall, but the nature of this particular one is no longer familiar.

Many Yiddish words, phrases, and expressions hardly need translation anymore, words like *bagel, ganef, glitsh, kosher, khutspe, megilla, mishmash, shtik, shmo, shmooze, tsores,* to say nothing of the ubiquitous vulgarisms. Certain expressions frequently heard in English are pure Yiddish translations, for instance: what's doing? (*vos tut zikh?*); talk to the wall! (*red tsu der vant!*); on one foot (*oyf eyn fus*); don't ask! (*freg nisht!*); I should worry! (*zol ikh zikh zorgn!*); I need it like a hole in the head! (*Ikh darf es vi a lokh in kop!*); It should happen to me! (*Oyf mir gezogt gevorn!*); break one's head (*brekh zikh dem kop*); Take a look! (*Gib a kuk!*); the end was... (*der sof iz geven...*). A popular expression, especially in business circles, is "the bottom line," a straight translation from Yiddish—*di untershte shure.* Most people would be surprised to learn that these words and phrases, now so common in English, originated in Yiddish. Inversions of word order which are unexceptional in Yiddish, and which used to be rare in English, are now frequently heard. One thinks of: again with... (*nokh amol... [un vider amol...]*); do me something! (*tu mir epes!*); enough already! (*genug shoyn!*); go know...! (*gey veys...*); from that he makes a living? (*fun dem makht men a lebn?*); give me a for instance (*gib mir a moshl*).

In addition to words, phrases, and expressions which are now in general use, there is a category of Yiddish terms used almost exclusively by Jews who don't necessarily read or even understand Yiddish but who nevertheless incorporate these Yiddish expressions into English usage. For instance; to *shep nakhes* (reap pleasure); to *bentsh likht* (bless the candles); to *badek* the *kale* (veil the bride); to *daven* (pray); and so on. It has been suggested that a fusion process has already begun which is fashioning a new Jewish language whose base is English and upon which are superimposed Hebrew and Yiddish, in much the same way that Yiddish originally developed from a Germanic base. Cynthia Ozick, in *Art and Ardor*, has proposed establishing what she calls a "New Yiddish." Like old Yiddish before its massacre by Hitler, New Yiddish will be the language of multitudes of Jews: spoken to Jews by Jews, written by Jews for Jews." It will be interesting to see this idea of a new Jewish language being fashioned onto an English root explored further.

It used to be said that translation from Yiddish into English was impossible, most likely because early translations of the writings of Mendele Mokher Sforim, Sholem Aleichem, I. L. Peretz and other classical Yiddish writers were poor. Many of the works of these writers contained significant amounts of folk material and occasional Russian words and phrases, or were laced with biblical and Talmudic references which confounded early translators. Even so, successful translations of Sholem Asch and I. J. Singer were already in print in the 1930s. With the translations by Julius and Frances Butwin of Sholem Aleichem stories in 1946, Yiddish literature became accessible to the general reader in literate and idiomatic English. (Their translations of the Tevye stories were the basis for the popular Broadway musical *Fiddler on the Roof*). Since that time, many of the masterpieces of Yiddish literature have been successfully translated and made available to the general reader. My own book, *Words Like Arrows*, has been translated into German, retitled *Erlekh ist beshwerlikh* (loosely, *Honesty is Difficult*), and is now in its second printing.

In some respects, the job of translating Yiddish into English has been made easier in recent years because there has been a pronounced infusion of Yiddish into English over the last several decades. There are several factors to explain this acceleration into English. With the maturing of the American Jewish community at the end of World War II, a generation of Jewish authors emerged, among them Saul Bellow, Norman Mailer, Bernard Malamud, Cynthia Ozick, Grace Paley, and Philip Roth. While these authors might not have known Yiddish (Saul Bellow and Cynthia Ozick are fluent), nonetheless they were imbued with and influenced by the Eastern European tradition, and their writings resonate with the word structures and intonations which derive directly from Yiddish. In this connection, Franz Kafka once stated: "I would tell you how much better you understand Yiddish than you suppose." On another occasion, he said: "Although I could not speak Yiddish, it was not a *foreign* language. A little Yiddish goes a long way."

The rise of the Jewish comedians in vaudeville and later on television also helped to popularize many Yiddish words, phrases, and expressions. These are now in general usage by English speakers and create an atmosphere of familiarity with Yiddish syntax and vocabulary, which facilitates its translation into English. These confluences have given the translator a context within which to work and have added an inestimable dimension to the ability of the translator to transmit into English the flavor of the Yiddish language, its ideas, and the world it represents. For these reasons, translation from Yiddish into English is easier today than ever before. Nevertheless, substantial difficulties remain.

There was a time when the expression *fartaytsht un farbesert* (translated and improved) was appended to translations from other languages into Yiddish; even the frontispieces of translations of Shakespeare contained it. It is hard to imagine that translators of Shakespeare actually believed the Bard could be improved upon. What this expression really means is that translation should not be a literal, word-for-word rendering but a transference from one language to another of the sense of the work, the literary quality. It reinforces the idea that translation is a complex art. A good translator is always concerned to retain the flavor of the original: the playfulness of the language, the contrasts, the mood, the occasional peculiarities of speech, the regional differences, and so on. The translator strives to maintain the brevity and the rhyme and must constantly weigh the desire to be faithful to the content and meaning against considerations of structure, diction, and style. A Yiddish folk saying states the case bluntly: "He who translates literally is a liar and he who alters a text is a blasphemer and a libeler." This is the dilemma and is sometimes a veritable nightmare for the translator. While it is necessary to consider the *pshat*, that is, the simple literal translation, as a starting point and to refer back to it frequently, one must at the same time keep in mind the context of the English into which it is being translated. Each and every word must be carefully weighed, bearing in mind the importance of every sentence in both languages. The Argentinian writer Jorge Luis Borges once said: "Don't translate what I say, but what I *wanted to* say." Since Yiddish is a richly descriptive and idiomatic language, loquacious and argumentative, striking a balance between what the author intended and what is actually said is the stuff of artistic creativity for a translator. The Hebrew writer Chaim Nachman Bialik liked to say that reading a work of literature in translation is comparable to viewing a beautiful woman through a veil. If that is so, it is to be hoped that such a reading will lead to an appreciation of the beauty that lies beyond the veil and that further, it will lead to a study of Yiddish as a means of penetrating that veil.

Language is the key to a culture, and embedded within Yiddish literature and lore lies the thousand-year experience of Jewish life in Eastern Europe. It was in this culture that the literature, both sacred and secular, and the very institutions which constitute present-day Jewry worldwide were formed and refined. The study of Yiddish—the language, the literature, and the history— is integral to an understanding of this world as it truly was and not as our nostalgia would imagine it. When the early Zionists were struggling to restore Hebrew as a spoken language, they would say: "To speak Hebrew is like riding a noble horse; at first, it's exhilarating, then rather uncomfortable, and finally, it's a torture. Dropping into Yiddish is like getting off the horse and onto your own two feet. *Oy, s'a mekhaye!* Oh, what a pleasure!" This is echoed in the once popular Yiddish folk saying *Hebreyish ret men, yidish ret zikh aleyn* (Hebrew one learns, Yiddish speaks by itself, that is, it comes naturally). These statements no longer hold true today following the annihilation of millions of Yiddish-speaking Jews in the Holocaust and, subsequently, the recognition of Hebrew as the official language of the State of Israel. Nevertheless, embedded in this saying is the acknowledgment that Yiddish is an organic and vibrant expression of the thousand-year experience of Jewish life in Eastern Europe and immigrant North America. When one considers that until World War II, 80 percent of the world's Jews spoke Yiddish, it is not hard to understand the influence Yiddish has exerted on Jewish culture.

Translation is the art of re-creating in another language and through other eyes what a culture appears to be saying. Ideally, it must fulfill several criteria. It must be true to the original while reading as if it were written in the language into which it has been translated. It must never call attention to itself, and the translator must never come between writer and reader. Skilled translators may differ in their interpretations and some readings may even be considered controversial. The art of translation may be compared to a journey. Although the destination is known, one nevertheless encounters unexpected twists and turns along the route; detours may have to be taken and digressions dealt with. The skilled translator tries to achieve a degree of clarity and sparkle. In spite of the greatest efforts, some nuances will be lost in translation, but it is hoped that this loss is offset by the pleasure of accessibility.

This process of rendering Yiddish into English is rife with frustrations and headaches, but it is also a source of the greatest pleasure and satisfaction. A translator is like a messenger who returns from another country bringing good news from abroad. Studying Yiddish folk expression is, in and of itself, deeply gratifying. Translating this very rich vein of Jewish experience and bringing the good news to future generations is its own reward.

JEWISH EASTERN EUROPE
1830-1914

○ Provincial Capital   ★ Major City   • Settlement

·········· Border   ·········· Provincial Border

▨▨▨ Congress Poland   ▨▨ Pale of Settlement

0   100   200
                          km
© Carta, JERUSALEM

MORE WORDS
MORE ARROWS

א גוטער אויסדרוק מאכט א גוטן איַינדרוק

A Fitting Expression Makes A Good Impression

A Guter Oysdruk Makht A Gutn Ayndruk

ABILITY

אַלע ייִדן זײַנען חזנים אָבער מערסטנס
זײַנען זיי הייזעריק

Any Jew can be a cantor, but most of the time he's hoarse
Ale yidn zaynen khazonim ober merstns zaynen zey heyzerik P

אַז מען קען גוט קריכן קריכט מען אויבן
אָן

If you can crawl well, you crawl right to the top
Az men ken gut krikhn krikht men oybn on NS

דער בעסטער פֿידל קען אַליין ניט שפּילן

The best violin can't make music all by itself
Der bester fidl ken aleyn nit shpiln AC

פֿאַראַן קינסטלערישע הענט מיט
פֿערדישע קעפּ

It's possible to have capable hands and a horse's head
Faran kinstlerishe hent mit ferdishe kep NS

האָסטו – האַלט; וויסטו – שווײַג,
קענסטו – טו!

You have?—hold; you know?—keep silent; you can?—do!
Hostu—halt; veystu—shvayg; kenstu—tu! AC

33

קענסטו ניט נייען – דאָרפֿסטו ניט
טרענען

If you can't sew—don't unravel
Kenstu nit neyen—darfstu nit trenen NS

טאַנצן קען איך נאָר ווי איך קען

I can only dance as well as I'm able
Tantsn ken ikh nor vi ikh ken AC

טרינקען און פֿײַפֿן קען מען ניט אין
איינעם

You can't drink and whistle at the same time
Trinken un fayfn ken men nit in eynem AC

ABSURDITY

אַ בחורס ווײַב און אַן אַלטע מוידס
קינדער זײַנען שטענדיק גער34טן

A bachelor's wife and an old maid's children always turn out well
A bokhers vayb un an alte moyds kinder zaynen shtendik gerotn IB

אַ טויבער האָט געהערט ווי אַ שטומער
האָט דערצײַלט אַז אַ בלינדער האָט
געזען ווי אַ קרומער איז געלאָפֿן

A deaf man heard a mute tell that a blind man saw a cripple run
A toyber hot gehert vi a shtumer hot dertseylt az a blinder hot gezen vi a krumer is gelofn IB

דעריבער גייען די גענדז באָרוועס און די
קאַטשקעס אין רויטע שיכעלעך

That's why geese go barefoot and ducks wear red shoes
[Commentary on a non sequitur]
Deriber geyen di gendz borves un di katshkes in royte shikelekh NS

זי איז אויסגעפּוצט ווי חוהלע צום גט

She is decked out like little Eve for the divorce
Zi iz oysgeputzt vi khavele tsum get P

ADVICE

באראָט זיך מיט וועמען דו ווילסט און
טו מיטן אייגענעם שכל

Consult whom you will, but act according to your own counsel
Barat zikh mit vemen du vilst un tu mitn eygenem seykhl IB

דאָס גרינגסטע איז צו געבן יענעם אַן
עצה, דאָס שווערסטע זיך אליין

It's easier to give someone else advice; hardest, to take it yourself
Dos gringste iz tsu gebn yenem an eytse, dos shverste zikh aleyn IB

פֿרעג אַן עצה בײַ דעם שונה און טו
פֿאַרקערט

Ask your enemy for advice and do the opposite
Freg an eytse bay dem soyne un tu farkert P

ראָט מיר גוט אָבער ראָט מיר ניט אָפּ

Advise me well, but don't talk me out of it
Rot mir gut ober rot mir nit op NS

AGING

אַ יונג ביימעלע בייגט זיך, אַן אלטער
ברעכט זיך

A young tree bends, an old one breaks
A yung beymele beygt zikh, an alter brekht zikh IB

אַלטע לײַט טראָגן די אויגן אין קעשענע,
די אויערן אין שיפֿלאָד און די ציין אין
גלאָז

Old people keep their eyes in their pockets, their ears in the drawer, and their teeth in the glass
Alte layt trogn di oygn in keshene, di oyern in shuflod un di tseyn in gloz AC

אַלטע לײַט זעצט מען אין דער זײַט

Old people get shoved aside
Alte layt zetst men in der zayt NS

אַלט זאָל מען ווערן אָבער ניט זיַין

Grow old, but don't act old
Alt zol men vern ober nit zayn P

אַן אַלטן איז גוט צו באַהאַלטן

Its okay to hide old people away
An altn iz gut tsu bahaltn NS

אַז מען וויל ניט אַלט ווערן זאָל מען זיך
יונגערהייַט אויפֿהענגען

If you want to avoid old age, hang yourself while still young
Az men vil nit alt vern zol men zikh yungerheyt oyfhengen IB

בעסער פֿריִער שטאַרבן אין דעם היַים
איַידער אויף דער עלטער אין הקדש

Better to die sooner in one's own home than later in the poorhouse
Beser fri'er shtarbn in der heym eyder oyf der elter in hekdesh NS

ביז וואַנען מען לערנט זיך אויס זיַין אַ
מענטש איז מען שוין עובֿר-בטל

By the time you learn to be a human being, you're already in your dotage
Biz vanen men lernt zikh oys zayn a mentsh iz men shoyn oyverbotl! AC

די אַלטע קיַיען און די יונגע שפּיַיען

What the old chew, the young spew
Di alte kayen un di yunge shpayen IB

עס איז ניטאָ דער פֿערד און וואָגן וואָס
זאָל די יונגע יאָרן דעריאָגן

No horse and wagon can go so fast as to overtake one's youthful past
Es iz nito der ferd-un-vogn vos zol di yunge yorn deryogn NS

פֿון פֿאַרטריקנטע ביימער קומען קיין
פּרות ניט אַרויס

You can't get fruit from withered trees
Fun fartrikente beymer kumen keyn peyres nit aroys IB

אין דער יוגנט אַ בהמה, אויף דער
עלטער – אַ פֿערד

In youth—a cow, in old age—a horse
In der yugnt a beheyme, oyf der elter—a ferd IB

אין דער יוגנט גיט מען אַוועק און אויף
דער עלטער קלײַבט מען צונויף

In youth you give away, in old age you gather together
In der yugnt git men avek un oyf der elter klaybt men tsunoyf NS

קיין אַלטע ייִדענע גיט מען ניט קיין
פֿעטע יויך

You don't give an old woman a rich broth
Keyn alte yidene git men nit keyn fete yoykh NS

כאָטש די אַלטע פֿאַרבן זיך די האָר
בלײַבן די וואָרצלען אַלץ ווײַס

Old people may die their hair, but the roots remain white
Khotsh di alte farbn zikh di hor blaybn di vortslen alts vays AC

מיט אַלטע זאַכן קען מען ניט פֿיל מאַכן

With old things you can't do anything
Mit alte zakhn ken men nit fil makhn NS

ווי מען יונגערהייט זיך האַלט, אַזוי
ווערט מען אלט

As in youth, so in age
Vi men yungerheyt zikh halt, azoy vert men alt IB

וויל מען אלט ווערן זאָל מען אויף דער
נשמה און גוף אַכטונג געבן

If you want to grow old, take care of your body and your soul
Vil men alt vern zol men oyf der neshome un guf akhtung gebn IB

וואָס אַלט איז טאַקע ניט נײַ אָבער
ס'איז מער געטרײַ

What's old isn't new, but it's loyal and true
Vos alt iz take nit nay ober s'iz mer getray NS

וואָס קומט אַרויס פֿון גרויען קאָפּ אַז
דער שכל איז אַלץ גרין?

What's the use of grey hair if the brains are still green?
Vos kumt aroys fun groyen kop az der seykhl iz alts grin? AC

וואָס מען מאַכט קאַליע אין דער יוגנט
קען מען אויף דער עלטער ניט פֿאַרריכטן

What one spoils in youth can't be repaired in old age
Vos men makht kalye in der yugnt ken men oyf der elter nit far'rikhtn P

ווייל איז דעם וואָס ווערט באַגליקט
אויף דער עלטער

Happy are the aged on whom good fortune shines
Voyl iz dem vos vert baglikt oyf der elter IB

יונגע שפּילערס – אַלטע בעטלערס

Young gamblers—old beggars
Yunge shpilers—alte betlers IB

AGREEMENT

בעסער יאָ איידער לא

Better yea than nay
Beser yo eyder lo IB

ער זאָגט אמן אויף אַלץ

He says "amen" to everything
Er zogt omeyn oyf alts AC

פֿאַר אמן קומט קיין פּאַטש ניט

Saying "amen" doesn't merit a slap
Far omeyn kumt keyn patsh nisht P

ניט אַלע מענטשן האָבן איין דעה

Not everyone has the same opinion
Nit ale mentshn hobn eyn deye IB

צוויי בל-מלאכות שטימען זעלטן

Two craftsmen seldom agree
Tsvey balmelokhes shtimen zeltn IB

ווען אַלע מענטשן זאָלן ציען אויף איין
זייַט וואָלט זיך די וועלט איבערגעדרייט

If everyone pulled together at one end, the whole world would tip over
Ven ale mentshn zoln tsi'en oyf eyn zayt volt zikh di velt ibergedrayt NS

וען אַלע ייִדן וואָלטן גלײַך געגלייבט | **If all Jews were in agreement, the**
וואָלט משיח שוין לאַנג געוווען געקומען | **Messiah would have arrived long ago**
Ven ale yidn voltn glaykh gegleybt volt meshi'ekh shoyn lang geven gekumen NS

AMBITION

אַז אַ ייִד קען ניט ווערן אַ שוסטער | **If a Jew can't become a shoemaker,**
טרוימט ער כאָטש פֿון ווערן אַ | **he dreams of becoming a professor**
פּראָפֿעסאָר | *Az a yid ken nit vern a shuster, troymt er khotsh fun vern a profesor* NS

אַז מען שפּאַרט זיך אײַן פֿירט מען אויס | **If you're determined, you'll succeed**
Az men shpart zikh ayn firt men oys P

אַז מען זוכט געפֿינט מען | **If you seek, you find**
Az men zukht gefint men P

די קרוי פֿליט הויך און זעצט זיך אויף אַ | **The crow flies high and settles on a**
חזיר | **pig**
Di kroy flit hoykh un zetst zikh oyf a khazer AC

מען טאָר ניט פֿאַרלאַנגען וואָס מען קען | **Don't desire what you can't acquire**
ניט דערלאַנגען | *Men tor nit farlangen vos men ken nit derlangen* NS

וויל נאָר וועסטו זײַן אַ ווילנער | **Will it and you can become a great scholar**
[Play on words: *vilner* refers to the great sage, the Gaon of Vilna]
Vil nor vestu zayn a vilner NS

ANGER

אַ טשײַניק װאָס קאָכט לױפֿט איבער

A boiling kettle overflows
A tshaynik vos kokht loyft iber AC

אַז מען בײיזערט זיך אָפּ גײיט אָפּ דער
כעס

When you vent your feelings, anger subsides
Az men beyzert zikh op, geyt op der kas NS

ביסט אין כעס? – רײַב דעם תחת אין אַ
שטײין װעט דײַן כעס איבערגײין

You're angry?—On a stone rub your ass and your anger will pass
Bist in kas?—rayb dem tokhes in a shteyn vet dayn kas ibergeyn NS

דער כעסניק שלאָפֿט אַלײין

An angry man sleeps alone
Der kasnik shloft aleyn AC

דער צאָרן איז אין האַרצן אַ דאָרן

Anger is a thorn in the heart
Der tsorn iz in hartsn a dorn NS

פֿון בײיזע לײַט גײיט מען אין דער זײַט

From people in heat beat a retreat
Fun beyze layt geyt men in der zayt NS

כהנים זײַנען רגזנים

Kohens are hotheads
Koyenim zaynen ragzunim IB

ANIMALS

אַ פֿערד האָט אַ גרױסן קאָפּ – זאָל ער
זיך זאָרגן

A horse has a big head—so let him worry!
A ferd hot a groysn kop—zol er zikh zorgn! NS

אַ הונט איז אַמאָל געטרײַער װי אַ קינד

A dog is sometimes more dependable than a child
A hunt iz amol getrayer vi a kind NS

אַלע גוטע פֿערד זײַנען משוגע

All good horses are crazy
Ale gute ferd zaynen meshuge NS

דער אײזל זאָל האָבן הערנער און דער
אָקס װאָלט געװוּסט פֿון זײַן כּוח װאָלט
די װעלט קיין קיום ניט געהאַט

If the ass had horns and the ox knew its own strength, the world would be done for
Der eyzl zol hobn herner un der oks volt gevust fun zayn koyekh volt di velt keyn ki'em nit gehat NS

APPEARANCE

אַ מאַן איז אַזױ אַלט װי די װײַב זײַנע
זעט אױס

A man is as old as his wife looks
A man iz azoy alt vi di vayb zayne zet oys AC

אַ שײנע באָרד און פּאות אָבער װײניק
דעות

A fine beard and sidecurls on display, but little sense does he convey
A sheyne bord un peyes ober veynik deyes IB

אַ ציג האָט אױך אַ באָרד און איז פֿאָרט
אַ ציג

A goat also has a beard, but it's still only a goat
A tsig hot oykh a bord un iz fort a tsig AC

אַלע הינט און אַלע יוונים האָבן אײן
פנים

All dogs and all soldiers look alike
Ale hint un ale yevonim hobn eyn ponem NS

אַז די פּאַװע קוקט אױף אירע פֿעדערן
קװעלט זי, אַז זי קוקט אױף אירע פֿיס
װײנט זי

When the peacock looks at his feathers, he beams; when he looks at his feet, he grieves
Az di pave kukt oyf ire federn kvelt zi, az zi kukt oyf ire fis veynt zi IB

41

בײַ נאַכט זײַנען אַלע קי שװאַרץ | **At night all cows are black**
Bay nakht zaynen ale ki shvarts IB

דער מיטװאָך איז לענגער װי דער דאָנערשטיק | **Wednesday is longer than Thursday**
[Comment on a slovenly person whose underclothes hang out]
Der mitvokh iz lenger vi der donershtik IF

דאָס פּנים זאָגט אױס דעם סוד | **The face reveals the secret**
Dos ponim zogt oys dem sod IB

ער האָט אַ פּנים װי אַ משומד אין אַ קלײן שטעטל | **He looks like an apostate in a small town**
[Everyone knows him for what he really is]
Er hot a ponim vi a meshumed in a kleyn shtetl IF

ער זעט אױס װי אַן אלמן נאָך שלשים | **He looks like a widower after the 30th day of mourning**
[All decked out looking for a new wife]
Er zet oys vi an almen nokh shloyshim IB

עס איז גרוי די פּאה און נאַריש די דעה | **The temples are grey, but the mind has gone astray**
Es iz groy di peye un narish di deye NS

פֿון אַ באָרד האָט מען לײַז נישט חכמה | **A beard breeds lice, not wisdom**
Fun a bord hot men layz nisht kokhme AC

פֿון װײַטן נאַרט מען לײַטן | **From a distance you can fool anyone**
Fun vayt nart men laytn AC

האָניק אויפֿן צונג – גאַל אויפֿן לונג

On the tongue—honey; in the heart—acrimony
Honik oyfn tsung—gal oyfn lung NS

כאָטש שוואַרץ אַבי אַ גוט האַרץ

Even homely as long as you're good-hearted
Khotsh shvarts abi a gut harts IB

קליידער מאַכן דעם מענטשן

Clothes make the person
Kleyder makhn dem mentshn NS

מיט וואָס פֿאַר אַן אויג מען קוקט אויף אײנעם אַזאַ פּנים האָט ער

The way you look at a person, that's how they appear
[Beauty is in the eyes of the beholder]
Mit vos far an oyg men kukt oyf eynem aza ponem hot er AC

ניט יעדערער אויף וועמען הינט בילן איז אַ גנבֿ

Not everyone dogs bark at is a thief
Nit yederer oyf vemen hint biln iz a ganef NS

ס׳איז דער זעלבער גוי נאָר אין אַן אַנדער היטל

Its the same goy but in a different cap
S'iz der zelber goy nor in an ander hitl NS

ס׳איז די זעלבע יענטע נאָר אַנדערש געשלייַערט

Its the same old busybody but differently veiled
S'iz di zelbe yente nor andersh geshlayert P

ווען די באָרד וואָלט געווען אַלעס וואָלט די ציג אויך געקענט האַלטן אַ דרשה

If the beard were enough, even a goat could deliver the sermon
Ven di bord volt geven ales volt di tsig oykh gekent haltn a droshe IB

43

זײַ אַ ייִד אין דער הײם און אַ מענטש אין | **Be a Jew at home and a person**
גאַס | **outside**

Zay a yid in der heym un a mentsh in gas IF

AUTHORITY

אַ פּאַרעך טאָר ניט זײַן אַ | **A scabhead shouldn't be a**
ראש-הקהל — ער האָט גענוג אויפֿן קאָפּ | **community leader—he has enough**
| **on his head**

[Scabhead: a person of tainted character]

A parekh tor nit zayn a roshakol—er hot genug oyfn kop AC

דער פּריץ איז גוט און אין האַנט איז די | **The master is kind, but in his hand**
רוט | **is the whip**

Der poretz iz gut un in hant iz di rut NS

דער וואָס האַלט דעם האָק גיט דעם | **The one with the axe delivers the**
קנאַק | **whacks**

Der vos halt dem hak git dem k'nak P

עס ווענדט זיך וווּ דער חמור שטייט | **It depends on where the donkey is**
| **located**

[*Khamer* has three meanings: if in a stall, it's a donkey; if in the cellar, it's wine; and if in a pit, it's lime. Play on words]

Es vent zikh vu der khamer shteyt AC

אין דעם שטעטל בין איך דער | **In this town I'm the boss!**
בעל-הבית! | *In dem shtetl bin ikh der balebos!* NS

מען טאָר ניט בעטן אויף אַ נײַעם מלך

One should not pray for a new king
[The new one may be worse]
Men tor nit betn oyf a nayem
meylekh P

ווי דער האַר האַלט דאָס הינטל אַזוי
האַלט ער דאָס גאַנצע געזינדל

How the master treats his dog is
how he treats all his possessions
Vi der har halt dos hintl azoy halt er
dos gantse gezindl NS

יעדער הונט איז אויף זײַן מיסט גרויס

Every dog is a big shot over his own
droppings
Yeder hunt iz oyf zayn mist groys IF

BARGAINS

דאָס לעבן איז די גרעסטע מציאה – מען
קריגט עס אומזיסט

Life is the biggest bargain—you get it for free
Dos lebn iz di greste metsi'e—men krigt es umzist AC

ער האָט אויסגעטוישט אַ בהמה פֿאַר אַן
אייזל

He traded a cow for a donkey!
Er hot oysgetoysht a beheyme far an eyzl! IB

מען האָט עס צעכאַפֿט ווי מצה-וואַסער

It sold like matzah-water!
[That is, like hot-cakes]
Men hot es tsekhapt vi matse-vaser! IB

BEAUTY

אַ שיין פּנים קאָסט געלט

A pretty face costs money
A sheyn ponem kost gelt IB

אַ שיין מיידל איז אַ קאָראַנטע שטיקל
סחורה

A pretty girl is a nice piece of merchanise
A sheyn meydl iz a karante shtikl skhoyre IB

ניט דאָס איז שיין וואָס איז שיין נאָר
דאָס וואָס געפֿעלט

That which pleases is more beautiful than beauty itself

Nit dos iz sheyn vos iz sheyn nor dos vos gefelt NS

וואָס טויג שיינקייט אָן מזל?

What use is beauty without luck?

Vos toyg sheynkeyt on mazl? IB

BEGINNINGS

אַ ספֿר אָן אַ הקדמה איז וי אַ גוף אָן אַ
נשמה

A book without a preface is like a body without a soul

A seyfer on a hakdome iz vi a guf on a neshome NS

אַז די ערשטע שורה איז קרום טויג דער
גאַנצער בריוו אויף כּפּרות

If the first line is badly written, the whole letter is worthless

Az di ershte shure iz krum toyg der gantser briv oyf kapores AC

ווער עס זאָגט אלף מוז זאָגן בית

Whoever says "A" must follow with "B"

Ver es zogt aleph muz zogn beyz IB

BELIEF

אַ זאַטער גלייבט ניט דעם הונגעריקן

A sated person doesn't believe the hungry

A zater gleybt nit dem hungerikn AC

אַז די וועלט זאָגט זאָל מען גלייבן

If the whole world says so, better believe it

Az di velt zogt zol men gleybn AC

47

בטחון ציט צום הימל, כבֿוד ציט ציט צו דער
ערד

Faith draws you to heaven; coveting
honor drags you down to the ground
*Bitokhn tsit tsum himl, koved tsit tsu
der erd* NS

ווען אלע ייִדן זאָלן גלײַך גלייבן וואָלט
משיח שוין לאַנג געווען געקומען

If all Jews believed the same, the
Messiah would long ago have
arrived
*Ven ale yidn zoln glaykh gleybn volt
meshi'ekh shoyn lang geven
gekumen* IB

BETTER AND WORSE

אַ סמאַגלער רעגן איז גוט פֿאַר די
פֿעלדער און שלעכט פֿאַר די וועגן

A heavy downpour is good for the
fields and bad for the roads
*A smagler regn iz gut far di felder un
shlekht far di vegn* NS

אַז עס ווערט ניט בעסער – ווערט
ממילא ערגער

If things don't get better, then of
course they'll get worse
*Az es vert nit beser—vert mimeyle
erger* AC

בעסער אַ ביסל און רעכטס איידער אַ סך
און שלעכטס

Better a little bit and good than a
whole lot and bad
*Beser a bisl un rekhts eyder a sakh un
shlekhts* NS

בעסער גוטס פֿון ווײַטן איידער שלעכטס
פֿון נאָענט

Better good news from afar than
bad news close by
*Beser guts fun vaytn eyder shlekhts fun
no'ent* IB

ערגערס דאַרף מען ניט און בעסערס
האָט קיין שעור ניט

Worse one doesn't need, and better
has no limits
*Ergers darf men nit un besers hot keyn
shir nit* AC

"משנה מקום משנה מזל" – אַ מאָל צום
גליק אַמאָל צום שלימזל

"He who changes his place, changes his luck"—sometimes for the better, sometimes for the worse
"Meshane mokem, meshane mazl"—a mol tsum glik a mol tsum shlimazl P

ווען ניט די שײַן וואָלט קיין שאָטן ניט
געווען

If not for the light there would be no shadow
Ven nit di shayn volt keyn shotn nit geven IB

BOASTING

אַ גאון דאַרף זיך ניט באַרימען אַז ער איז
אַ גאון

A genius shouldn't boast that he's a genius
A go'en darf zikh nit barimen az er iz a go'en AC

אַ גרויסער וואָלקן – אַ קליינער רעגן

A big cloud—a little shower!
A groyser volkn—a kleyner regn! IB

אַ גראָשן אין אַ ליידיקע פֿאַס הילכט אַ
סך

Even one coin in an empty barrel reverberates loudly
A groshn in a leydike fas hilkht a sakh NS

אַז גאָט טוט אַ טובֿה באַרימט ער זיך ניט

When God does a favor, He doesn't boast of it
Az got tut a toyve barimt er zikh nit NS

עס איז אַלץ פּיסק-מלאכה!

Its all jaw-work!
Es iz alts pisk-melokhe! AC

גענייט און געשטעפּט, געשפּינט און
געוועבט – און אַלץ מיט דער צונג

Sewed and basted, spun and woven—and all with the tongue
Geneyt un geshtept, geshpint un gevebt—un alts mit der tsung AC

מיך גלײַכט מען, מיך טראָגט מען אויף די
העַנט – ביז צו דער טיר

I am well liked. People carry me on their shoulders—right out the door
Mikh glaykht men, mikh trogt men oyf di hent—biz tsu der tir AC

ניט פֿון בלאָזן זיך ווערט דער אינדיק
פֿעט

Not from puffing itself up does the turkey become fattened
Nit fun blozn zikh vert der indik fet AC

יעדער שענקער לויבט זײַן ביר

Every innkeeper praises his own beer
Yeder shenker loybt zayn bir IB

BODY AND SOUL

דער גוף איז אַ שוואָם, די נשמה איז אַ
תּהום

The body is a sponge, the soul an abyss
Der guf iz a shvom, di neshome iz a t'hom NS

דער מאָגן איז ווי אַ וואָגן, וואָס מען זאָל
ניט אַרײַנלייגן מוז מען פֿאַרטראָגן

The stomach is like a wagon of hay—whatever goes in gets carted away
Der mogn iz vi a vogn, vos men zol nit araynleygn muz men fartrogn NS

די נשמה ליגט טיף

The soul lies deeply buried
Di neshome ligt tif NS

דער בויך פֿאַרשלינגט דעם קאָפּ מיטן
שׂכל

The stomach devours the head and the brains
Der boykh farshlingt dem kop mitn seykhl NS

די אויגן זײַנען גרעסער פֿון מויל (מאָגן)

The eyes are bigger than the mouth (stomach)
Di oygn zaynen greser fun moyl (mogn) P

50

אין בויך זעט קיינער ניט

No one sees inside the stomach
In boykh zet keyner nit AC

אָפפֿרירן פֿרירט מען אָפ אַ הינטן ניט אַ קאָפ

One freezes one's behind, not one's head
Opfrirn frirt men op a hintn nit a kop NS

יעדער ווילן האָט זיַין צילן

Every soul has its goal
Yeder viln hot zayn tsiln AC

BOREDOM

אַז עפעס וואַקסט פֿון אַ בוים זאָגט מען:
"בורא פרי העץ" און אַז ס'וואַקסט פֿון
דער ערד זאָגט מען: "בורא פרי האדמה"
אָבער אַז ס'וואַקסט שוין פֿון גאָרגל
וואָס פֿאַר אַ ברכה מאַכט מען?

Before eating fruit which comes from a tree, one says: "Creator of the fruit of the tree," and for that which comes out of the earth, one says: "Creator of the fruit of the earth," but what kind of blessing do you make when it comes out of your ears?
[Literally, throat]
Az epes vakst fun a boym, zogt men: "borey pri ho'eyts," un az s'vakst fun der erd, zogt men: "borey pri hodomo," ober az s'vakst shoyn fun gorgl, vos far a brokhe makht men? LMF

קרעפּלעך עסן ווערט אויך נימאס

Eating nothing but dumplings is also boring
Kreplekh esn vert oykh nimes P

אויסגעוואַשן די שיסל און ווייַטער באָרשט

Washed out the bowl and again it's borsht
Oysgevashn di shisl un vayter borsht AC

BORROWING AND LENDING

אַז מען באָרגט די המוציא איז מען מיט
אַ ברכה ניט יוצא

When you borrow to buy bread, you can't pay it back with a blessing
Az men borgt di hamoytse iz men mit a brokhe nit yoytse IB

דער בעסטער בטוח איז די אייגענע
קעשענע

The best security is your own pocket
Der bester botu'ekh iz di eygene keshene IB

קראַצן און באָרגן איז נאָר גוט אויף אַ
ווײַל

Scratching and borrowing are only good for a while
Kratsn un borgn iz nor gut oyf a vayl P

אויף קאָרטן און אויף אַ טאַנץ באָרגט
מען ניט קיין געלט

Don't borrow money for gambling or for dancing
Oyf kortn un oyf a tants borgt men nit keyn gelt IB

וווויל איז דעם וואָס האָט ניט קיין געלט
צו באָרגן זיינע פריינד, ער שאַפט זיך ניט
קיין שונאים

Good for him who has no money to lend his friends; he won't make any enemies
Voyl iz dem vos hot nit keyn gelt tsu borgn zayne fraynd, er shaft zikh nit keyn sonim NS

BRAINS

אַ ממזר קען מען זײַן אָבער קלוג זאָל
מען זײַן

Be a bastard if you must, but be clever
A mamzer ken men zayn ober klug zol men zayn P

אַ ייִד אַ למדן גיט זיך אַן עצה – אַז ער
האָט ניט קיין שטיוול גייט ער באָרוועס

A learned person manages—if he has no boots, he goes barefoot
A yid a lamdn git zikh an eytse—az er hoy nit keyn shtivl geyt er borves NS

אַז גאָט וויל איינעם דאָס האַרץ
אָפּשטויסן גיט ער אים אַ גרויסן שׂכל

When God wants to break a person's heart, He gives him a lot of brains
Az got vil eynem do harts opshtoysn git er im a groysn seykhl IB

אַז מען האָט ניט קיין שׂכל דאַרף מען
קיין קאָפּ ניט האָבן

If you don't have brains, you don't need a head
Az men hot nit keyn seykhl darf men keyn kop nit hobn AC

בעסער אַ קרומער פֿוס איידער אַ
קרומער קאָפּ

Better a lame foot than a lame brain
Beser a krumer fus eyder a krumer kop NS

דאָס ביסל שׂכל איז ווערט געלט

A bit of brains is worth money
Dos bisl seykhl iz vert gelt P

געשמדט און געהאַנגען זאָל מען זײַן און
שׂכל זאָל מען האָבן

Whatever one's fate, one should have brains
Geshmad un gehangen zol men zayn un seykhl zol men hobn NS

כּוח איז נאָך ניט מוח

Brawn is not yet brain
Koyekh iz nokh nit moyekh P

מיט פֿרעמדן שׂכל קען מען ניט לעבן

You can't live on borrowed brains
Mit fremdn seykhl ken men nit lebn P

מיט שׂכל וועסטו פֿאַנגען אַפֿילו אַ לייב, | With brains you can outsmart even a lion, with strength alone not even a fly
מיט גבֿורה אַפֿילו ניט קיין פֿליג

Mit seykhl vestu fangen afile a leyb,
mit gvure afile nit keyn flig NS

אויגן קוקן – שׂכל זעט | Eyes look—brains see

Oygn kukn—seykhl zet NS

ניט יעדער איז צופֿרידן מיט זײַן פנים | Not everyone is content with their looks, but everyone is content with their brains
אָבער מיט זײַן שׂכל איז יעדער צופֿרידן

Nit yeder iz tsufridn mit zayn ponim
ober mit zayn seykhl is yeder
tsufridn AC

שׂכל ברענגט אַמאָל מער אײַן ווי געלט | Brains are sometimes worth more than money

Seykhl brengt amol mer ayn vi gelt AC

שׂכל אָן מזל איז אַ רויער ברילִיאַנט | Brains without luck is a diamond in the rough

Seykhl on mazl iz a royer brilyant IB

צום גליק באַדאַרף מען קיין חכמה ניט | With luck you don't need brains

Tsum glik badarft men keyn khokhme
nit NS

ווען מען דאַרף האָבן מוח העלפֿט ניט | When brains are needed, brawn won't do
קיין כוח

Ven men darf hobn moyekh helft nit
keyn koyekh P

ווער עס האָט שׂכל דעם איז גאָט מוחל | If you're really smart, God will forgive you

Ver es hot seykhl dem iz got meykhl NS

BRIBERY

אַ געשמירט מויל זאָגט ניט ניין

A greased mouth won't say "no"
A geshmirt moyl zogt nit neyn AC

אַ הונט אַז מען וואַרפֿט אים אַ ביין,
שוויַיגט ער

A dog, if you throw it a bone, shuts up
A hunt az men varft im a beyn, shvaygt er AC

אַז דער אדון ווייסט פֿון כל דבֿר שורש
העלפֿט ניט קיין חורש

If the boss knows all the details, hush money won't help
Az der odon veyst fun kol dover shoyresh helft nit keyn khoyresh IB

אַז מען שמירט פֿאָרט מען

If you grease [palms], you ride
Az men shmirt, fort men P

BUSINESS

אַז מען האַנדלט גענוג ווערט מען קלוג

If lots you buy and sell, they'll think you smart as well
Az men handlt genug vert men klug NS

אַז מען האַנדלט מיט טאַבעק האָט מען
אַ שמעק, אַז מען האַנדלט מיט האָניק
האָט מען אַ לעק און אַז מען האַנדלט
מיט גאָרנישט האָט מען דרעק

If you deal in tobacco you get a sniff, if you deal in honey you get a lick, but if you deal in nothing, all you get is shit
Az men handlt mit tabek hot men a shmek, az men handlt mit honik hot men a lek un az men handlt mit gornisht hot men drek AC

אַז מען האָט סחורה האָט מען ניט קיין
מורה

If you have the wares, you have no cares
Az men hot skhoyre hot men nit keyn moyre NS

אַז מען לייגט ניט אַרײַן טאַקע נעמט מען אַרויס אַ מכה

If an effort you won't make, a plague you'll take
Az men leygt nit arayn take nemt men aroys a make P

די ערגסטע סחורה איז 'לא'

The worst merchandise is "no"
Di ergste skhoyre is 'loy' IB

דער הלוך ילך'ט ניט

The going didn't go
[The merchandise didn't move]
Der hulokh yaylekht nit IB

דרײַ ווײַבער מיט אַ גאַנדז הייסט שוין אַ יריד

Three women and a goose constitute a market
Dray vayber mit a gandz heyst shoyn a yarid AC

עס האָט זיך אויסגעלאָזט אַ בוידעם!

The attic caved in!
[It came to nothing]
Es hot zikh oysgelozt a boydem! P

פֿון האַנדלען אין גאַס מיט קלײַנע זאַכן קען מען קיין גרויסע זאַכן ניט מאַכן

Peddling small won't bring much at all
Fun handlen in gas mit kleyne zakhn ken men keyn groyse zakhn nit makhn NS

כל-זמן דאָס געלט איז אויפֿן פּאַפּיר איז דאָס פּאַפּיר

As long as the money is on paper, it's only paper
Kolzman dos gelt iz oyfn papir is dos papir AC

מען האָט עס צעכאַפּט ווי מצה-וואַסער

It sold like *matzah*-water!
[That is, like hot cakes]
Men hot es tsekhapt vi matse-vaser! IB

נאָר אויף צרות איז ניטאָ קיין קונה | **Only for troubles are there no customers**
Nor oyf tsores iz nito keyn koyne AC

אויף ניט אַרויס און ניט אַרײַן קען קיין ערגערס ניט זײַן | **No way out and no way in—there's no worse position to be in**
Oyf nit aroys un nit arayn ken keyn ergers nit zayn IB

וואָס גרעסער דער סוחר אַלץ קלענער דער ייִד | **The greater the merchant, the smaller the Jew**
Vos greser der soykher alts klener der yid P

CANTORS

אַ חזן נעמט געלט פֿאַר שרײַען און אַ
רבי פֿאַר שװײַגן

A cantor is paid to shout and a rabbi to keep silent

A khazn nemt gelt far shrayen un a rebe far shvaygn AC

אַ חזן אױף דער עלטער בילט װי אַ הונט
און עסט װי אַ פֿערד

A cantor past his prime howls like a dog and eats like a horse

A khazn oyf der elter bilt vi a hunt un est vi a ferd NS

אַלע ייִדן זײַנען חזנים אָבער מערסטנס
זײַנען זײ הײזעריק

Any Jew can be a cantor, but most of the time he's hoarse

Ale yidn zaynen khazonim ober merstns zaynen zey heyzerik P

ער איז אַ גרױסער נאַר, װאָלט חוץ מיר
קײנער ניט געװוּסט, איז ער אָבער אַ
חזן, װײסט די גאַנצע קהילה

He's a big fool; if only no one but myself knew, but he's the cantor, so the entire community knows

Er iz a groyser nar, volt khuts mir keyner nit gevust, iz er ober a khazn, veyst di gantse kehile AC

ביסט אַ חזן? – זינג זשע, ביסט אַ
גלח? – קלינג זשע

If you're a cantor, sing; if you're a
priest, ring the bells
Bist a khazn? zing zhe, bist a
galekh?—kling zhe IB

לויטן פנים דאַרף ער זיַין אַ חזן, לויטן
קול מוז ער זיַין אַ גרויסער חכם

According to his face he should be a
cantor; according to his voice he
must be a towering intellect
Loytn ponem darf er zayn a khazn,
loytn kol muz er zayn a groyser
khokhem AC

צוויי מאָל זאָגט אַ חזן

Twice repeated is for the cantor
[Refers to the practice of repeating
the same passage before concluding
the prayer]
Tsvey mol zogt a khazn NS

CAUTION

אַז אַ לייב שלאָפֿט, לאָז אים שלאָפֿן

Let sleeping lions be
Az a leyb shloft, loz im shlofn P

אַז דו וועסט פֿאָרן פּאַמעלעך וועסטו
שנעלער אָנקומען

The slower you drive, the quicker
you'll arrive
Az du vest forn pamelekh vestu shneler
onkumen NS

אַז מען עפֿנט ניט דאָס מויל כאַפּט מען
ניט קיין פֿליגן

Don't open your mouth and you'll
catch no flies
Az men efnt nit dos moyl khapt men
nit keyn flign AC

אַז מען ליגט אויף דער ערד קען מען ניט
פֿאַלן

If you lie on the ground, you can't
fall down
Az men ligt oyf der erd ken men nit
faln IB

אַז מען זאָגט ביסט טויט – ליג
אײַנגעלייגט

If people say you're dead—lie low!
Az men zogt bist toyt—lig ayngeleygt! P

דער גרעסטער שווימער קען זיך טרענקן

Even the best swimmer can drown
Der grester shvimer ken zikh trenken IB

די שלאַנג פֿון לאָך זאָל מען אַרויסציִען
מיט פֿרעמדע הענט

**Draw the snake out of the hole with
someone else's hands**
*Di shlang fun lokh zol men aroystsi'en
mit fremde hent* AC

פֿאַר אַ צאַפּ האָט מען מורה פֿון פֿאָרנט,
פֿאַר אַ פֿערד פֿון הינטן און פֿאַר אַ נאַר
פֿון אַלע זײַטן

**Beware a goat from the front, a
horse from the rear, and a fool from
all sides**
*Far a tsap hot men moyre fun fornt, far
a ferd fun hintn un far a nar fun ale
zaytn* NS

האַלט מיך פֿאַר אַ רבֿ און היט מיך ווי אַ
גנבֿ

**Treat me like a rabbi, but watch me
like a thief**
*Halt mikh far a rov un hit mikh vi a
ganef* NS

היט זיך פֿאַר אַ פֿײַער און גלייב ניט דאָס
וואַסער

**Guard against fire and don't trust
water**
*Hit zikh far a fayer un gleyb nit dos
vaser* NS

מיט געפֿאַר און מיט געפֿילן טאָר מען זיך
ניט צו פֿיל שפּילן

**With danger and with feelings there
should be no trifling dealings**
*Mit gefar un mit gefiln tor men zikh nit
tsu fil shpiln* AC

שפּײַ ניט אין ברונעם, וועסט נאָך פֿון
אים דאַרפֿן וואַסער טרינקען

**Don't spit into the well, you might
have to drink from it later**
*Shpay nit in brunem, vest nokh fun im
darfn vaser trinken* NS

וואַרף ניט אַרויס די שמוציקע איידער דו האָסט די ריינע

Don't throw out the soiled before you have the clean
Varf nit aroys di shmutsike eyder du host di reyne IB

וואָס מער געוואָרט, מער גענאַרט

The more you hesitate, the more you'll be deceived
Vos mer gevart, mer genart NS

CERTAINTY

אַ טאַפּ אין וואָגן שאַט נישט

A poke into the wagon does no harm
[Refers to the practice of lazy guards conducting superficial searches for contraband]
A tap in vogn shat nisht IB

אַז מען זוכט אַ באָדנער געפֿינט מען אַ גלעזער, אַז מען זוכט חלה פֿאַרלירט מען דערווייַל דאָס ברויט

Look for a cooper, you find a glazier; look for challah, and meanwhile, you lose ordinary bread
Az men zukht a bodner gefint men a glezer, az men zukht khale farlirt men dervayl dos broyt NS

בעסער אַ האָן אין האַנט איידער אַן אָדלער אין הימל

Better a rooster in the hand than an eagle in the sky
Beser a hon in hant eyder an odler in himl NS

בעסער הייַנט אַן איי איידער מאָרגן אַן אָקס

Better an egg today than an ox tomorrow
Beser haynt an ey eyder morgn an oks AC

גלייַכער מיט אַ היימישן גנבֿ איידער מיט
אַ פֿרעמדן רבֿ

Better with a hometown thief than with an imported rabbi
Glaykher mit a heymishn ganef eyder mit a fremdn rov IB

ווען צוויי שפּילן מוז איינער געווינען און
איינער פֿאַרלירן

When two play, one wins and the other loses
Ven tsvey shpiln muz eyner gevinen un eyner farlirn NS

זיכער איז אַ קריכער

Certainty is a loser
[Slow and easy wins the race]
Zikher iz a krikher NS

זאָל דער פֿערד געבוירן ווערן – אַ
רייַטער וועט זיך שוין געפֿינען

Let the horse be born—a rider will be found soon enough
Zol der ferd geboyrn vern—a rayter vet zikh shoyn gefinen IB

CHARACTER

אַ דרים געפֿינט מען שטענדיק בייַ אַ
שנייַדער

A thread is always found on a tailor
A drim gefint men shtendik bay a shnayder AC

אַ גוטער דאַרף נייט קיין בריוו, אַ
שלעכטן העלפֿט ניט קיין בריוו

A good person doesn't need a recommendation; a bad person won't benefit from one
A guter darf nit keyn briv, a shlekhtn helft nit keyn briv IB

אַ גוטן וועט דער שענק ניט קאַליע מאַכן
און אַ שלעכטן וועט דער בית-המדרש
ניט פֿאַרריכטן

A good person won't be corrupted by the tavern nor a bad person reformed by the synagogue
A gutn vet der shenk nit kalye makhn un a shlekhtn vet der beysmedresh nit far'rikhtn IB

אַ הונט אָן ציין איז אויס הונט **A dog without teeth is no longer a dog**
A hunt on tseyn is oys hunt NS

אַ קנויל האָט אויך אַן עק **A ball of twine also unwinds**
A k'noyl hot oykh an ek IB

אַ מענטש איז שטאַרקער פֿון אײַזן און שוואַכער פֿון אַ פֿליג **A human being is stronger than iron and weaker than a fly**
A mentsh iz shtarker fun ayzn un shvakher fun a flig IF

אַ מוכר-סמֿרים איז קיין למדן ניט, אַ חלפֿן איז קיין עושר ניט און אַ קבֿרות-מאַן איז קיין צדיק ניט **A bookseller is no scholar, a money changer no millionaire, and a gravedigger no saint**
A moykher-sforim iz keyn lamdn nit, a khalfn iz keyn oysher nit un a kvoresman iz keyn tsadik nit NS

אַ ייִדישע קישקע קען מען ניט אָפּשאַצן **A Jewish gizzard can't be measured**
A yidishe kishke ken men nit opshatsn P

אַן אָדלער כאַפּט ניט קיין פֿליגן **An eagle doesn't catch flies**
An odler khapt nit keyn flign NS

אַז דער פּאַלאַץ פֿאַלט אײַן איז עס אַלץ פּאַלאַץ, זאָל מען אויפֿהייבן דעם הקדש בלײַבט עס אַלץ הקדש **If the castle totters, it's still a castle; fix up the poorhouse and it's still a poorhouse**
Az der palats falt ayn iz es alts palats, zol men oyfheybn dem hegdesh blaybt es alts hegdesh AC

אַז עס קומט אַרויס פֿון אַ קאַץ כאַפּט עס מײַז (מאַכט עס מיאַאָו) **If it's born of a cat it'll catch mice (miaow)**
Az es kumt aroys fun a kats khapt es mayz (makht es miaow) NS

אַז מען האָט אַן אלטע מויד אין שטוב
דאַרף מען ניט האָבן קיין הונט

With an old maid in the house a
watchdog is unnecessary
*Az men hot an alte moyd in shtub darf
men nit hobn keyn hunt* AC

אַז מען שפּײַט די זונה אין פנים זאָגט זי
אַז עס רעגנט

Spit in the whore's face and she'll
say it's raining
*Az men shpayt di zoyne in ponim zogt
zi az es regnt* P

בלאָטע איז גלײַך צו כריין, ניט מען
אַקערט ניט מען זייט, עס וואַקסט פֿון
זיך אַליין

Mud is like horseradish: it's neither
sown nor cultivated but grows by
itself
*Blote iz glaykh tsu khreyn: nit men
akert, nit men zeyt, es vakst fun zikh
aleyn* NS

דער בעסטער פֿערד דאַרף האָבן אַ
בײַטש, דער קלוגסטער מענטש אַן עצה
און די פֿרומסטע נקבֿה אַ מאַן

The best horse needs a whip, the
smartest person needs advice, and
the most virtuous of women needs
a man
*Der bester ferd darf hobn a baytsh, der
klugster mentsh an eytse un di frumste
nekeyve a man* NS

דער פּראָסטער שטופּט זיך אויבן אָן

A coarse person pushes himself
forward
Der proster shtupt zikh oybn on P

די קלענסטע נקמה פֿאַרסמט די נשמה

The smallest vengeance poisons the
soul
*Di klenste nekome farsamt di
neshome* IB

עס זײַנען ניטאָ קיין מיאוסע ליבעס און
קיין שיינע תּפֿיסות

No loves are homely, no prisons are
comely
*Es zaynen nito keyn mi'ese libes un
keyn sheyne tfises* AC

פֿון איין טיפֿער גרוב האָט מען מער
וואַסער ווי פֿון צען פֿלאַכע

**One deep ditch holds more water
than ten shallow ones**
*Fun eyn tifer grub hot men mer vaser vi
fun tsen flakhe* NS

גאָלדענע כּלים ווערן קיין מאָל ניט
שוואַרץ

Golden utensils never turn black
*Goldene keylim vern keyn mol nit
shvarts* NS

אין אַ קרומען שפּיגל איז די נאָז אין אַ
זייט

**In a warped mirror the nose is
askew**
*In a krumen shpigl iz di noz in a
zayt* AC

מזל און חן קויפֿט מען ניט אין קרעמל

**Luck and charm can't be bought at
the store**
*Mazl un kheyn koyft men nit in
kreml* IB

אָרעם איז ניט רייַך, קרום איז ניט גלייַך

Poor isn't rich, crooked isn't straight
*Orem iz nit raykh, krum iz nit
glaykh* NS

אויף מיסט איז קאָרן געראָטן

Corn grows on manure
Oyf mist iz korn gerotn NS

ווען אַ שיכּור האָט ניט קיין בראָנפֿן
רעדט ער כאָטש פֿון בראָנפֿן

**Even when a drunkard has no
whiskey, he still talks of whiskey**
*Ven a shiker hot nit keyn bronfn ret er
khotsh fun bronfn* IB

וואָס מער קען מען פֿון אַן אָקס
פֿאַרלאַנגען ווי אָקסנפֿלייש?

**What more can you expect from an
ox besides oxmeat?**
*Vos mer ken men fun an oks farlangen
vi oksnfleysh?* NS

ווו דו זאָלסט ניט וואַרפֿן אַ שטעקן
בלייַבט ער אַלץ שטעקן

**No matter where you throw the
stick, it remains a stick**
*Vu du zolst nit varfn a shtekn, blaybt er
alts shtekn* NS

יעדער זאַק איז שטאַרק ביז ער צעריַיסט
זיך

Every sack is strong until it rips
*Yeder zak iz shtark biz er tserayst
zikh* P

CHARITY

אַ טובֿה קאָסט טייַער

A favor is expensive
A toyve kost tayer IB

אַז מען עפֿנט ניט די טיר פֿאָרן אָרעמאַן
וועט זי זיך אַליין עפֿענען פֿאַרן דאָקטער

**If you don't open the door to the
pauper, it will open itself to the
doctor**
*Az men efnt nit di tir farn oreman vet
zi zikh aleyn efenen farn dokter* NS

בעסער מיטן קאָפּ דורך דער וואַנט
איידער אויסשטרעקן אַ האַנט

**Better to knock your head through
the wall than to hold out your hand**
*Beser mitn kop durkh der vant eyder
oys'shtrekn a hant* NS

ער איז אַ גוטער ב'צדק – ביז צו דער
קעשענע

**He is a kind man—but his charity
ends at his pocket**
[A play on words involving an
anagram]
*Er iz a guter BeTzeDek—Biz Tsu Der
Keshene* P

גיבן זאָלסטו מיט אַ וואַרעמער האַנט
ניט מיט קיין קאַלטער

**Give with a warm hand, not a cold
one**
[Give while still alive]
*Gibn zolstu mit a varemer hant nit mit
keyn kalter* P

66

ניט קיין מיצווה, ניט קיין תּורה, מיט
וואָס זשע קומט מען פֿאַרן בורא?

No good deeds, no Torah education, how do you appear before the Lord of Creation?
Nit keyn mitsve, nit keyn toyre, mit vos zhe kumt men farn boyre? IB

אויף צדקה איז אויך דאָ חזקה

Charity is also a right
Oyf tsedoke iz oykh do khazoke IB

צדקה צו געבן און ליב צו האָבן קען מען
קיינעם ניט נייטן

You can't force anyone to give charity or love
Tsedoke tsu gebn un lib tsu hobn ken men keynem nit neytn P

ווען מען לעבט פֿון דער פּושקע איז
ליידיק די קישקע

When you live off the dole, in your belly there's a hole
Ven men lebt fun der pishke iz leydik di kishke IB

CHARM

אַז מען טוט אָן אַ שטעקן שיין האָט ער
אויך חן

Dress up a stick and it will also have charm
Az men tut on a shtekn sheyn hot er oykh kheyn NS

חן גייט איבער שיין

Charm is better than beauty
Kheyn geyt iber sheyn NS

מזל און חן קויפֿט מען ניט אין קרעמל

Luck and charm can't be bought at the store
Mazl un kheyn koyft men nit in kreml P

אָן חן איז מען ניט שיין

Without charm there is no beauty
On kheyn iz men nit sheyn NS

CHILDREN

אַ קינדס וועלט איז קליין אָבער שווער
צו פֿאַרשטיין

**A child's world, though small, is
hard to understand at all**
*A kinds velt iz kleyn ober shver tsu
farshteyn* NS

אַלע פֿינגער טוען גלײַך וויי, אַלע קינדער
זײַנען גלײַך טײַער

**All fingers hurt alike; all children
are equally precious**
*Ale finger tu'en glaykh vey, ale kinder
zaynen glaykh tayer* NS

בעסער נישט צו האָבן איידער צו
באַגראָבן

**Better not to have had them than to
bury them**
*Beser nisht tsu hobn eyder tsu
bagrobn* NS

איינס איז קיינס

One is none
Eyns iz keyns IF

פֿאַר טאַטע-מאַמעס זינד לײַדט דאָס
קינד

**The child pays for parents' sinning
ways**
Far tate-mames zind layt dos kind NS

איטלעכעס קינד ברענגט זיין אייגענע
ברכה אויף דער וועלט

**Every child brings its own blessing
into the world**
*Itlekhes kind brengt zayn eygene
brokhe oyf der velt* AC

קליינע לײַט גייען ניט ווײַט

Little people don't travel far
Kleyne layt geyen nit vayt AC

לאָז עס זײַן פֿון טײַוול אַבי עס הייסט
פֿײַוול

**Even if it's sired by the Devil, as
long as it has a Jewish name**
*Loz es zayn fun tayvl abi es heyst
fayvl* NS

68

נאָך אַ קינד, נאָך אַ ברויט
Another child, another bread
Nokh a kind, nokh a broyt NS

BIG AND LITTLE CHILDREN

אַז ניטאָ קיין קלײנע איז ניטאָ קיין
גרויסע
If there are no little ones, there can't be big ones
Az nito keyn kleyne iz nito keyn groyse NS

קלײנע קינדער קלײנע פֿריידן (צרות),
גרויסע קינדער גרויסע לײַדן (צרות)
Little children, little joys (woes); big children, big sorrows
Kleyne kinder, kleyne fraydn (tsores); groyse kinder, groyse laydn (tsores) P

קלײנע קינדער לאָזן ניט שלאָפֿן, גרויסע
קינדער לאָזן ניט לעבן
Little children don't let you sleep; big ones don't let you live
Kleyne kinder lozn nit shlofn, groyse kinder lozn nit lebn AC

CLEVER CHILDREN

בײַ יעדער מאַמען זײַנען אירע קינדער די
געראָטנסטע
To every mother her children are the brightest
Bay yeder mame zaynen ire kinder di gerotenste IB

מײַנע קינדער זײַנען גאָטס ווונדער
My children, big and small, are wonders all
Mayne kinder zaynen gots vinder IB

ווען אַ קינד זאָגט אַ חכמה שטופ עס
אַרויס ווײַל עס קען באַלד זאָגן אַ
נאַרישקייט
When a child says something clever, pay no attention; it can just as easily say something foolish
Ven a kind zogt a khokhme shtup es aroys vayl es ken bald zogn a narishkeyt IB

GRANDCHILDREN

אַן אייניקל האָט מען ליבער ווי אַן אייגן
קינד

A grandchild is more beloved than one's own child
An eynikl hot men liber vi an eygn kind NS

אַז מען האָט אַן אייניקל האָט מען צוויי
קינדער

When you have a grandchild you have two children
Az men hot an eynikl hot men tsvey kinder NS

MARRYING OFF CHILDREN

אֲפֿילו אַ קינד איז ערגער ווי אַ גזלן
דאַרף מען אויך טאַנצן אויף זײַן חתונה

Even if a child is worse than a thief, the parents are obliged to dance at his wedding
Afile a kind iz erger vi a gazlen darf men oykh tantsn oyf zayn khasene P

אַז מען גיט אויס אַ טאָכטער איז אַראָפּ
אַ שטיין פֿון האַרץ

When you marry off a daughter, a stone is lifted from your heart
Az men git oys a tokhter iz arop a shteyn fun harts NS

נדן קענען עלטערן געבן אָבער ניט מזל

Parents can provide dowry but not luck
Nadn kenen eltern gebn ober nit mazl P

אַז די עלטערן געבן ניט די קינדער אין
שיך, נעמען זיך די קינדער שפּעטער אין
די זאָקן

If the parents don't provide shoes, the children will later help themselves in their stockinged feet
[Refers to the practice of shiveh when mourners sit shoeless]
Az di eltern gebn nit di kinder in shikh, nemen zikh di kinder shpeter in di zokn IB

די אייער לערנען די הינער | The eggs teach the hens
Di eyer lernen di hiner P

איידער מען איז מגדל אַ קינד ווערט מען | Rearing children costs you your
אָן דאָס געזינט | health
Eyder men iz megadl a kind vert men on dos gezint IB

אין דעם בעסטן קינד פֿאַרגעסט מען | The least demanding child is easily neglected
In dem bestn kind fargest men P

קינדער האָבן איז שווער אָבער זיי מגדל | Bearing children is difficult, raising
צו זײַן איז נאָך מער | them even more so
Kinder hobn iz shver ober zey megadl tsu zayn iz nokh mer NS

JOY FROM CHILDREN

אַ קינד אין שטוב, פֿול אין אַלע | With a child in the house, all the
ווינקעלעך | corners are full
A kind in shtub, ful in ale vinkelekh NS

קינדער און גלעזער האָט מען קיין מאָל | There's no such thing as too many
ניט צו פֿיל | drinking glasses or too many children
Kinder un glezer hot men keyn mol nit tsu fil IB

נחת פֿון קינדער איז טײַערער פֿאַר געלט | Joy from children is more precious than money
Nakkhes fund kinder iz tayerer far gelt P

71

אַ בת-יחידה זאָל מען זוכן

Look for a one-and-only daughter
[She will likely have household
skills]
A bas-yekhide zol men zukhn NS

אַ טאָכטער אין דער נויט, אַ זון נאָכן טויט

**A daughter when in need, a son for
after one's death**
*A tokhter in der noyt, a zun nokhn
toyt* NS

אַז דער זון האָט חתונה גיט ער דער ווײַב
אַ כתובה און דער מאַמען אַ גט

**When a son marries, he gives his
wife a contract and his mother a
divorce**
*Az der zun hot khasene git er der vayb
a ksube un der mamen a get* IB

אַז עס ווערט געבוירן אַ מיידל איז עס
אַ הצלחה אין דער משפחה

**When a girl is born it's a good sign
for the family**
*Az es vert geboyrn a meydl iz es a
hatslokhe in der mishpokhe* NS

אַז מען פֿאַרלירט אַ טאָכטער וויינט מען
ניט אויפֿן נדן

**When you lose a daughter, you
don't grieve for the dowry**
*Az men farlirt a tokhter veynt men nit
oyfn nadn* NS

בעסער אַ זון אַ בעדער איידער אַ
טאָכטער אַ רביצין

**Better to have a son who is a
bathhouse attendant than a
daughter who is a rabbi's wife**
[This reflects the assets a family
would need in order provide a
dowry sufficient to acquire a rabbi
as a son-in-law]
*Beser a zun a beder eyder a tokhter a
rebetsin* IB

פֿון אַ גוטן איידעם האָט מען אַ זון, פֿון אַ
שלעכטן פֿאַרלירט מען די טאָכטער אויך

With a good son-in-law, you gain a
son; with a bad one, you lose your
daughter also
*Fun a gutn eydem hot men a zun, fun a
shlekhtn farlirt men di tokhter oykh* AC

האָט מען זין איז ווייל, האָט מען
טעכטער מאַכן זיי הויל

Sons are nice but daughters will
clean you out
*Hot men zin iz voyl, hot men tekhter
makhn zey hoyl* NS

CHOICE

אַז מען האָט ניט קיין ברירה מוז מען
טאָן אָן אַ ברירה

If you don't have a choice, do it
without a choice
*Az men hot nit keyn breyre muz men
ton on a breyre* P

אַז מען קען ניט טאָן ווי מען וויל מוז
מען זיצן שטיל

If you can't do as you will, you
must sit still
*Az men ken nit ton vi men vil muz men
zitsn shtil* NS

אַז מען קען ניט זיין קיין איבער מוז מען
זיַין אַן אונטער

If you can't be a master, be a servant
*Az men ken nit zayn keyn iber muz
men zayn an unter* NS

אַז ס׳איז ניטאָ קיין מיידן טאַנצט מען
מיט שיקסעס

If there are no Jewish girls about,
then one takes Gentile girls out
*Az s'iz nito keyn meydn tantst men mit
shikses* NS

בעסער מיט אַ קלוגן אין גיהנום איידער
מיט אַ נאַר אין גן-עדן

Better with a wise man in hell than
with a fool in paradise
*Beser mit a klugn in gehenem eyder
mit a nar in gan-eydn* IB

"במקום שאין איש" – איז א הערינג
אויך א פֿיש

"When men are scarcer than one can wish"—even a herring will do for a fish
"Bimkoym she'eyn ish"—iz a hering oykh a fish IB

איינער האָט ליב סמעטענע און דער
אנדערער – מפֿטיר

One person likes cream and another likes prayer
Eyner hot lib smetene un der anderer—maftir AC

האָב ניט קיין מורה ווען דו האָסט ניט
קיין אַנדערע ברירה

Don't be afraid when you have no other choice
Hob nit keyn meyre ven du host nit keyn andere breyre IB

קיין ברירה איז אויך אַ ברירה

To say "no choice" is also a choice
Keyn breyre iz oykh a breyre P

מען קען ניט טאַנצן אויף צוויי חתונות
מיט איין מאָל

You can't dance at two weddings at the same time
Men ken nit tantsn oyf tsvey khasenes mit eyn mol P

וואָס דאַרפֿסטו דעם גאָנער אַז די גאַנדז
גיט שמאַלץ?

Who needs the gander when the goose provides the fat?
Vos darfstu dem goner az di gandz git shmalts? NS

CHUTSPEH

אַן עזות-פנים קומט גלײַך אין גן-עדן
אַרײַן

An insolent person goes straight to heaven
An azes-ponim kumt glaykh in gan-eydn arayn IB

אַז מען פֿאַרטשעפּעט אַ ייִדן אַ העקעלע וויל ער מען זאָל אים אָפּמאַכן אַ גאַנצן קאַפֿטן

If you snag a Jew's coat, he demands that you get him a new one
Az men fartshepet a yidn a hekele vil er men zol im opmakhn a gantsn kaftn NS

אַז מען שפּײַט די זונה אין פּנים זאָגט זי אַז עס רעגנט

Spit in the whore's face and she says it's raining
Az men shpayt di zoyne in ponim zogt zi as es regnt P

דער ייִד שלאָגט און שרײַט געוואַלד

A Jew flogs you and himself shouts "help!"
Der yid shlogt un shrayt gevald! NS

ער וויל מיר אָנהענגען אַ לונג און לעבער אויף דער נאָז!

He wants to hang a lung and liver on my nose!
Er vil mir onhengen a lung un leber oyf der noz! NS

חוצפּה גילט

Chutspeh succeeds
Khutspe gilt NS

CLEVERNESS

אַלע קענערס גייען אָן שטיוול

All smart people go without boots
[A virtue is made out of necessity]
Ale keners geyen on shtivl P

אַז מען האָט מזל דאַרף מען קיין חכם ניט זײַן

With luck you don't have to be clever
Az men hot mazl darf men keyn khokhem nit zayn P

בעסער זײַן אונטער קלוגע אונטערטעניק אײדער איבער נאַראָנים אַ קעניג

Better under a wise man's rules than to be a king over fools
Beser zayn unter kluge untertenik eyder iber naronim a kenig IB

ניט אַלע קלוגע זײַנען גלײַך – אײנער
איז קלוג פֿאַר דער צײַט, אַ צווייטער נאָך
דער צײַט און אַ דריטער, צו דער צײַט

**Not all smart people are equal—
some are smart too soon, some too
late, and some at the right time**
*Nit ale kluge zynen glaykh—eyner iz
klug far der tsayt, a tsveyter nokh der
tsayt un a driter, tsu der tsayt* AC

צווײי קלוגע מאַכן דעם דריטן צום נאַר

**Two smart people can make a fool
out of a third**
*Tsvey kluge makhn dem dritn tsum
nar* P

וויבאַלד דו פֿאַרשטייסט דײַן נאַרישקייט
ביסטו אַ קלוגער

**As long as you understand your
foolishness, you're smart**
*Vibald du farshteyst dayn narishkeyt
bistu a kluger* AC

COMMON SENSE

אַ קעכן פֿאַרדאַרבט זיך ניט

A cook doesn't poison herself
A kekhn fardarbt zikh nit IB

אַז עס ברענט איז אַ פֿײַער

If it's burning, there's fire
[Where there's smoke, there's fire]
Az es brent iz a fayer P

אַז מען האָט נעכטן געגעסן איז מען
הײַנט ניט זאַט

**What you ate yesterday won't
satisfy you today**
*Az men hot nekhtn gegesn iz men
haynt nit zat* P

אַז מען שפּײַט אין דער לופֿט פֿאַלט עס
צוריק אין פּנים

**If you spit upwards it will fall back
in your face**
*Az men shpayt in der luft falt es tsurik
in ponim* NS

פֿרעג ניט בײַ אַ בלינדן דעם ריכטיקן
וועג

Don't ask directions from a blind person

Freg nit bay a blindn dem rikhtikn veg IB

פֿון וואַנען זאָל אַ גוטער ייד וויסן אַז
באָרשט איז רויט?

How should a learned Jew know that borsht is red?

Fun vanem zol a guter yid visn az borsht iz royt? IB

COMPARISON

אַ מענטש צו אַ מענטש איז ניט גלײַך

One person cannot be compared to another

A mentsh tsu a mentsh iz nit glaykh P

אַן אַלטער צעברעכט און אַ יונגער בויט
איז נאָך ניט גלײַך

An old man wrecks and a young one builds; they're still not equal

An alter tsebrekht un a yunger boyt iz nokh nit glaykh IB

אַז מען זעט ניט שרה די בלינדע איז
רבֿקה די שוואַרצע שענער

Compared to blind Sarah, swarthy Rivke is better looking

Az men zet nit sore di blinde iz rivke di shvartse shener IB

דער רבי איז גרויס ווען ער האָט אַ סך
קליינע ייִדעלעך

The rabbi is a giant when surrounded by small people

Der rebe iz groys ven er hot a sakh kleyne yidelekh NS

ס׳איז בעסער צו טראָגן די וואָכעדיקע
מלבושים יום-טובֿ איידער די
יום-טובֿדיקע מלבושים אין דער וואָכן

It's better to wear weekday clothing on a holiday than holiday clothing midweek

[That is, to a funeral]

S'iz beser tsu trogn di vokhedike malbushim yontev eyder di yontevdike malbushim in der vokhn IB

77

ווען פֿרייט זיך אַ הויקער? ווען ער זעט אַ
גרעסטערן הויקער פֿאַר זיך

When does a hunchback rejoice?
When he sees a bigger hump than
his own
Ven freyt zikh a hoyker? ven er zet a
gresern hoyker far zikh IB

CONCEIT

אַליין איז די נשמה ריין

Only one's own soul is unblemished
Aleyn iz di neshome reyn P

דאָס ווערעמל נאַרט אָפּ און ניט דער
פֿישער אָדער די ווענדקע

It's the bait that lures, not the
fisherman or the tackle
Dos vereml nart op un nit der fisher
oder di vendke NS

עס לויבט זיך אַליין, עס שמעט זיך אַליין

Praise yourself, shame yourself
Es loybt zikh aleyn, es shemt zikh
aleyn NS

גאווה און אַ ליידיקער טײַסטער זײַנען
ניט קיין פֿאָר

Conceit and an empty wallet are
not fit companions
Gayve un a leydiker tayster zaynen nit
keyn por NS

מיט עניוות זאָל מען זיך ניט גרויסן

Don't boast about your modesty
Mit anives zol men zikh nit groysn IB

יעדער מענטש איז אויף זיך אַליין בלינד

Everyone is blind to his own faults
Yeder mentsh iz oyf zikh aleyn blind P

CONFUSION

ער רעדט אין דער וועלט אַרײַן!

He talks to no point!
Er ret in der velt arayn! P

עס איז נישט אויף קידוש און נישט אויף
הבֿדלה

It's not for Sabbath eve or Sabbath end
Es iz nisht oyf kidesh un nisht oyf havdole IB

מען גיסט און מען פּישט און עס טוט זיך
אַ וועלט!

There's pouring and peeing and the world's in a spin!
Men gist un men pisht un es tut zikh a velt! NS

מען קען פֿאַרפֿאָרן קיין מצרים!

We could blunder right back into ancient Egypt!
Men ken farforn keyn mitsrayim! NS

CONSEQUENCE

אַ הונט בילט ניט אויף זיך אַליין

A dog doesn't bark at itself
A hunt bilt nit oyf zikh aleyn IB

אַ סעודה אָן אַ פֿאָרץ איז װי אַ חתונה אָן
כלי־זמרים

A feast without a fart is like a wedding without musicians
A sude on a forts iz vi a khasene on klezmorim AC

אַז אַ פֿייגעלע פֿליט דורך לאָזט זי אויך
עפּעס איבער

Even a little bird flying by leaves something behind
Az a feygele flit durkh lozt zi oykh epes iber IB

אַז אַ ייִדיש װײַבל שלאָפֿט מיט אַ גוי
קומט אַרויס אַ פֿאַרטיקער משומד

When a Jewish woman sleeps with a Gentile, out comes a ready-made convert
Az a yidish vaybl shloft mit a goy kumt aroys a fartiker meshumed WZ

אַז דער תּלמיד איז אַ וווילער איז דער
רבי אויך אַ וווילער

If the pupil is apt, the rabbi is a good teacher
Az der talmed iz a voyler iz der rebe oykh a voyler IB

אַז עס ברענט איז אַ פֿײַער

If it burns, there's fire
[Where there's smoke, there's fire]
Az es brent iz a fayer P

אַז עס איז דאָ אַ פֿוטער וועט שוין זײַן אַ
טשוואָק עס אויפֿצוהענגען

If there's a fur, you'll find a peg to hang it on
Az es iz do a futer vet shoyn zayn a tshvok es oyftsuhengen IB

אַז אין דרויסן איז אַ ווינט פֿליט דאָס
מיסט הויך

When the wind blows, garbage flies
Az in droysn iz a vint flit dos mist hoykh NS

אַז מען עסט ניט קיין קנאָבל שטינקט
ניט פֿון מויל

If you don't eat garlic, your mouth won't smell
Az men est nit keyn k'nobl shtinkt nit fun moyl P

אַז מען האַקט האָלץ פֿליט שפּענער

If you chop wood, chips fly
Az men hakt holts flit shpener IB

אַז מען האָט ניט קיין אתרוג דאַרף מען
קיין פּושקע ניט האָבן

If you don't have the citron, you don't need the container
[Refers to Succoth observance]
Az men hot nit keyn esreg darf men keyn pushke nit hobn IB

אַז מען קלינגט איז אָדער אַ חגא, אָדער
אַ פּגר אָדער אַ שׂרפֿה

When church bells peal, it's either a [Gentile] holiday, a funeral, or a fire
Az men klingt iz oder a khoge, oder a peyger, oder a sreyfe NS

אַז מען לייגט נישט אַרײַן טאַקע נעמט
מען אַרױס אַ מכה

**If an effort you don't make, a
plague you will take**
*Az men leygt nisht arayn take nemt
men aroys a make* P

אַז מען שלאָפֿט מיט הינט שטייט מען
אױף מיט פֿליי

**If you sleep with dogs, you rise
with fleas**
*Az men shloft mit hint shteyt men oyf
mit fley* IB

אַז ס'איז דאָ אױף פֿיש איז דאָ אױף
פֿעפֿער אױך

**If there's enough for fish, there's
enough for pepper, too**
Az s'iz do oyf fish iz do oyf fefer oykh IB

אַזױ װי מען שפּילט אַזױ טאַנצט מען

**The way they play, that's how
you'll dance**
Azoy vi men shpilt azoy tantst men P

דאָרט װוּ ס'איז אַ רױך איז אַ פֿײַער אױך

Where's there's smoke, there's fire
Dort vu s'iz a roykh iz a fayer oykh NS

אין שיסל קען ניט זײַן מער װי אין טאָפּ

**You can't have more on the plate
than is in the pot**
In shisl ken nit zayn mer vi in top NS

מען קען ניט זײַן אַ בעזעם און ניט װערן
באַשמוצט

**You can't be a broom without
getting soiled**
*Men ken nit zayn a bezem un nit vern
bashmutst* AC

אױף אַזאַ קידוש געהערט אַזאַ ברכו

Each blessing according to its prayer
Oyf aza kidesh gehert aza borkhu NS

װען די קאַץ שלאָפֿט טאַנצן די מײַז

**When the cat's asleep, the mice
dance**
[When the cat's away, the mice will
play]
Ven di kats shloft tantsn di mayz NS

וואָס פֿאַר אַ כּלי-זמר – אַזאַ חתונה | As the musicians—so the wedding
Vos far a klezmer—aza khasene P

װוּ האָניק – דאָרט פֿליגן | Where honey—there flies
Vu honik—dort flign P

יעדער כּלל האָט אַ יציא מן הכּלל | Every rule has its exception
Yeder klal hot a yoytse min haklal NS

CORRUPTION

אַלע מיאוסע פרנסות האָבן שיינע | Shady pursuits bear rich fruits
מזלות | *Ale mi'ese parnoses hobn sheyne mazoles* IB

אַז דער אדון װײסט פֿון כּל דבר שורש | If the boss knows all the details,
העלפֿט ניט קיין חורש | bribery won't help
Az der odon veyst fun kol dover shoresh helft nit keyn khoresh IB

בעסער צען מאָל פֿאַרדאָרבן איידער איין | Better ten times corrupted than one
מאָל געשטאָרבן | time dead
Beser tsen mol fardorbn eyder eyn mol geshtorbn AC

דער גבאי האָט די בעסטע מילכיג װײַל | The trustee has the best of dairy
ער מעלקט די שול | dishes because he milks the synagogue
Der gabay hot di beste milkhig vayl er melkt di shul IB

דער רויטסטער עפל קען אויך האָבן אַ | The reddest apple can contain a
װאָרעם | worm
Der roytster epl ken oykh hobn a vorem NS

COURAGE

אַז מען פֿאַרלירט מוט פֿאַרלירט מען די
מלחמה
If you lose courage you lose the war
*Az men farlirt mut farlirt men di
milkhome* AC

באַראָט זיך ניט מיט אַ פּחדן וועגן
מלחמה
Don't consult a coward about war
*Barat zikh nit mit a pakhdn vegn
milkhome* AC

דער וואָס האָט גאָרניט צו פֿאַרלירן מעג
אַלץ פּרובירן
**If you have nothing to lose, you can
anything choose**
*Der vos hot gornit tsu farlirn meg alts
prubirn* NS

דער וואָס וואַגט ניט קריגט ניט זײַן חלק
**If you don't dare, you won't get
your share**
*Der vos vagt nit krigt nit zayn
kheylek* AC

דער יוון ווערט געמוטיקט נאָך וואַרעמס
**Soldiers become brave after eating
cooked food**
*Der yovn vert gemutikt nokh
varems* NS

געלט פֿאַרלוירן, גאָרניט פֿאַרלוירן; מוט
פֿאַרלוירן, אַלץ פֿאַרלוירן
**Money lost, nothing lost; courage
lost, all is lost**
*Gelt farloyrn, gornit farloyrn; mut
farloyrn, alts farloyrn* IB

CRITICISM

אַליין טוט מען און אויף אַנדערע זאָגט
מען
**You do it yourself but criticize it in
others**
*Aleyn tut men un oyf andere zogt
men* P

עס איז לײַכטער בײַ אַנדערער חסרונות
צו געפֿינען ווי בײַ זיך מעלות

It's easier to find fault in others than virtues in oneself
Es iz laykhter bay andere khasroynes tsu gefinen vi bay zikh mayles NS

אײן מויז עסט קעז און אויף אַנדערע
זאָגט מען

One mouse eats the cheese and the others get the blame
Eyn moyz est kez un oyf andere zogt men IB

גאָט זאָל וועלן אויסהערן דעם פּאַסטעך
וואָלטן אַלע שאָף אויסגעפגרט

If God would listen to the shepherd's complaint, all the sheep would perish
Got zol veln oys'hern dem pastekh voltn ale shof oysgepeygert NS

שעמען זאָלסטו זיך אין ווײַטן האַלדז
אַרײַן!

You should be ashamed right down to your gut!
Shemen zolstu zikh in vaytn haldz arayn! NS

ווען מענטשן זאָלן וויסן וואָס איינער
אויף דעם אַנדערן טראַכט, וואָלטן זיי
זיך אומגעבראַכט

If people knew what others thought of them, the result would be murder and mayhem
Ven mentshn zoln visn vos eyner oyf dem andern trakht, voltn zey zikh umgebrakht AC

ווי אַזוי דער חזן זאָל ניט זינגען קריגט
ער אַלץ אין טאַטן אַרײַן

No matter how well the cantor sings, he'll still be cursed
Vi azoy der khazn zol nit zingen krigt er alts in tatn arayn NS

CURSES

אַ קללה שטעקט ניט אויס אַן אויג אַז אַ
פֿויסט גייט ניט מיט

A curse won't put out an eye unless accompanied by a fist

A klole shtekt nit oys an oyg az a foyst geyt nit mit NS

בעסער זיך צו ווינטשן איידער יענעם צו
שעלטן

Better to wish yourself well than to curse others

Beser zikh tsu vintshn eyder yenem tsu sheltn NS

פֿון אַ קאַץ אַ קראַץ און פֿון אַ ווײַב אַ
קללה

From a cat a scratch, and from a wife a curse

Fun a kats a krats un fun a vayb a klole NS

ניט מיט שעלטן, ניט מיט לאַכן, קען מען
די וועלט איבערמאַכן

Neither ridicule, nor swearing will bring about the world's repairing

Nit mit sheltn, nit mit lakhn, ken men di velt ibermakhn NS

ווי אַזוי דער חזן זאָל ניט זינגען קריגט
ער אַלץ אין טאַטן אַרײַן

No matter how well the cantor sings, he'll still be cursed

Vi azoy der khazn zol nit zingen krigt er alts in tatn arayn IB

EXAMPLES

אַ דאָקטער זאָל אים דאַרפֿן!

May a doctor need him!

A dokter zol im darfn! AC

אַ משוגענעם זאָל מען אויסשרײַבן און
אים אַרײַנשרײַבן!

May a lunatic be released and he committed!

A meshugenem zol men oys'shraybn un im araynshraybn! NS

אַ שיינע ריינע כּפּרה אויף אים!	**May he become a beautiful pure sacrifice!** *A sheyne reyne kapore oyf im!* P
אַרויסשלעפֿן זאָל מען אים די קישקעס פֿון בויך און אַרומוויקלען זיי איבערן האַלדז!	**May his guts be torn out of his belly and wrapped around his neck!** *Aroys'shlepn zol men im di kishkes fun boykh un arumviklen zey ibern haldz!* AC
ברענען זאָל דאָס אָרט וווּ דער חסיד שטייט!	**May the spot on which a Hassid stands be consumed by fire!** *Brenen zol dos ort vu der khosid shteyt!* NS
דער מלאך-המוות זאָל זיך אין אים פֿאַרליבן!	**May the Angel of Death take a fancy to him!** *Der malekhamoves zol zikh in im farlibn!* NS
דאָס מויל זאָל אים נאָר פֿון הינטן שטיין!	**May his mouth be repositioned in his rear!** *Dos moyl zol im nor fun hintn shteyn!* NS
עס זאָל אים דונערן אין בויך און בליצן אין די הויזן!	**May it thunder in his belly and flash lightning in his pants!** *Es zol im dunern in boykh un blitsn in di hoyzn!* NS
עס זאָל דיר וואַקסן אַ געשוויר אויפֿן פּופּיק אַזוי גרויס ווי אַ וואָדערמעלאָן!	**May you develop an abscess on your belly button as big as a watermelon!** *Es zol dir vaksn a geshvir oyfn pupik azoy groys vi a vodermelon!* AC
איין אומגליק איז פֿאַר אים ווייניק!	**One misfortune is too few for him!** *Eyn umglik iz far im veynik!* AC

געגוג צו לעבן צו לאַנגע יאָר!	**Enough of living to a long life!**
	Genug tsu lebn tsu lange yor! NS
גיין זאָל ער מיטן רויך!	**May he go with the smoke!**
	Geyn zol er mitn roykh! NS
גיין זאָל ער וווּ דער רוח זאָגט: 'גוט	**May he go where the devil says**
מאָרגן'!	**"good morning!"**
	Geyn zol er vu der ru'ekh zogt: 'gut
	morgn'! NS
גאָט זאָל אים בענטשן מיט דרײַ	**May God bless him with three**
מענטשן – איינער זאָל אים האַלטן, דער	**people—one to lash him, a second**
צווייטער זאָל אים שפּאַלטן און דער	**to smash him, and a third to stash**
דריטער זאָל אים באַהאַלטן	**him!**
	Got zol im bentshn mit dray mentshn—
	eyner zol im haltn, der tsveyter zol im
	shpaltn un der driter zol im bahaltn! IB
גאָט זאָל אים העלפֿן ער זאָל אַלצדינג	**God help him to see everything**
זען מיט די אויגן און ניט האָבן פֿאַר	**with his eyes and not have enough**
וואָס צו קויפֿן!	**money to buy!**
	Got zol im helfn er zol altsding zen mit
	di oygn un nit hobn far vos tsu
	koyfn! AC
גאָט זאָל אים שיקן פֿון די צען מכּות די	**May God send him the choicest of**
בעסטע!	**the ten plagues!**
	Got zol im shikn fun di tsen makes di
	beste! AC
גויים זאָלן האָבן צו טאָן מיט ייִדן!	**May Goyim have to deal with Jews!**
	Goyim zoln hobn tsu ton mit yidn! AC
הונטס יאָרן און ציין זאָלסטו האָבן!	**May you have dog's years and dog's**
	teeth!
	Hunts yorn un tseyn zolstu hobn! NS

אין די זומערדיקע טעג זאָל ער זיצן
שבעה און אין די ווינטערדיקע נעכט
זאָל אים רייַסן אויף די ציין!

**May he sit in mourning during the
days of summer, and may he suffer
toothache during the long winter
nights!**
*In di zumerike teg zol er zitsn shive un
in di vinterdike nekht zol im raysn oyf
di tseyn!* NS

כאַפֿט אים דער רוח!

The Devil take him!
Khapt im der ru'ekh! P

קאָפֿ אין דר'ערד, פֿיס אין קלויסטער!

**Head in the ground, feet in the
church!**
Kop in dr'erd, fis in kloyster! NS

לאַכן זאָל ער מיט יאַשטשערקעס!

May he laugh with tears in his ears!
[May he laugh out of the wrong side
of his mouth]
Lakhn zol er mit yashtsherkes! AC

מייַנע שׂונאים זאָלן האָבן און באַגראָבן!

May my enemies bear and bury!
[That is, children]
*Mayne sonim zoln hobn un
bagrobn!* NS

מען זאָל שוין נאָך אים אַ נאָמען געבן!

**May a child soon be named after
him!**
[Traditionally, babies are named
after deceased relatives]
*Men zol shoyn nokh im a nomen
gebn!* NS

מיט בלוט, מיט גליק, מיט שטריק, מיט
בענדעלעך געבונדן!

**With blood, with luck, with rope,
and with fetters bound!**
*Mit blut, mit glik, mit shtrik, mit
bendelekh gebundn!* AC

ניט דערלעבן זאָל ער עלטער צו ווערן!

May he not live to grow any older!
Nit derlebn zol er elter tsu vern! P

אויף דעם בלאָטער אַ פּרישטש און אויף
דער מכה אַ בלאָטער!

On the boil a blister, and on the blister a pimple!
Oyf dem bloter a prishtsh un oyf der make a bloter! NS

אויסקרענקען זאָל ער דער מאַמעס
מילך!

May he sicken and spew forth his mother's milk!
Oyskrenken zol er der mames milkh! IB

רעדן זאָל ער פֿון היץ!

May he speak from delirium!
Redn zol er fun hits! IB

שרײַבן זאָל מען אים רעצעפּטן!

May prescriptions be written for him!
Shraybn zol men im retseptn! IB

צו געזונט, צו לעבן, צו קורצע יאָר!

To health, to life, to few years!
[A play on words of a traditional greeting]
Tsu gezunt, tsu lebn, tsu kurtse yor! AC

וויפֿל יאָר ער איז געגאַנגען אויף די פֿיס
זאָל ער גיין אויף די הענט און די
איבעריקע זאָל ער זיך שאַרן אויפֿן הינטן

As many years as he walked on his feet may he walk on his hands, and the rest may he slither on his behind!
Vifl yor er iz gegangen oyf di fis zol er geyn oyf di hent un di iberike zol er zikh sharn oyfn hintn! NS

ווינען זאָל ער אין אַ פּאַלאַץ, דער
פּאַלאַץ זאָל האָבן הונדערט צימערן, אין
יעדן צימער זאָל שטיין אַ גאָלדענע בעט
און דער קדחת זאָל אים וואַרפֿן פֿון איין
בעט ביזן אַנדערן!

May he live in a palace; the palace
should have a hundred rooms; in
every room should stand a golden
bed, and may he suffer convulsions
and be tossed from one bed to
another!

*Voynen zol er in a palats, der palats
zol hobn hundert tsimern, in yedn
tsimer zol shteyn a goldene bet un der
kadokhes zol im varfn fun eyn bet bizn
andern!* AC

זײַן נאָמען זאָל אַהיימקומען!

May his name come home!
[That is, without him]
Zayn nomen zol aheymkumen! IB

זאָל דער זייגער בײַ אים קריכן, דאָס
האַרץ לויפֿן, די גאַל איבערגיין, די ווײַב
אַנטלויפֿן און דער נאָז שטענדיק רינען!

May his clock run slow, his heart
fast, his bile over, his wife away,
and his nose always!

*Zol der zeyger bay im krikhn, dos harts
loyfn, di gal ibergeyn, di vayb antloyfn,
un der noz shtendik rinen!* NS

זאָל ער פֿאַרשפּאָרן פֿון פֿאָרנט און פֿון
הינטן!

May he be spared from the front
and from the rear!
[Refers to urination and defecation]
*Zol er farshporn fun fornt un fun
hintn!* NS

זאָל ער קרענקען אין נחת!

May he sicken from pleasure!
Zol er krenken in nakhes! AC

זאָל ער זיך אַזוי מאַטערן מיטן טויט ווי
איך מאַטער זיך מיטן לעבן!

May he suffer from death as much
as I suffer from life!
*Zol er zikh azoy matern mitn toyt vi
ikh mater zikh mitn lebn!* AC

זָאל אים וואָקסן ציבעלעך פֿון פּופּיק! May onions sprout from his belly button!

Zol im vaksn tsibelekh fun pupik! AC

זאָלסט זײַן ווי אַן אויוון – ווען דער קאָפּ ברענט זאָל דיר דער בויך גליען! May you be like a stove—when your head burns, may your belly glow!

Zolst zayn vi an oyvn—ven der kop brent zol dir der boykh gli'en! AC

CUSTOM

אַ מינהג ברעכט אַ דין Custom supercedes law

A minheg brekht a din AC

דער אָקס איז געוווינט צום חלף The ox is accustomed to the knife

Der oks iz gevoynt tsum khalef NS

ער איז אַן אָנגענומענער מענטש – ווּ ער קומט אָן נעמט מען אים פֿאַרן קאָלנער He is a customary caller—wherever he goes he's tossed out by the collar!

Er iz an ongenumener mentsh—vu er kumt on nemt men im farn kolner! AC

מען זאָל ניט געפּרוווט ווערן צו וואָס מען קען געוווינט ווערן May one never be tested as to what one can endure

Men zol nit gepruft vern tsu vos men ken gevoynt vern P

צו גוטס געוווינט מען זיך גיך צו One quickly becomes accustomed to the good

Tsu guts gevoynt men zikh gikh tsu AC

ווען מען קומט אין אַ שטאָט זאָל מען נאָכפֿאָלגן זייערע מינהגים When you come to a town, follow its customs

Ven men kumt in a shtot zol men nokhfolgn zeyere minhogim AC

ווי די שול אַזוי שפרינגט מען קדוש

As the congregation, so the custom
*Vi di shul, azoy shpringt men
koydesh* NS

ווי עס מאַכט זיך איז רעכט

The way things go is rightly so
Vi es makht zikh iz rekht NS

Cynicism

אַ ריין האַרץ איז בײַ אַ מת

A pure heart is found on a corpse
A reyn harts iz bay a mes NS

אַז מען וויל זיך העננגען דאַרף מען נעמען
אַ הויכן בוים

**If you want to hang yourself—pick
a tall tree**
*Az men vil zikh hengen darf men
nemen a hoykhn boym* NS

פֿריער זײַנען די מלאכים אַרומגעגאַנגען
אויף דער ערד, הײַנט זײַנען זיי אין הימל
אויך ניטאָ

**Once angels walked on earth;
nowadays, they're not found in
heaven, either**
*Fri'er zaynen di malokhim
arumgegangen oyf der erd, haynt
zaynen zey in himl oykh nito* NS

ווען אַ טויזנט חסידים זאָלן זיך דרייען
אַרום אַ קלאָץ וואָלט עס אויך באַוויזן
נסים

**If a thousand Hassidim circled a
block of wood, it too would
perform miracles**
*Ven a toyznt khsidim zoln zikh dreyen
arum a klots volt es oykh bavizn
nisim* AC

זײַ אַ מענטש וועסטו זיצן פורים אין
סוכה

**Be honorable and you'll sit in the
Succah on Purim**
*Zay a mentsh vestu zitsn purim in
suke* AC

DANGER

אַז די נאַסע ביימער ברענען וואָס זאָלן
די טרוקענע זאָגן?

If the wet trees burn, what should the dry ones say?
Az di nase beymer brenen vos zoln di trukene zogn? NS

אַז מען אַנטלויפֿט פֿון אַ ברענענדיק הויז
שטעלט מען זיך ניט אָפּ קושן די מזוזה

When you flee a burning house you don't stop to kiss the mezzuzah
Az men antloyft fun a brenendik hoyz shtelt men zikh nit op kushn di mezuze AC

מיט פֿרעמדע הענט איז גוט פֿײַער צו
שאַרן

With someone else's hands it's good to stoke the fire
Mit fremde hent iz gut fayer tsu sharn P

DEATH

אַ לעבן אין נויט איז אַלץ בעסער ווי דער
שענסטער טויט

Better a life of trial than death in the finest style
A lebn in noyt iz alts beser vi der shenster toyt NS

אַלץ דרייט זיך אַרום ברויט און טויט

Everything revolves around being dead or fed
Alts dreyt zikh arum broyt un toyt NS

אַראָפ דער קאָפ, אַראָפ דער ווייטיק!

Off with the head, off with the ache!
Arop der kop, arop der veytik! NS

אַז מען זאָגט געשטאָרבן איז מען
באַגראָבן

If they say you're dead, you're buried
Az men zogt geshtorbn iz men bagrobn AC

בעסער אַ זיסער טויט איידער אַ ביטער
לעבן

Better a sweet death than a bitter life
Beser a ziser toyt eyder a biter lebn NS

דעם מענטשנס יאָרן פֿליען איבער ווי אַ
חלום און כאַפט מען זיך אויף ליגט מען
גאָר אין דר'ערד

A person's years fly by like a dream, and when you wake up, you're dead and buried
Dem mentshns yorn fli'en iber vi a kholem un khapt men zikh oyf ligt men gor in dr'erd NS

דער מלאך-המוות, קלאַפֿט ניט ביי דער
טיר

The Angel of Death doesn't knock at the door
Der malekhamoves klapt nit bay der tir NS

דער מלאך-המוות שטעכט און בלייבט
גערעכט

The Angel of Death slaughters and is always right
Der malekhamoves shtekht un blaybt gerekht IB

דער 'וויאָ' העלפֿט ניט אַז די פֿערד זיינען
פגרות

"Giddyap" won't help if the horses are corpses
Der 'v'yo' helft nit az di ferd zaynen p'gires NS

עס איז ניטאָ קיין שלעכטע מוטער און
קיין גוטער טויט

There's no such thing as a bad mother or a good death
Es iz nito keyn shlekhte muter un keyn guter toyt NS

פֿאַראַן טויזנטער קראַנקייטן און נאָר
איין טויט

There are thousands of diseases, but only one death
Faran toyznter krankaytn un nor eyn toyt AC

פֿאַרזאָרג דאָס לעבן און געדענק דעם
טויט

Provide for life, but remember death
Farzorg dos lebn un gedenk dem toyt NS

פֿון וואָס מען רעדט קומט מען אַלץ
אַרויס אויפֿן טויט

No matter what you talk about, you still end up dead
Fun vos men ret kumt men alts aroys oyfn toyt IB

קיינער ווייסט ניט וועמענס מאָרגן עס
וועט זײַן

No one knows whose tomorrow it will be
Keyner veyst nit vemens morgn es vet zayn P

כּל-זמן עס רירט זיך אַן אבֿר קלערט מען
ניט פֿון קבֿר

As long as one limb stirs, thoughts of the grave are deferred
Kolzman es rirt zikh an eyver, klert men nit fun keyver NS

גאָלד און זילבער לאָזט מען שטיין – אַז
מען רופֿט מוז מען גיין

Gold and silver must stay—when called, you must away
Gold und zilber lozt men sheyn—az men ruft muz men geyn IF

קיין מענטש גייט ניט פֿאַרלאָרן ביז עס
ענדיקן זיך ניט זײַנע יאָרן

No person is done until his time has come
Keyn mentsh geyt nit farlorn biz es endikn zikh nit zayne yorn NS

מען שטאַרבט אָן אַ דאָקטער אויך	**One can die even without a doctor** *Men shtarbt on a dokter oykh* AC
מען זאָל גאָרניט דערלעבן צו שטאַרבן	**One shouldn't live long enough to die** *Men zol gornit derlebn tsu shtarbn* NS
מיטן מלאך-המוות טרייבט מען ניט קיין קאַטאָוועס	**Don't make jokes with the Angel of Death** *Mitn malekhamoves traybt men nit keyn katoves* IB
ניפֿטר-פֿיפֿטער, אַ לעבן מאַכט ער?	**Dead-shmed; is he earning a living?** *Nifter-pifter, a lebn makht er?* P
נאָכן טויט ווערט מען חשובֿ	**After death you become honorable** *Nokhn toyt vert men khoshev* AC
אויף דער מצבֿה זייַנען אַלע ייִדן שיין	**According to the gravestones, all Jews were honorable** *Oyf der matseyve zaynen ale yidn sheyn* NS
אויף מתים טאָר מען זיך ניט פֿאַרלאָזן	**Don't rely on the dead** *Oyf meysim tor men zikh nit farlozn* NS
שטאַרבן שטאַרבט מען נאָר איין מאָל	**You only die once** *Shtarbn shtarbt men nor eyn mol* P
שטאַרבן האָט מען אַלע מאָל ציַיט	**There's always time for dying** *Shtarbn hot men ale mol tsayt* NS
שטאַרבט מען יונגערהייט איז עס אויף דער עלטער ווי געפֿונען	**If you die young you won't have to worry about old age** *Shtarbt men yungerheyt iz es oyf der elter vi gefunen* NS

96

צום שטאַרבן דאַרף מען קיין לוח ניט
האָבן

You don't need a calendar to die
Tsum shtarbn darf men keyn lu'ekh nit hobn NS

צוויי מאָל שטאַרבט מען ניט

You don't die twice
Tsvey mol shtarbt men nit P

יעדער מענטש טאַנצט זיך זײַן טאַנץ און
אַלע קומען צום זעלבן טאַנץ

Everyone dances his own dance, and ends up with the same dance
Yeder mentsh tantst zikh zayn tants un ale kumen tsum zelbn tants AC

יעדער מענטש וווייסט אַז ער וועט
שטאַרבן אָבער קיינער וויל עס ניט
גלייבן

Everyone knows you must die, but nobody wants to believe it
Yeder mentsh veyst az er vet shtarbn ober keyner vil es nit gleybn AC

זיכער איז מען נאָר מיטן טויט

Death is the only certainty
Zikher iz men nor mitn toyt P

זאָל איך אזוי לעבן ווי איך וויל שטאַרבן!

I should live so long if I want to die!
Zol ikh azoy lebn vi ikh vil shtarbn! AC

BURIAL

אַ מת פֿון בית־חיים טראָגט מען ניט
צוריק

A corpse is not carried back from the cemetery
A mes fun beyskhayim trogt men nit tsurik IB

אַ ווײַב באַגראָבן איז ווי ציבעלעס
עסן – די אויגן וויינען אָבער דאָס האַרץ
לאַכט

Burying a wife is like eating onions—the eyes weep but the heart rejoices
A vayb bagrobn iz vi tsibeles esn—di oygn veynen ober dos harts lakht NS

אַז מען זאָגט געשטאָרבן איז מען
באַגראָבן

If they say you're dead, you're busied

Az men zogt geshtorbn iz men bagrobn AC

בעסער צו לעבן און וייניק האָבן
איידער צו זיין אין גאַנצן באַגראָבן

Better alive with little around than to be buried in the ground

Beser tsu lebn un veynik hobn eyder tsu zayn in gantsn bagrobn NS

מען קען אומעטום באַגראָבן ווערן

You can be buried anywhere

Men ken umetum bagrobn vern AC

שטאַרבן איז נאָך ווי עס איז אָבער דאָס
אַריינלייגן אין דר'ערד דאָס באַגראָבט אַ
מענטשן

Dying isn't so bad, it's laying the person in the ground that really buries him

Shtarbn iz nokh vi es iz, ober dos araynleygn in dr'erd dos bagrobt a mentshn NS

DEBT

בעסער טאָן טובֿות איידער זיין שולדיק
חובֿות

Better to do favors than to owe debts

Beser ton toyves eyder zayn shuldik khoyves NS

די האָר פֿונעם קאָפּ זיינען נישט זיינע

Even the hairs on his head aren't his own

Di hor funem kop zaynen nisht zayne IF

פֿאַר דער קלענסטער טובֿה ווערט מען אַ
בעל-חובֿ

For the smallest favor you become a debtor

Far der klenster toyve vert men a bal-khoyv NS

חובֿות זײַנען ניט קיין טובֿות
A debt is not a good bet
Khoyves zaynen nit keyn toyves IB

מיט טרערן (אַ קרעכץ) באַצאָלט מען ניט קיין חובֿ
You can't pay off a debt with tears (a sigh)
Mit trern (a khrekhts) batsolt men nit keyn khoyv AC

אויף 'וואָלט איך' און 'זאָלט איך' באָרגט מען ניט קיין געלט
Don't lend money on "I would have" or "I should have"
Oyf 'volt ikh' un 'zolt ikh' borgt men nit keyn gelt NS

וווֹיל איז דעם וואָס האָט ניט קיין געלט צו באָרגן זײַנע פֿרײַנד, ער שאַפֿט זיך ניט קיין שונאים
Happy is he who has no money to lend his friends, he won't make any enemies
Voyl iz dem vos hot nit keyn gelt tsu borgn zayne fraynd, er shaft zikh nit keyn sonim NS

DECEPTION

דער גלײַכסטער וועג איז פֿול מיט שטיינער
The smoothest road is full of stones
Der glaykhster veg iz ful mit shteyner NS

דער שפּיגל נאַרט קיינעם ניט אָפּ נאָר דעם מיאוסן
The mirror deceives none but the ugly
Der shpigl nart keynem nit op nor dem mi'esn NS

גיי רעד זיך אײַן אַ קינד אין בויך!
Go convince yourself you're pregnant!
Gey red zikh ayn a kind in boykh! P

לייג זיך ניט קיין פֿייגעלעך אין בוזעם!

Don't nestle little birds in your bosom!
Leyg zikh nit keyn feygelekh in buzem! IB

DEFECTS

אַ מויד מיט אַ הויקער מאַכט זאָרג ערבֿ ובוקר

A girl with a blight makes worry day and night
A moyd mit a hoyker makht zorg erev vaboyker IB

אַ צעבראָכענער כּלי קען מען ניט גאַנץ מאַכן

A broken vessel can't be mended
A tsebrokhene keyle ken men nit gants makhn AC

עס וועט ניט שאַטן צום שידוך

It won't interfere with the wedding plans
Es vet nit shatn tsum shidekh P

איבער אַ צוויקל מאַכט מען ניט קאַליע קיין העמד

Over one flaw you don't discard the whole shirt
Iber a tsvikl makht men nit kalye keyn hemd NS

חסרונות זעט מען נאָר ביַי יענעם

Flaws are found only in others
Khasroynes zet men nor bay yenem P

מער חסרון – מער נדן

More blemish—more dowry
Mer khisorn—mer nadn AC

צוליב צוויי פֿענצטער מאַכט מען ניט חורבֿ דעם גאַנצן בנין

Over two faulty windows you don't raze the entire structure
Tsulib tsvey fenster makht men nit khorev dem gantsn binyen NS

DESTINY

אַ קאַץ קען אויך קאַליע מאַכן

Even a cat can spoil your plans
A kats ken oykh kalye makhn P

אַז עס איז באַשערט אַ צרה קומט עס
אַליין אין שטוב אַרײַן

If troubles are destined, they arrive by themselves
Az es iz bashert a tsore kumt es aleyn in shtub arayn IB

אַז עס איז באַשערט איז קיין חכמה ניט

If it's fated, brains won't help
Az es iz bashert iz keyn khokhme nit AC

אַז גאָט וויל, מאַכט קאָמעץ בית באָ

If God wills it, it's as easy as ABC
Az got vil, makht kometz beyz bo P

דאָס ברויט פאַלט שטענדיק מיט דער
פּוטער אַראָפּ

Bread always falls buttered-side down
Dos broyt falt shtendik mit der puter arop P

ערשט געלעבט, שוין געשטאָרבן —
ערשט געשטאָרבן, שוין באַגראָבן

Just now alive, already dead—hardly dead, already buried
Ersht gelebt, shoyn geshtorbn—ersht geshtorbn, shoyn bagrobn AC

פֿאַר איינעם אַ טובה, פֿאַרן צווייטן אַן
אומגליק

For one a favor, for another a misfortune
Far eynem a toyve, farn tsveytn an umglik NS

גאָט באַשערט דעם טרינקער זײַן ווײַן,
דעם שפּינער זײַן פֿלאַקס און דעם נגיד
אַ ברית אויף יום-כיפּור

God destines the drinker his wine, the spinner his flax, and the rich man a feast on Yom Kippur
Got bashert dem trinker zayn vayn, dem shpiner zayn flaks un dem noged a bris oyf yomkiper NS

קיינער וויסט ניט וואָס דער מאָרגן
ברענגט

No one knows what tomorrow will bring
Keyner veyst nit vos der morgn brengt P

מען קען ביַים ברעג אויך דערטרונקען
ווערן

One can drown even close to shore
Men ken baym breg oykh dertrunken vern NS

צופֿאַל איז אַמאָל אַ גוטער גאַסט און
אַמאָל אַ שווערע לאַסט

Sometimes chance brings a welcome guest or a troublesome pest
Tsufal iz amol a guter gast un amol a shvere last NS

ווער עס דאַרף הענגען ווערט ניט
דערטרונקען

Whoever is destined to hang won't drown
Ver es darf hengen vert nit dertrunken NS

וואָס עס וועט זיַין מיט דער כלה וועט
זיַין מיט אונדז אַלע

Whatever happens to the bride will happen on every side
Vos es vet zayn mit der kale vet zayn mit undz ale NS

וואָס מער פֿלייש, אַלץ מער ווערעם

The more flesh—the more worms
Vos mer fleysh, alts mer verem AC

DISBELIEF

דעם ליגנערס נאמנות איז ווי דעם
מוסרס רחמנות

The liar's pledge is like the informer's pity
Dem ligners nemones iz vi dem musers rakhmones IB

די קו איז געפֿלויגן איבערן דאַך און
געלייגט אַן איי!

The cow flew over the roof and laid an egg!
Di ku iz gefloygn ibern dakh un geleygt an ey! P

ער האָט דאָס ביַי זיַין מאַמען אין
קאָמפּעט ניט געזען!

He didn't see that when his mother
gave birth to him!
*Er hot dos bay zayn mamen in kimpet
nit gezen!* AC

עס הייבט זיך ניט אָן, עס לאָזט זיך ניט
אויס!

It didn't start, it didn't finish!
*Es heybt zikh nit on, es lozt zikh nit
oys!* P

עס איז ניט דאָס דאָרף און ניט די
קרעטשמע!

It's not the town and not the tavern!
[It's neither fish nor fowl]
Es iz nit dos dorf un nit di kretshme! IB

עס קלעבט זיך ניט אַ וואָרט צו אַ
וואָרט!

One word doesn't stick to another
Es klebt zikh nit a vort tsu a vort P

עס וועט דויערן פֿון היַינט ביז מאָרגן!

It will last from today until
tomorrow!
Es vet doyern fun haynt biz morgn! P

גאָטס נסים – דריַי לאָקשנטעפּלעך אין
איינעם!

God's miracle—three noodle pots
together!
*Gots nisim—dray lokshnteplekh in
eynem!* IB

גאָטס ווונדער – אַ פּץ מאַכט קינדער!

God's miracle—a prick makes
children!
Gots vinder—a pots makht kinder! WZ

אדם נאַקעט, חוה באָרוועס!

Adam naked, Eve barefoot!
Odem naket, khave borves! IB

פּורים איז דאָ לאָקשן אין באָד אויך!

On Purim you get noodles at the
bathhouse too!
Purim iz do lokshn in bod oykh! IF

DIVORCE

אַז אַ גענעטער מאַן האָט חתונה מיט אַ
גענעטער פֿרוי ליגן פֿיר אויפֿן בעט

When a divorced man marries a divorced woman there are four in the bed
Az a gegeter man hot khasene mit a gegeter froy lign fir oyfn bet AC

מע שלאָפֿט פֿיר אין אַ בעט

They sleep four in a bed
Me shloft fir in a bet LMF

צו אַ חתונה גייט מען, צו אַ גט לויפֿט
מען

To the wedding one walks, to the divorce one runs
Tsu a khasene geyt men, tsu a get loyft men IB

DOCTORS

אַ דאָקטער און אַ קבֿרות-מאַן זײַנען
שותפֿים

Doctors and gravediggers are partners
A dokter un a kvures-man zaynen shutfim NS

אַ רבי און אַ דאָקטער ווערן רײַך נאָר פֿון
ווײַבער

Rabbis and doctors get rich from women
A rebe un a dokter vern raykh nor fun vayber NS

אַז די דאָקטוירים נעמען זיך באַראָטן
קען דער חולה דערווײַל אַוועקשטאַרבן

When doctors start consulting, meanwhile the patient dies
Az di doktoyrim nemen zikh baratn ken der khoyle dervayl avekshtarbn AC

אַז מען דערזעט דעם דאָקטער דערמאָנט
מען זיך אַז מ'איז קראַנק

At sight of the doctor you remember you're ill
Az men derzet dem dokter dermont men zikh az m'iz krank AC

אײן רופֿה מאַכט אַרבעט פֿאַר אַ צווייטן

One doctor makes work for another
Eyn royfe makht arbet far a tsveytn NS

פֿרעג ניט בײַם רופֿה, פֿרעג בײַם חולה

Ask the patient, not the doctor
Freg nit baym royfe, freg baym khoyle P

מען האָט מער מורה פֿאַרן דאָקטער ווי פֿאַר קרענק

The doctor is more to be feared than the disease
Men hot mer moyre farn dokter vi far krenk AC

מיט אַ גרויסן רופֿה גייט אַ גרויסער מלאך

A great doctor is accompanied by a great angel
Mit a groysn royfe geyt a groyser malekh AC

DREAMS

דאָס לעבן איז ניט מער ווי אַ חלום אָבער וועק מיך ניט אויף

Life is no more than a dream, but don't wake me up
Dos lebn iz nit mer vi a kholem ober vek mikh nit oyf NS

קרעפּלעך אין חלום איז ניט קיין קרעפּלעך נאָר אַ חלום

Dumplings in a dream are not dumplings, but a dream
Kreplekh in kholem iz nit keyn kreplekh nor a kholem P

נאָר אין חלום זײַנען מערן ווי בערן

Only in dreams are carrots as big as parrots
Nor in kholem zaynen mern vi bern IB

וואָס טויג מיר דער שיינער חלום ווען דער פֿרימאָרגן איז קאַלט?

What's the use of a beautiful dream when the dawn is chilly?
Vos toyg mir der sheyner kholem ven der frimorgn iz kalt? NS

EFFORT

אַז מען שפּאַרט זיך אײַן פֿירט מען אויס   **If you're determined, you will succeed**
Az men shpart zikh ayn firt men oys   P

גייט עס, גייט עס, קוועטשן זיך דאַרף מען ניט   **If it works, don't force it**
Geyt es, geyt es, kvetshn zikh darf men nit   AC

מע דאַרף זיך אונטערגאַרטלען   **You have to gird yourself**
Me darf zikh untergartlen   AC

EMISSARIES

אַ קאַץ שיקט מען ניט נאָך פּוטער און אַ הונט נאָך פֿלייש   **You don't send a cat for butter or a dog for meat**
A kats shikt men nit nokh puter un a hunt nokh fleysh   NS

בעסער גיין אַליין איידער שיקן יענעם   **Better to go yourself than to send someone else**
Beser geyn aleyn eyder shikn yenem   P

מען שיקט דעם שמשׂ און מען גייט אַליין **Send the sexton and you end up going yourself**
Men shikt dem shames un men geyt aleyn NS

EMOTIONS

אַ טשייניק װאָס קאָכט לויפֿט איבער **A boiling kettle overflows**
A tshaynik vos kokht loyft iber AC

די טױערן פֿון טרערן זײַנען קיין מאָל ניט פֿאַרשלאָסן **The gates of tears are never closed**
Di toyern fun trern zaynen keyn mol nit farshlosn NS

עס איז ניט אַזױ טײַער דער געשאַנק װי דער געדאַנק **The intent means more than the present**
Es iz nit azoy tayer der geshank vi der gedank NS

פֿון רחמנות און פֿון פּחדנות קען מען זיך ניט אױסהײלן **There's no cure for compassion or cowardice**
Fun rakhmones un fun pakhdones ken men zikh nit oys'heyln NS

שטיל װאַסער גראָבט טיף **Still waters run deep**
Shtil vaser grobt tif IB

ENDS

אַז דער סוף איז גוט איז אַלץ גוט **All's well that ends well**
Az der sof iz gut iz alts gut P

דעם לעצטן בײַסן די הינט **The last one gets bitten by the dog**
Dem letstn baysn di hint NS

אָפּגעטאָן איז אָפּגעטאָן **What's done is done**
Opgeton iz opgeton P

ENDURANCE

אַז מען קען ניט איבערהאַרן דאָס
שלעכטע קען מען דאָס גוטע ניט
דערלעבן

If you can't endure the bad, you won't survive to see the good
Az men ken nit iberharn dos shlekhte ken men dos gute nit derlebn AC

דער קאָפּ קען ניט איַינזאַפן וואָס דער
הינטן קען ניט אויסהאַלטן

The head can't absorb what the seat can't endure
Der kop ken nit aynzapn vos der hintn ken nit oys'haltn P

מען זאָל אים אַפֿילו ברענען און בראָטן!

Even if he should be burned and roasted!
[That is, at the stake]
Men zol im afile brenen un brotn! P

מיט געדולד שעפּט מען אויס אַ קוואַל

With patience you can drain a brook
Mit geduld shept men oys a kval P

ניט אין איין טאָג איז דער בית-המיקדש
געבויט געוואָרן

The Holy Temple wasn't built in just one day
Nit in eyn tog iz der beysamigdesh geboyt gevorn IB

ווער עס קען קיין פּולווער ניט שמעקן
דער זאָל אין דער מלחמה ניט גיין

If you can't stand the smell of gunshot, don't wage war
Var es ken keyn pulver nit shmekn der zol in der milkhome nit geyn IB

ENEMIES

אַ סך המנס און נאָר איין פּורים!

So many Hamans and only one Purim
A sakh homens un nor eyn purim! P

אַלע אונדזערע שׂונאים זאָלן האָבן איין אויג, איין קינד און איין העמד

All our enemies should have only one eye, one child, and one shirt
Ale undzere sonim zoln hobn eyn oyg, eyn kind un eyn hemd NS

אַז מען כאַפּט אַ פּאַטש באַקומט מען אַ שׂונא דערצו

If you get slapped, you acquire an enemy as well
Az men khapt a patsh bakumt men a soyne dertsu NS

בעסער אַ גוטער שׂונא איידער אַ שלעכטער פֿרײַנד

Better a good enemy than a bad friend
Beser a guter soyne eyder a shlekhter fraynd NS

די גרעסטע שׂונאים ווערן די נאָענסטע מחותנים

The worst enemies become the closest-in-laws
Di greste sonim vern di no'enste mekhutonim AC

עס איז אַ מיצווה אַ חזיר אַ האָר אַרויסצורײַסן

It's a good deed to pull a hair out of a pig
Es iz a mitsve a khazer a hor aroystsuraysn IB

איידער מען דערלעבט די נחמה קען אַרויס די נשמה

Before comfort comes, the soul succumbs
Eyder men derlebt di nekhome ken aroys di neshome NS

איין שׂונא איז איבעריק און הונדערט פֿרײַנט ניט גענוג

One enemy is superfluous, and a hundred friends not enough
Eyn soyne iz iberik un hundert fraynd nit genug AC

גוטע פֿרײַנד זאָלן זיך מחיה זײַן, שונאים
זאָלן פּלאַצן

**Friends should have pleasure,
enemies should burst**
*Gute fraynd zoln zikh mekhaye zayn,
sonim zoln platsn* AC

מײַנע שונאים זאָלן ניט אַלט ווערן!

May my enemies never grow old!
Mayne sonim zoln nit alt vern! AC

נאָך נעילה ווערט מען ווידער ברוגז

**After the Day of Atonement is done,
enmity is again begun**
Nokh nile vert men vider broyges AC

שונאים קענען ניט טאָן דאָס וואָס דער
מענטש טוט זיך אַליין

**Enemies can't do the harm a person
does to himself**
*Sonim kenen nit ton dos vos der
mentsh tut zikh aleyn* P

וואָס דער מענטש טוט זיך אַליין וואָלטן
אים צען שונאים ניט געטאָן

**What a person is capable of doing
to himself, ten enemies couldn't do**
*Vos der mentsh tut zikh aleyn voltn im
tsen sonim nit geton* P

ENVY

אַז מען האָט ברויט וויל מען קוילעטש

**If you have bread, you want the
holiday loaf**
Az men hot broyt vil men koyletsh AC

דעם ייִדן שאַט ניט אַזוי זײַן אייגענער
דלות ווי דעם אַנדערנס עשירות

**A Jew isn't bothered so much by his
own poverty as by another's wealth**
*Dem yidn shat nit azoy zayn eygener
dales vi dem anderns ashires* NS

פֿון קינאה ווערט שינאה

Envy breeds hatred
Fun kine vert sine IB

אין יענעמס מויל צײלט מען ניט די צײן

Don't count the teeth in someone else's mouth

In yenems moyl tseylt men nit di tseyn AC

EQUALITY

אַ מאַן װי אַ מויז און אַ װײב װי אַ הויז
איז נאָך ניט גלײך

A man like a mouse and a wife like a house, they're still not equal

A man vi a moyz un a vayb vi a hoyz iz nokh nit glaykh IB

בײמער אין װאָלד זײַנען אויך ניט גלײך

Trees in the forest are also not identical

Beymer in vald zaynen oykh nit glaykh NS

די זון שײַנט גלײַך פֿאַר אָרעם און רײַך

The sun shines the same for rich and for poor

Di zun shaynt glaykh far orem un raykh NS

אין באָד זיך צו שעמען איז ניטאָ פֿאַר װעמען

In the bathhouse no shame—everyone's the same

In bod zikh tsu shemen iz nito far vemen NS

אָרעם און רײַך זײַנען אין קבֿר גלײַך

Rich and poor are equal in the grave

Orem un raykh zaynen in keyver glaykh IB

ERROR

אַ געלער מאַכט ניט קײן פֿעלער

Those with red hair never err

A geler makht nit keyn feler NS

111

אַז דער קלוגער פֿײלט פֿײלט ער וויַיט

When a clever person makes a mistake, it's a big one
Az der kluger feylt, feylt er vayt NS

פֿון דרוק פֿעלער קריגט מען האַרץ פֿעלער

From a printing error you get heart failure
Fun druk feler krigt men harts feler AC

טויטע מאַכן ניט קיין טעותים

The dead don't make mistakes
Toyte makhn nit keyn to'isim IB

ETHICS

אַ שלעכטער געוויסן ווערט פֿון זיך אַליין געביסן

A bad conscience gnaws away at itself
A shlekhter gevisn vert fun zikh aleyn gebisn NS

אַז מען גייט גליַיך פֿאַלט מען ניט

If you walk the straight path, you won't stumble
Az men geyt glaykh falt men nit P

אַז מען האָט אַ געהאַנגענעם אין דער משפחה זאָגט מען ניט: הענג מיר אויף דעם מאַנטל

If a member of the family was hanged, don't ask anyone to hang up your coat
Az men hot a gehangenem in der mishpokhe zogt men nit: heng mir oyf dem mantl AC

בעסער אַ וויַיטיק אין האַרץ איידער אַ חרפה אין פנים

Better pain in your heart than shame thrown in your face
Beser a veytik in harts eyder a kharpe in ponim IB

בעסער צו שטאַרבן שטייענדיק איידער צו לעבן אויף די קני

Better to die upright than to live on one's knees
Beser tsu shtarbn shteyendik eyder tsu lebn oyf di k'ni NS

דער מענטש האָט צוויי אויגן, צוויי
אויערן און נאָר איין מויל

A human being has two eyes, two ears, but only one mouth
Der mentsh hot tsvey oygn, tsvey oyern un nor eyn moyl NS

די גאַנצע וועלט איז פֿול מיט שדים,
טרײַב זיי כאָטש פֿון זיך אַרוס

The world is full of demons; at least drive them out of yourself
Di gantse velt iz ful mit sheydim, trayb zey khotsh fun zikh aroys NS

ערלעך איז שווערלעך

Straight is a weight
Erlekh iz shverlekh P

גאונים פֿעלן ניט אָבער כאַראַקטער איז
אַ ריכטיקער חפֿץ

There's no lack of genius, but character is a rare article
Geyonim feln nit ober kharakter iz a rikhtiker kheyfets AC

מיט פֿאַסטן אַליין איז מען נאָך קיין
צדיק ניט

From fasting alone you don't become a saint
Mit fastn aleyn iz men nokh keyn tsadik nit AC

ניט אַלע מאָל ווען מען איז שלעכט איז
מען אומגערעכט

Sometimes when one acts bad, one isn't necessarily a cad
Nit ale mol ven men iz shlekht iz men umgerekh NS

ניט קיין מיצווה, ניט קיין תּורה, מיט
וואָס זשע קומט מען פֿאַרן בורא?

No good deeds, no Torah education, how do you appear before the Lord of Creation?
Nit keyn mitsve, nit keyn toyre, mit vos zhe kumt men farn boyre? IB

אויף אַ וווּנד טאָר מען קיין זאַלץ ניט
שיטן

Don't pour salt on a wound
Oyf a vund tor men keyn zalts nit shitn P

רוף מיך בער נאָר יאָג מיך ניט אין וואַלד
אַרײַן

Call me a bear, but don't chase me into the woods
Ruf mikh ber nor yog mikh nit in vald arayn NS

שטופּ זיך ניט וווּ מען דאַרף ניט

Don't push yourself where you don't belong
Shtup zikh nit vu men darf nit P

צו ליב טאָן קאָסט תּמיד טײַער

Trying to please is always expensive
Tsu lib ton kost tomed tayer NS

טו ניט דאָס וואָס דו וועסט דאַרפֿן
געפֿינען אַ תירוץ

Don't do anything for which you will later need an excuse
Tu nit dos vos du vest darfn gefinen a terets AC

יענער האָט אויך אַ נשמה

The next person also has a soul
Yener hot oykh a neshome AC

זיבן זאַכן פֿאַרקירצן די יאָרן: כּעס און
קינאה, תּאווה און גאווה, רכילות, זונות
און לײדיקגײן

Seven things shorten life: anger and jealousy, lust and pride, gossip, debauchery, and idleness
Zibn zakhn farkirtsn di yorn: kas un kine, tayve un gayve, rekhiles, zoynes un leydikgeyn NS

EXAGGERATION

דער טײַוול איז ניט אַזוי שוואַרץ ווי מען
מאָלט אים

The devil is not as black as he's painted
Der tayvl iz nit azoy shvarts vi men molt im IB

פֿון אַ קלײנער פּעטרישקע מאַכט ער אַ
גאַנצן גאָרטן

From one little parsley he makes a whole garden!
Fun a kleyner petrishke makht er a gantsn gortn! IF

מען קען מאַכן דעם חלום גרעסער ווי די
נאַכט

You can make the dream longer
than the entire night
*Men ken makhn dem kholem greser vi
di nakht* IB

EXCESS

אַז דו ביסט אַ הונט זײַ זשע נישט קיין
חזיר אויך

Just because you're a dog, don't be a
pig, too
*Az du bist a hunt zay zhe nisht keyn
khazer oykh* P

בײַ אַ נאַר זײַנען הענט און פֿיס איבעריק

To a fool, hands and feet are
superfluous
Bay a nar zaynen hent un fis iberik P

בײַ אַ סך ניאַנקעס ווערט דאָס קינד
דערשטיקט

Too many nannies kill the baby
[Too many cooks spoil the broth]
*Bay a sakh ni'ankes vert dos kind
dershtikt* IB

ער קען אַ קייסער אָרעם מאַכן

He can impoverish even a tsar
Er ken a keyser orem makhn IF

פֿון איבערעסן חולה'ט מען מער ווי פֿון
ניט דערעסן

Overindulgence causes more
suffering than hunger
*Fun iberesn khoylet men mer vi fun nit
deresn* NS

מען דאַרף אים ווי אַ פֿינפֿטן צום וואָגן!

We need him like a fifth wheel on
the wagon!
Men darf im vi a finftn tsum vogn! IB

טויזנטער שיכּורן זיך אָן צום טויט
איידער איינער שטאַרבט פֿון דאָרשט

Thousands drink themselves to
death before one person dies of
thirst
*Toyznter shikern zikh on tsum toyt
eyder eyner shtarbt fun dorsht* AC

115

צו הערינג באַדאַרף מען ניט קיין זאַלץ
און צו גריוון ניט קיין שמאַלץ

You don't need salt for herring or fat for cracklings
Tsu hering badarf men nit keyn zalts
un tsu grivn nit keyn shmalts NS

צווישן אַ סך באָבעס ווערט דאָס קינד
זאַדישעט

Among a lot of old women the infant suffocates
Tsvishn a sakh bobes vert dos kind
zadishet IF

ווו עס איז איבעריק דאָרטן פֿעלט

Where there's too much, it's not enough
Vu es iz iberik dortn felt IB

EXCUSE

אַז אַ מויד איז מיאוס זאָגט זי אַז דער
שפיגל איז שולדיק

If a girl is ugly, she says the mirror is at fault
Az a moyd iz mi'es zogt zi az der shpigl
iz shuldik NS

דער מענטש איז דאָך נאָר אַ בשר-ודם

A human being is only flesh and blood
Der mentsh iz dokh nor a boser
v'dam IB

דער תירוץ איז: עבֿדים היינו!

The excuse is: "We were slaves"
[Refers to the Passover story]
Der terets iz: "ovadim hayinu" IB

עס איז אַ ראיה פֿון דער אַלטער באָבע
חיה

This testimony believe, it comes from great grandma Eve
Ez iz a raye fun der alter bobe khaye IB

גאָט, שענק מיר אַן אויסרייד!

God, give me a good excuse!
Got, shenk mir an oysreyd! IB

אָן קיין תירוץ איז גאָר קיין דרך-ארץ

Without an explanation there's no consideration
On keyn terets iz gor keyn derekh-eretz NS

טו ניט דאָס וואָס דו וועסט דאַרפֿן געפֿינען אַ תירוץ

Don't do that for which you'll need an excuse
Tu nit dos vos du vest darfn gefinen a terets AC

זאָל איך אזוי וויסן פֿון בייז ווי איך וייס וואָס בײַ מיר טוט זיך!

May evil befall me if I know what's really going on
Zol ikh azoy visn fun beyz vi ikh veys vos bay mir tut zikh! P

EXPECTATIONS

אַז מען קומט נאָך ירושה מוז מען אָפֿט באַצאָלן קבורה-געלט

If you come for the legacy, you may end up paying for the funeral
Az men kumt nokh yerushe muz men oft batsoln kvure-gelt NS

בעסער אַ האָן אין האַנט איידער אַן אָדלער אין הימל

Better a rooster in the hand than an eagle in the sky
Beser a hon in hant eyder an odler in himl NS

בעסער הײַנט אַן איי איידער מאָרגן אַן אָקס

Better an egg today than an ox tomorrow
Beser haynt an ey eyder morgn an oks NS

עס זאָל זיך ניט טרעפֿן וואָס קען זיך טרעפֿן

What could happen shouldn't happen
Es zol zikh nit trefn vos ken zikh trefn P

פֿון איטלעכער גוטע זאַך וויל מען אַ סך   **From good things to be got, we want a lot**
Fun itlekher gute zakh vil men a sakh NS

האָפֿן און האַרן מאַכן מענטשן צו נאַרן   **If you only wait and hope, you're a dope**
Hofn un harn makhn mentshn tsu narn AC

כּל-זמן מען לעבט וויל מען אַלץ האָבן   **As long as one lives, one wants everything**
Kolzman men lebt vil men alts hobn AC

מיט אַלע מעלות איז ניטאָ   **Nothing is perfect**
Mit ale mayles iz nito P

EXPERTS

אַלע ייִדן זײַנען חזנים אָבער מערסטנס זײַנען זיי הייזעריק   **Any Jew can be a cantor, but most of the time he's hoarse**
Ale yidn zaynen khazonim ober merstns zaynen zey heyzerik P

איין נאַר איז אַ מבֿין אויפֿן צווייטן   **One fool is an expert on another**
Eyn nar iz a meyvn oyfn tsveytn P

אויף גוטס איז איטלעכער אַ מבֿין   **Everyone is an expert on quality**
Oyf guts iz itlekher a meyvn IB

FALSEHOOD

אַ האַלבער אמת איז אַ גאַנצער ליגן

Half a truth is a whole lie
A halber emes iz a gantser lign NS

אַ ליגנער דאַרף האָבן אַ גוטן זכרון

A liar should have a good memory
A ligner darf hobn a gutn zikorn ACf

אַ ליגנער גלייבט מען ניט אפילו ווען ער
זאָגט דעם אמת

No one believes a liar even when he tells the truth
A ligner gleybt men nit afile ven er zogt dem emes AC

אַז מען קען קיין ליגן ניט זאָגן זאָל מען
קיין שדכן ניט זיַן

If you can't tell a lie don't become a matchmaker
Az men ken keyn lign nit zogn zol men keyn shadkhn nit zayn IB

דער אמת האָט פֿיס איז ער אַנטלאָפֿן,
דער שקר האָט קיין פֿיס ניט איז ער
געבליבן

The truth has legs and ran away; the lie has no legs and must stay
Der emes hot fis iz er antlofn, der sheker hot keyn fis nit iz er geblibn NS

אײנער איז אַ ליגן, צװײי איז אַ ליגן, דרײַ
איז שון פּאָליטיק

One is a lie, two are lies, three is already politics
Eyner iz a lign, tsvey iz a lign, dray iz shoyn politik P

מען דרײט מיט יענעם אַזױ לאַנג ביז מען
פֿאַרדרײט זיך אַלײן

Lie to others long enough and you end up confusing yourself
Men dreyt mit yenem azoy lang biz men fardreyt zikh aleyn AC

מיט אַ מעשׂה און מיט אַ ליגן קען מען
נאָר קינדער פֿאַרװיגן

Only children can be lulled to sleep with fairy tales and lies
Mit a mayse un mit a lign ken men nor kinder farvign NS

אױף דעם װאָס מען שװערט איז אָפֿט
פּונקט פֿאַרקערט

What you swear to is often just the opposite
Oyf dem vos men shvert iz oft punkt farkert NS

אױף זײַנע רײד קען מען שטעלן אַ
קלױסטער

On the strength of his word you could build a church
Oyf zayne reyd ken men shteln a kloyster NS

FASHION

אַזױ װי די צײַטן אַזױ די לײַטן

Like the times, so the people
Azoy vi di tsaytn azoy di laytn P

שװאַרץ גײט קײן מאָל ניט אַרױס פֿון
מאָדע

Black never goes out of style
Shvarts geyt keyn mol nit aroys fun mode NS

וויַיבער בייזערן זיך ניט אויף דעם
שנײַדער ווען ער נייט זייערער תכריכים

Women don't get mad at the tailor when he sews their shrouds
Vayber beyzern zikh nit oyf dem shnayder ven er neyt zeyere takhrikhim NS

ווי אַ צרה, דאָרט אַ מאָדע

No matter how stupid, that's the style
Vi a tsore, dort a mode AC

FEAR

אַ ייִדנס שׂימחה איז מיט אַ ביסל שרעק

A Jew's celebration is laced with trepidation
A yidns simkhe iz mit a bisl shrek NS

אַלע נעבעכעס עסן געדיכטע לאָקשן

Every sissy eats thick noodles
Ale nebekhes esn gedikhte lokshn AC

אַז מען שערט די שאָף ציטערן די לעמער

When the sheep are shorn the lambs tremble
Az men shert di shof tsitern di lemer IB

עס זאָל זיך ניט טרעפֿן וואָס עס קען
טרעפֿן

What could happen, shouldn't
Es zol zikh nit trefn vos es ken trefn P

ווען ניט די מורה וואָלט געוועון זיס די
עבֿירה

If not so frightful, sinning would be delightful
Ven nit di meyre volt geven zis di aveyre NS

FIRE

אַז מען דאַרף האָבן פֿײַער זוכט מען עס
אין אַש

If you need fire, look for it in the ashes
Az men darf hobn fayer zukht men es in ash NS

עס איז שלעכט די מגפֿה אָבער זיס די
שׂרפה

The plague is terrible but the fires are warming
Es iz shlekht di mageyfe ober zis di sreyfe NS

צען מײַל פֿון אָדעס ברענט דער גיהנום

Ten miles from Odessa, hell fires burn
Tsen mayl fun odes brent der gehenem NS

FOOD AND DRINK

אַ הון איז גוט צו עסן זאַלבענאַנד – איך
און די הון

It's good to have two at the feast— me and the chicken
A hun iz gut tsu esn zalbenand—ikh un di hun NS

אַ לעבעדיקע זאַך בעט עסן

Every living thing must eat
A lebedike zakh bet esn P

אַ שטיקל ברויט פֿאַרטרײַבט די נויט

Feed drives out need
A shtikl broyt fartraybt di noyt NS

אכילה איז די בעסטע תפֿילה

Eating is the best kind of praying
Akhile iz di beste tfile IB

אַז דער יעגער קען ניט שיסן בלײַבט דער
הונט אָן אַ ביסן

If the hunter has nothing in his sight, the dog will not get a bite
Az der yeger ken nit shisn blaybt der hunt on a bisn NS

אַז גאָט גיט ברויט גיבן מענטשן פּוטער

When God gives bread, people supply butter
Az got git broyt gibn mentshn puter NS

אַז מען עסט שבת קוגל איז מען די גאַנצע וואָך זאַט

If you eat Shabbes pudding you will be full for a week
Az men est shabes kugl iz men di gantse vokh zat IB

אַז ס'איז ניטאָ קיין פֿיש איז מען יוצא מיט הערינג

If there's no fish, you have to be satisfied with herring
Az s'iz nito keyn fish iz men yoytse mit hering AC

ברויט אונטערוועגנס איז קיין משׂא ניט

Carrying bread on the road is not a heavy load
Broyt untervegns iz keyn mase nit SK

דער הונט בילט ניט אַז מען שלאָגט אים מיט אַ ביין

The dog won't complain if you beat him with a bone
Der hunt bilt nit az men shlogt im mit a beyn AC

די ווייַב עסט גוט בשעת זי ליגט אין קימפּעט, דער מאַן בשעת ער עסט אין סוכּה, ביידע עסן גוט ווען זיי זייַנען בייַ יענעם אויף אַ שׂימחה, ביידע עסן קרענק בשעת ס'איז בייַ זיי אַ שׂימחה

The wife eats well in childbirth, the husband when he sits in the Succah, and both eat well as guests at someone else's celebration; but both eat aggravation at their own celebration
Di vayb est gut b'shas zi ligt in kimpet, der man b'shas er est in suke, beyde esn gut ven zey zaynen bay yenem oyf a simkhe, beyde esn krenk b'shas s'iz bay zey a simkhe AC

ערשט פֿון דעם דריטן בייגל ווערט מען
זאַט

Only from the third bagel is one's
hunger satisfied
*Ersht fun dem dritn beygl vert men
zat* NS

עס איז גוט צו זײַן אַ קאַץ ווען די
בעל-הביתטע לאָזט לעקן פֿון טאַץ

Being a cat is great when the
housewife lets it lick the plate
*Es iz gut tsu zayn a kats ven di
baleboste lozt lekn fun tats* NS

עס און בענטש און זײַ אַ מענטש!

Eat and pray and act in an ethical
way!
Es un bentsh un zay a mentsh! NS

איידער דעם דאָקטער אַ צווייער איז
בעסער זיך אַ שאָק אייער

Rather than pay a doctor's bill, it's
better to eat your fill!
*Eyder dem dokter a tsveyer iz beser
zikh a shok eyer* NS

איידער צו לייגן אין פּושקע איז בעסער
צו לייגן אין קישקע

Rather than stuff the alms-box it's
better to stuff the stomach
*Eyder tsu leygn in pishke iz beser tsu
leygn in kishke* NS

איין מאָלצײַט קען מען מיט דעם קייסער
אויך מיטהאַלטן

You can afford to prepare at least
one meal fit for a king
*Eyn moltsayt ken men mit dem keyser
oykh mit'haltn* AC

פֿון ברויט מיט קרויט ווערן די באַקן
רויט

From cabbage and bread the cheeks
get red
*Fun broyt mit kroyt vern di bakn
royt* NS

ג="האקטע לעבער איז בעסער ווי
געהאקטע צרות

Chopped liver is better than
chopped troubles
[Good food is better than
unremitting troubles]
*Gehakte leber iz beser vi gehakte
tsores* P

געזונט זאָל זײַן דער וואָס האָט
אויסגעטראַכט בייגל צו עסן!

A toast to him who invented the
eating of bagel!
*Gezunt zol zayn der vos hot
oysgetrakht beygl tsu esn!* NS

האָבן מיר ניט געוואָלט עסן מן אין דער
מידבר מוזן מיר אַצינד עסן ציבעלע

Because we wouldn't eat mannah
in the desert, we now have to eat
onions
[And suffer heartburn]
*Hobn mit nit gevolt esn man in der
midber muzn mir atsind esn tsibele* NS

"אים אין קמחה אין תורה" – וואָס פֿאַר
אַן עסער אַזאַ טוער

"Where there's no flour, there can't
be Torah"—as the eater, so the
worker
*"Im eyn kemakh eyn toyre"—vos far
an eser aza tu'er* NS

כרײן איז גוט פֿאַר די צײן און יויך איז
גוט פֿאַרן בויך

Bitters are good for the teeth, and
broth for the stomach beneath
*Khreyn iz gut far di tseyn un yoykh iz
gut farn boykh* NS

מען מעג עסן אָבער ניט פֿרעסן

One should eat, not devour
Men meg esn ober nit fresn AC

שלאָג שטיקער וועסטו ווערן דיקער

Beat wicker and you'll get thicker
Shlog shtiker vestu vern diker NS

125

צו באָרשט דאַרף מען ניט האָבן קיין ציין

For borsht you don't need teeth
Tsu borsht darf men nit hobn keyn tseyn NS

צו לייד און צו פֿרייד מוז מען עסן

Sad or glad, one must eat
Tsu layd un tsu frayd muz men esn NS

ווען זינגט אַ ייד? ווען ער איז הונגעריק

When does a Jew sing? When he's hungry
[That is, to forget his hunger]
Ven zingt a yid? ven er iz hungerik IB

ווער עס עסט לאַנג קוגל דער לעבט לאַנג

Eat pudding for many years and you'll live a long time
Ver es est lang kugl der lebt lang NS

FOOLS AND FOLLY

אַ גדולה וואָס די מאַמע האָט אים געהאַט און ניט קיין פרעמדע יידענע!

He rejoices that his mother bore him and not some strange female!
A gedule vos di mame hot im gehat un nit keyn fremde yidene! P

אַ נאַר, אַ נאַר, און שאָקלט זיך!

A fool, a fool, though he sways like a scholar!
A nar, a nar un shoklt zikh! NS

אַ נאַר דאַרף האָבן אַ סך שיך

A fool needs a lot of shoes
A nar darf hobn a sakh shikh P

אַ נאַר פֿילט ניט

A fool feels nothing
A nar filt nit NS

אַלע נאַראָנים האָבן דאָס חתונה פנים

All fools wear a wedding face
Ale naronim hobn dos khasene ponim IB

126

א נאַר איז אַן אומגליק (תמיד אַ
בעל-גאווה)

A fool is a misfortune (always puts on airs)
A nar iz an umglik (tomed a bal-gayve) NS

א נאַר קען אַמאָל זאָגן אַ גלײַך וואָרט

A fool can sometimes utter a clever saying
A nar ken amol zogn a glaykh vort NS

א נאַר קלערט צו אַ פֿלוי האָט אַ פּופּיק

The fool wonders if a flea has a navel
A nar klert tsu a floy hot a pupik AC

א נאַר ווערט אין חלום רײַך

A fool gets rich in his dreams
A nar vert in kholem raykh NS

א נגיד אַ נאַר איז אויך אַ האַר

A rich man, even though a fool, is still master
A noged a nar iz oykh a har NS

אַז אַ נאַר וויל זיך הענגען כאַפּט ער אַ
מעסער

When a fool wants to hang himself he grabs a knife
Az a nar vil zikh hengen khapt er a meser NS

אַז דער קאָפּ איז אַ נאַר ליגט דער
גאַנצער גוף אין דר'ערד

When the head is a fool, the whole body can go to hell
Az der kop iz a nar ligt der gantser guf in dr'erd NS

אַז מען חכמה'ט זיך מיט אַ בהמה קריגט
מען דעם עק אין פנים

If you fool around with a cow, you'll get the tail in your face
Az men khokhmet zikh mit a beheyme krigt men dem ek in ponim AC

אַז מען שיקט אַ נאַר אויפֿן מאַרק פֿרייען
זיך די קרעמער

When you send a fool to market, the merchants rejoice
Az men shikt a nar oyfn mark freyen zikh di kremer P

אַז מען זייט געלט וואַקסן נאַראָנים

If you plant money, you raise fools
Az men zeyt gelt vaksn naronim IB

בײַ אַ נאַר זײַנען הענט און פֿיס איבעריק

To a fool, hands and feet are superfluous
Bay a nar zaynen hent un fis iberik P

בײַ אים איז תּורת משה

To him, it's the Torah straight from Moses
Bay im iz toyres moyshe AC

דער חמור טראָגט ספֿרים אָבער העלפֿן
העלפֿט עס ניט

The ass carries books, but it doesn't help
Der khamer trogt sforim ober helfn helft es nit AC

דער נאַר שפרינגט אַרײַן אין וואַסער,
פֿאַר מורא פֿונעם רעגן

A fool jumps into the water for fear of rain
Der nar shpringt arayn in vaser far moyre funem regn AC

דער נאַר זוכט דעם נעכטיקן טאָג

The fool searches for yesterday
Der nar zukht dem nekhtikn tog P

די גרעסטע נאַרישקייט פֿון אַ נאַר איז
וואָס ער מיינט אַז ער איז קלוג

The greatest folly of a fool is that he considers himself wise
Di greste narishkeyt fun a nar iz vos er meynt az er iz klug P

דאָס היטל פּאַסט, דער קאָפ איז נאָר אַ
ביסל צו קליין

The cap fits, it's only the head that's a little too small
Dos hitl past, der kop iz nor a bisl tsu kleyn P

דאָס מזל פֿון אַ נאַר איז אַז ער ווייסט ניט אַז ער ווייסט ניט

The luck of a fool is that he doesn't know that he doesn't know
Dos mazl fun a nar iz az er veyst nit az er veyst nit P

ער איז אַ חכם – ווען ער שלאָפֿט

He is wise—when he sleeps
Er iz a khokhem—ven er shloft P

ער איז אַן אינדיק בײַם כעלעמער חזן!

He is the Chelmer cantor's turkey
[He's a triple fool]
Er iz an indik baym khelemer khazn! NS

ער איז געוואָר געוואָרן אַז ער הייסט נאָך אַ טויטן

He discovered that he's named after a dead person
[Traditionally, babies are named after deceased kin]
Er iz gevor gevorn az er heyst nokh a toytn IF

ער איז ניט נאָענט צו אַ חכם און ניט ווײַט פֿון אַ נאַר

He's not close to being wise, and not far from being a fool
Er iz nit no'ent tsu a khokhem un nit vayt fun a nar NS

ער קלערט אַז ער הערט ווי אַ פֿלוי היסט און אַ וואַנץ ניסט

He thinks he hears a flea cough and a roach sneeze
Er klert az er hert vi a floy hist un a vants nist AC

ער קלערט ווו די רויכעס קומען אַהין

He wonders where smoke disappears to
Er klert vu di roykhes kumen ahin IB

איין נאַר איז אַ מבֿין אויפֿן צווייטן

One fool is an expert on another
Eyn nar iz a meyvn oyfn tsveytn P

פֿון אַ נאַר האָט מען צער

A fool gives you reason to grieve
Fun a nar hot men tsar P

גאָט האָט געגעבן דעם נאַר הענט און פֿיס און געלאָזט אים לויפֿן

God gave the fool limbs and let him run
Got hot gegebn dem nar hent un fis un gelozt im loyfn P

הויך און דאַר און שמעקט מיט נאַר!

Tall and skinny and what a ninny!
Hoykh un dar un shmekt mit nar! NS

איך רעד אַהין און אַהער, ער שטייט ווי אַ בער!

I talk here, I talk there, he stands there like a bear!
Ikh red ahin un aher, er shteyt vi a bear! IB

מען קען אים שיקן נאָך אַ סוכּה-שער!

You can send him to fetch a succah-scissors!
[That is, a pail of steam, a shore line]
Men ken im shikn nokh a suke-sher! P

מען מוז זיך אַמאָל מאַכן צום נאַר

Sometimes it's necessary to act the fool
Men muz zikh amol makhn tsum nar P

מיט אַ נאַר טאָר מען ניט האַנדלען

Don't do business with a fool
Mit a nar tor men nit handlen AC

אויף אַ נאַר איז קיין קשיא ניט צו פֿרעגן און קיין פּשט ניט צו זאָגן

Don't question a fool or give him an explanation
Oyf a nar iz keyn kashe nit tsu fregn un keyn p'shat nit tsu zogn NS

ווען ער איז צוויי מאָל אַזוי קלוג וואָלט ער געווען אַ גולם!

If he were twice as smart, he'd be an idiot!
Ven er iz tsvey mol azoy klug volt er geven a goylem! AC

ווען מען שיקט אַ נאַר מאַכן פֿײַער מאַכט ער גאָר אַ שרפֿה

Send a fool to light the fire and he ends up making an inferno
Ven men shikt a nar makhn fayer makht er gor a sreyfe NS

יעדער הויף (חדר) האָט זײַן נאַר

Every courtyard (classroom) has its fool
Yeder hoyf (kheyder) hot zayn nar P

זײַ ניט קיין נאַר וועט מען פֿון דיר ניט לאַכן

Don't be a fool and no one will poke fun at you
Zay nit keyn nar vet men fun dir nit lakhn P

CHARACTER OF FOOLS

אַ בהמה איז אַ בהמה אפֿילו אין אַ פּאַלאַץ

A cow is a cow even in a palace
A beheyme iz a beheyme afile in a palats AC

אַ גנבֿ בלײַבט אַ גנבֿ, אַ שיכּור בלײַבט אַ שיכּור און אַ נאַר בלײַבט אַ נאַר

A thief remains a thief, a drunkard remains a drunkard, and a fool remains a fool
A ganef blaybt a ganef, a shiker blaybt a shiker un a nar blaybt a nar NS

אַ קראַנקער וועט געזונט ווערן, אַ שיכּור וועט זיך אויסניכטערן, אַ שוואַרצער וועט ווײַס ווערן – און אַ נאַר בלײַבט אַ נאַר

A sick person will be healed, a drunkard will sober up, the swarthy will turn light—but a fool remains a fool
A kranker vet gezunt vern, a shiker vet zikh oysnikhtern, a shvartser vet vays vern—un a nar blaybt a nar NS

אַז אַ נאַר שווײַגט ווייסט מען ניט צי ער איז אַ נאַר צי אַ חכם

When a fool keeps quiet, you can't tell whether he's foolish or smart
Az a nar shvaygt veyst men nit tsi er iz a nar tsi a khokhem P

131

קאָך אים אין עסיק און אין האָניק
בלײַבט ער אַלץ אַ נאַר

Even if you cook him in sugar and
dill, he remains an idiot still
*Kokh im in esik un in honik blaybt er
alts a nar* NS

COMPARISON

אַ בלינדער לויפֿט און אַ נאַר קויפֿט
קומען בײַדע שלעכט אָן

When a blind man runs and a fool
goes shopping, both end up badly
*A blinder loyft un a nar koyft kumen
beyde shlekht on* NS

אַ פֿרעמדער נאַר איז אַ געלעכטער, אַן
אייגענער – אַ שאַנד

Someone else's fool is a joke; your
own—a disgrace
*A fremder nar iz a gelekhter, an
eygener—a shand* NS

אַ קלוגער גייט צו פֿוס און אַ נאַר פֿאָרט
אין אַ קאַרעטע

A wise man travels on foot and a
fool in a coach
[Wisdom is not necessarily rewarded]
*A kluger geyt tsu fus un a nar fort in a
karete* IB

אַ נאַר פֿאַרלירט און אַ קלוגער פֿאַרדינט

A fool loses and a clever person
earns
A nar farlirt un a kluger fardint NS

אַ נאַר גייט צוויי מאָל דאָרט וווּ אַ
קלוגער גייט ניט קיין איינציק מאָל

A fool goes twice where a wise
person won't go even once
*A nar geyt tsvey mol dort vu a kluger
geyt nit keyn eyntsik mol* NS

אַ נאַר קען פֿרעגן מער קשיאות אין אַ
שעה ווי אַ קלוגער קען ענטפֿערן אין אַ
יאָר

A fool can ask more questions in an
hour than a wise person can
answer in a year
*A nar ken fregn mer kashes in a sho vi
a kluger ken entfern in a yor* NS

132

אַ ייִד אַז ער איז קלוג איז ער קלוג און
אַז ער איז אַ נאַר איז ער אַ נאַר

A Jew, if he's wise, is wise indeed; if he's a fool, he's a real fool
A yid az er iz klug iz er klug un az er iz a nar iz er a nar AC

בעסער אַן איינגעוואַנדערטער נאַר
איידער אַ היימישן גנב

Better an imported fool than a home-grown thief
Beser an ayngevandertn nar eyder a heymishn ganef NS

בעסער פֿון אַ חכם אַ פּאַטש איידער פֿון
אַ נאַר אַ קוש

Better a slap from a wise man than a kiss from a fool
Beser fun a khokhem a patsh eyder fun a nar a kush IB

דער קלוגער דערציילט וואָס ער האָט
געזען, דער נאַר וואָס ער האָט געהערט

The wise person tells what he saw, the fool what he heard
Der kluger dertseylt vos er hot gezen, der nar vos er hot gehert NS

פֿאַר אַ צאַפּ האָט מען מורא פֿון פֿאָרנט,
פֿאַר אַ פֿערד פֿון הינטן און פֿאַר אַ נאַר
פֿון אַלע זייטן

Beware a goat from the front, a horse from the rear, and a fool from all sides
Far a tsap hot men moyre fun fornt, far a ferd fun hintn un far a nar fun ale zaytn NS

ווען אַ נאַר וואַרפֿט אַריין אַ שטיין אין
ברונעם קענען אים קיין צען חכמים ניט
אַרויסנעמען

When a fool throws a stone into a well, ten wise men can't recover it
Ven a nar varft arayn a shteyn in brunem kenem im keyn tsen khakhomim nit aroysnemen NS

וואָס אַ נאַר קען קאַליע מאַכן קענען צען
חכמים ניט פֿאַרריכטן

What a fool can wreck, ten wise men can't repair
Vos a nar ken kalye makhn kenen tsen khakhomim nit far'rikhtn NS

FORCE

דער שטאָרקער איז תמיד גערעכט	**Might is always right** *Der shtarker iz tomed gerekht* NS
ער האָט אים געגעבן אַ "מי שברך"!	**He gave him the "Prayer for Health"!** [When he got through with him he needed it!] *Er hot im gegebn a "mishebeyrekh"!* LMF
געצוווּנגען און גענייט טוט גאָט לייד	**Force and might offend God's sight** *Getsvungen un geneyt tut got layd* NS
נעם צו דעם של-יד!	**Take your tefillin-hand off me!** *Nem tsu dem shel-yad!* IB
שלעפּ מיך, איך גיי גערן!	**Drag me, I go gladly!** *Shlep mikh, ikh gey gern!* NS
וואָס מען רייַסט ניט אָפּ מיט גוואַלד, דאָס האָט מען ניט	**What you don't grab by force, you won't have** *Vos men rayst nit op mit gvald, dos hot men nit* AC

FORESIGHT

אַז ס'איז ניטאָ אין טאָפּ איז ניטאָ אין טעלער	**If there's nothing in the pot, there's nothing on the plate** *Az s'iz nito in top iz nito in teler* AC
בעסער פֿריִער באַוואָרנט איידער שפּעטער באַוויינט	**Better earlier warning than later mourning** *Beser fri'er bavornt eyder shpeter baveynt* NS

134

בעסער פֿריִער איין וואָרט איידער צוויי
דערנאָך

Better one word earlier than two words later
Beser fri'er eyn vort eyder tsvey dernokh NS

מיט אַ לייטער אויפֿן הימל קען מען זיך
ניט באַוואָרענען

You can't insure yourself with a ladder to the sky
Mit a leyter oyfn himl ken men zikh nir bavorenen NS

FRIENDSHIP

אַ פֿרײַנד באַקומט מען אומזיסט, אַ
שׂונא מוז מען זיך קויפֿן

A friend you get for nothing, an enemy has to be bought
A fraynd bakumt men umzist, a soyne muz men zikh koyfn NS

אַז מען קען ניט העלפֿן אַ פֿרײַנד מיט
געלט זאָל מען אים כאָטש העלפֿן מיט אַ
קרעכץ

If you can't help your friend with money, at least utter a sympathetic sigh
Az men ken nit helfn a fraynd mit gelt zol men im khotsh helfn mit a krekhts NS

בעסער איין פֿרײַנד מיט געקעכץ איידער
הונדערט מיט אַ קרעכץ

Better one friend with a pie than a hundred with a sigh
Beser eyn fraynd mit gekekhts eyder hundert mit a krekhts NS

איין שׂונא איז צו פֿיל און הונדערט
פֿרײַנד ניט גענוג

One enemy is too many, and a hundred friends not enough
Eyn soyne iz tsu fil un hundert fraynd nit genug P

גוטע פֿרײַנד פֿון ווײַטן

Good friends from a distance
Gute fraynd fun vaytn P

אין שפּיגל זעט איטלעכער זײַן בעסטן
פֿרײַנד

In the mirror everyone sees his best friend
In shpigl zet itlekher zayn bestn fraynd NS

מיט גוטע חבֿרים פֿאַרשפּאָרט מען אין
שלעכטע וועגן צו גיין

Good companions keep you from going astray
Mit gute khaveyrim farshport men in shlekhte vegn tsu geyn AC

אויף אַ צעריסענער פֿרײַנדשאַפֿט קען
מען קיין לאַטע ניט לייגן

You can't patch up a torn friendship
Oyf a tserisener frayndshaft ken men keyn late nit leygn AC

זאָג מיר ווער דײַנע חבֿרים זײַנען וועל
איך דיר זאָגן ווער דו ביסט

Tell me who your friends are, and I'll tell you who you are
Zog mir ver dayne khaveyrim zaynen vel ikh dir zogn ver du bist AC

FUTILITY

אַז דער דײן וויל ניט פּסקנען מעג דער
שולחן-ערוך צעזעצט ווערן

If the judge won't make a decision, then the whole Code of Laws can go to hell
Az der dayen vil nit paskenen meg der shulkhn-orekh tsezetst vern IF

אַז מען קלאַפּט אין טיש רופֿט זיך אָפּ די
שער

When you thump the table, the scissors jump
Az men klapt in tish ruft zikh op di sher IB

ער פֿירט שטרוי קיין מצרים!

He carries straw back to ancient Egypt
[He carries coal to Newcastle]
Er firt shtroy keyn mitsrayim! AC

עס העלפֿט ווי אַ טויטן "אל מלא
רחמים"!

It will help like chanting the
Memorial Prayer!
*Es helft vi a toytn "eyl mole
rakhamim"!* IB

עס וועט העלפֿן ווי אַ טויטן באַנקעס!

It will help like cupping a corpse
Es vet helfn vi a toytn bankes! P

פֿון איין אָקס קען מען קיין צוויי פֿעלן
ניט אַראָפּציִען

You can't pull two hides off one ox
*Fun eyn oks ken men keyn tsvey feln
nit aroptsi'en* NS

געווען שיין, געהאַט געלט, געקאָנט
זינגען – האָט אין גאַנצן קיין ווערט ניט

Was beautiful, had money, could
sing—is all worthless
*Geven sheyn, gehat gelt, gekont
zingen—hot in gantsn keyn vert nit* AC

גיי רעד צו דער וואַנט!

Go talk to the wall!
Gey red tsu der vant! P

גיי שרײַ "חי וקים"!

Go proclaim: "God is everlasting!"
Gey shray "khay v'kayam!" IB

מען קען דעם באַרג מיט אַ שפּענדל ניט
אַוועקטראָגן

You can't move a mountain with a
splinter
*Men ken dem barg mit a shpendl nit
avektrogn* NS

מען קען ניט אַריבערלויפֿן די לבֿנה

You can't jump over the moon
Men ken nit ariberloyfn di levone NS

מאָל אויס אַ טויבן אַ כלי-זמר און אַ
בלינדן אַ רעגנבויגן

Describe a musician to the deaf and
a rainbow to the blind
*Mol oys a toybn a klezmer un a blindn
a regn-boygn* NS

רעד כאָטש טאַטעריש און טערקיש!

Even if you talk Tatar and Turkish!
Red khotsh taterish un terkish! IB

שפּאָר, שפּאָר, קומט דער שוואַרץ יאָר
און נעמט צו גאָר!

Save, save, a black day comes and takes it all away!

Shpor, shpor, kumt der shvarts yor un nemt tsu gor! NS

וואָס קומט אַרויס פֿון דער גוטער קו
וואָס גיט אַ סך מילך אַז זי שלאָגט
דערנאָך דאָס שעפֿל אויס?

What use is a good cow that gives a lot of milk if afterwards she knocks over the pail?

Vos kumt aroys fun der guter ku vos git a sakh milkh az zi shlogt dernokh dos shefl oys? NS

138

GENTILES

א גוייש ווערטל איז להבֿדיל אויך א
תורה

A Goyish proverb can also contain wisdom
A goyish vertl iz lehavdil, oykh a toyre IB

אַלע חכמות קומען אַרויס פֿון
דײַטש – און אַליין בלײַבט ער אַ נאַר

Clever things come from the Germans—yet they themselves remain fools
Ale khokhmes kumen aroys fun daytsh—un aleyn blaybt er a nar NS

אַז מען קלינגט איז אָדער אַ חגא, אָדער
אַ פּגר, אָדער אַ שֹרפה

When church bells peal, it's either a [Gentile] holiday, a funeral, or a fire
Az men klingt iz oder a khoge, oder a peyger, oder a sreyfe IB

בעסער אַ ייִדיש האַרץ מיט אַ גוייִשן
קאָפּ איידער אַ גוייִש האַרץ מיט אַ
ייִדישן קאָפּ

Better a Jewish heart with a Goyish head, than a Goyish heart with a Jewish head
Beser a yidish harts mit a goyishn kop eyder a goyish harts mit a yidishn kop NS

139

בעסער אין גוייִשע הענט איידער אין
ייִדישע מײַלער

Better in Gentile hands than in Jewish mouths

Beser in goyishe hent eyder in yidishe mayler IB

דו ווילסט מען זאָל דיך ניט
באַגאַנוועננען? וווין צווישן ציגײַנער

You want to avoid being robbed? Live among gypsies

Du vilst men zol dikh nit baganvenen? voyn tsvishn tsigayner NS

גאָט זאָל אָפּהיטן פֿון גוייִשן כּוח און
ייִדישן מוח

God protect us from Goyish hands and Jewish wits

Got zol op'hitn fun goyishn koyekh un yidishn moyekh NS

צו וואָס דאַרף אַ גוי האָבן אַ קאָפּ? אַז
קיין שׂכל האָט ער ניט, קיין גמרא לערנט
ער ניט, קיין יאַרמולקע טראָגט ער ניט און
קיין תּפֿילין לייגט ער ניט. אַ גוי דאַרף
האָבן אַ קאָפּ כּדי אַ ייִד זאָל האָבן וואָס
צו פֿאַרדרייען

Why does a Goy need a head? Sense, he doesn't have, Talmud he doesn't study, a skull cap he doesn't wear, and tefillin he doesn't put on. A Goy needs a head so a Jew can confuse it

Tsu vos darf a goy hobn a kop? az keyn seykhl hot er nit, keyn gemore lernt er nit, keyn yarmulke trogt er nit un keyn tfilin leygt er nit. A goy darf hobn a kop kedey a yid zol hobn vos tsu fardreyen AC

וואָס מער גוי אַלץ מער מזל

The more Goy, the better the luck

Vos mer goy alts mer mazl! P

GIVING AND TAKING

אַ נעמער איז ניט קיין געבער

A taker is not a giver

A nemer iz nit keyn geber NS

140

אַז גאָט וויל ניט געבן טאָר מען זיך אַליין
ניט נעמען

If God doesn't give, one shouldn't take
Az got vil nit gebn tor men zikh aleyn nit nemen NS

אַז מען גיט ניט נעמט מען!

If they don't give, take!
Az men git nit nemt men! P

דער וואָס גלײַכט צו נעמען גלײַכט ניט
צו געבן

He who likes to take doesn't like to give
Der vos glaykht tsu nemen glaykht nit tsu gebn P

גאָט נעמט מיט איין האַנט און גיט מיט
דער אַנדערער

God takes with one hand and gives with the other
Got nemt mit eyn hant un git mit der anderer NS

"לעולם תקח" – דערווײַל קיק איך

"Always take"—so far, I'm just looking
"L'oylem tikekh"—dervayl kik ikh IB

ווער עס וועט כאַפּן דעם וועט מען
קלאַפּן

If you snatch, you'll get scratched
Ver es vet khapn, dem vet men klapn NS

וואָס מען נעמט זיך ניט אַליין דאָס האָט
מען ניט

What you won't take, you won't have
Vos men nemt zikh nit aleyn dos hot men nit NS

GOD

אַ גאָט האָבן מיר – אַזאַ יאָר אויף אונדז
און אַ פֿאָלק האָט ער – אַזאַ יאָר אויף
אים!

A God we have—woe to us; and a people He has—woe to Him!
A got hobn mir—aza yor oyf undz un a folk hot er—aza yor oyf im! IB

אַ מענטש טראַכט און גאָט לאַכט	**Man thinks and God laughs** [Man proposes, God disposes] *A mentsh trakht un got lakht* P
אַז גאָט וויל שיסט אַ בעזעם אויך	**If God wills it, even a broom can shoot** *Az got vil shist a bezem oykh* P
דער מענטש פֿאָרט און גאָט האַלט די לייצעס	**A person rides, but God holds the reins** *Der mentsh fort un got halt di leytses* NS
ער האָט דאָס לעבן פֿון גאָט און דאָס עסן פֿון מענטשן	**He owes his life to God and his sustenance to people** *Er hot dos lebn fun got un dos esn fun mentshn* NS
פֿאַר גאָט האָט מען מורא, פֿאַר מענטשן מוז מען זיך היטן	**Fear God, but be wary of people** *Far got hot men moyre, far mentshn muz men zikh hitn* NS
גאָט אַליין איז ניט רײַך – ער נעמט נאָר בײַ איינעם און גיט דעם אַנדערן	**God isn't rich—all He does is take from one and give to the other** *Got aleyn iz nit raykh—er nemt nor bay eynem un git dem andern* NS
גאָט פֿאַרשטייט ניט קיין קאַטאָװעס	**God doesn't understand jokes** *Got farshteyt nit keyn katoves* NS
גאָט האַנדלט ניט און גאָט װאַנדלט ניט	**God doesn't bargain and He doesn't make change** *Got handlt nit un got vandlt nit* NS
גאָט היט אָפּ די נאַראָנים – װער נאָך?	**God protects fools—who else would?** *Got hit op di naronim—ver nokh?* P

גאָט האָט מער וויפֿל ער האָט
אויסגעטיילט

God possesses more than He dispenses
Got hot mer vifl er hot oysgeteylt NS

גאָט איז אַ פֿאָטער: אַז ער גיט ניט אַ
מכה גיט ער אַ בלאָטער

God is a father: If He doesn't give you a boil He gives you a blister
Got iz a foter: az er git nit a make git er a bloter IB

גאָט איז גאָר קיין מענטש ניט

God Himself isn't honorable
Got iz gor keyn mentsh nit AC

גאָט שיקט די קעלט נאָך די קליידער

God sends the weather according to the clothing
Got shikt di kelt nokh di kleyder NS

גאָט שפּייַזט אפֿילו דעם װאָרעם אויף
דער ערד

God provides sustenance even for the lowly worm
Got shpayzt afile dem vorem oyf der erd NS

גאָט שטראָפֿט מיט איין האַנט און
בענטשט מיט דער אַנדערער

God punishes with one hand and blesses with the other
Got shtroft mit eyn hant un bentsht mit der anderer NS

גאָט װעט העלפֿן – װי העלפֿט נאָר גאָט
ביז װאַנען גאָט װעט העלפֿן

God will provide—if only God would provide until He provides
Got vet helfn—vi helft nor got biz vanen got vet helfn AC

גאָט זיצט אויבן און מיר מאַטערן זיך
אונטן

God sits on high and we suffer here below
Got zitst oybn un mir matern zikh untn NS

גאָט זאָל מיך בענטשן איך זאָל ניט
אָנקומען צו מענטשן

**God bless me so that I don't need
help from people**
*God zol mikh bentshn ikh zol nit
onkumen tsu mentshn* NS

מיט גאָט טאָר מען זיך ניט שפּילן,
ערשטנס טאָר מען ניט און צווייטנס
לאָזט ער ניט

**Don't trifle with God; first it's not
allowed, and second, He won't let
you**
*Mit got tor men zikh nit shpiln, ershtns
tor men nit un tsveytns lozt er nit* NS

אָן גאָטס וואָרט – קיין טריט פֿון אָרט

**Without God's word, no step is
heard**
On gots vort—keyn trit fun ort NS

וועמען גאָט וויל דערקוויקן קענען
מענטשן ניט דערשטיקן

**Whom God will sustain, people
can't disdain**
*Vemen got vil derkvikn kenen mentshn
nit dershtikn* NS

ווען גאָט נעמט איינעם צו דאָס געלט
נעמט ער אים דעם שׂכל אויך צו

**When God takes away someone's
money, He deprives him of his
brains, too**
*Ven got nemt eynem tsu dos gelt nemt
er im dem seykhl oykh tsu* NS

ווער עס גלייבט ניט אין גאָט קען צו אים
קיין טענות ניט האָבן

**He who doesn't believe in God can
have no complaints to Him**
*Ver es gleybt nit in got ken tsu im keyn
taynes nit hobn* AC

וואָלט דער מענטש אַזוי פֿיל ווערט
געווען ווי גאָט קען העלפֿן

**If only human beings would
deserve as much as God can help**
*Volt der mentsh azoy fil vert geven vi
got ken helfn* AC

144

וואָס גאָט טוט באַשערן קען קיין
מענטש ניט פֿאַרווערן

What God has sent no one can prevent

Vos got tut bashern ken keyn mentsh nit farvern NS

וואָס שווערער מען נעמט זיך פֿאַר אַלץ
לײַכטער העלפֿט גאָט

The harder the undertaking, the easier God's help

Vos shverer men nemt zikh for alts laykhter helft got NS

GOOD AND BAD

אַז מען שענקט דאָס שלעכטע
באַעוולהט מען דאָס גוטע

If you pardon the bad, you injure the good

Az men shenkt dos shlekhte ba'avlt men dos gute AC

בעסער גוט און אַ ביסל איידער
שלעכטס און אַ פֿולע שיסל

Better good and a little bit, than bad and a lot of it

Beser gut un a bisl eyder shlekhts un a fule shisl NS

דער וואָס האָט ניט פֿאַרזוכט דאָס
ביטערע ווייסט ניט וואָס זיס איז

Who has not tasted bitter doesn't know what sweet is

Der vos hot nit farzukht dos bitere veyst nit vos zis iz AC

דאָס גוטע און דאָס שלעכטע איז ניט
אויף אייביק

Both the good and the bad don't last forever

Dos gute un dos shlekhte iz nit oyf eybik AC

ניט אויף אַלע מאָל שלעכט און ניט אויף
אַלע מאָל גוט

Things can't always be bad or always good

Nit oyf ale mol shlekht un nit oyf ale mol gut NS

צום גוטן ווערט מען באַלד געוווינט

One quickly becomes accustomed to good
Tsum gutn vert men bald gevoynt P

יעדער באַרג אַרויף האָט זײַן באַרג אַראָפּ

Every uphill has its downhill
Yeder barg aroyf hot zayn barg arop NS

GOSSIP

אַן אַרײַנטראָגערקע איז אַן אַרויסטראָגערקע

One who carries in, carries out
An arayntrogerke iz an aroystrogerke IB

אַז מען גייט צווישן לײַטן ווייסט מען וואָס עס טוט זיך אין דער היים

When you mix with people, you find out what's going on at home
Az men geyt tsvishn laytn veyst men vos es tut zikh in der heym AC

די ערגסטע רכילות איז דער אמת

The worst gossip is the truth
Di ergste rekhiles iz der emes NS

פֿון פֿיל ריידן קומט אַרויס לײַדן

Much talk in the air brings on despair
Fun fil raydn kumt aroys laydn NS

פֿון ייִדישע רייד קען מען זיך ניט אָפּוואַשן אפֿילו אין צען וואַסערן

Ten washings cannot cleanse one of Jewish talk
Fun yidishe reyd ken men zikh nit opvashn afile in tsen vasern NS

האָב אין זינען זיך וועסטו פֿאַרגעסן אין יענעם

Watch what you do, and you'll forget about watching what others do
Hob in zinen zikh vestu fargesn in yenem AC

לשון-הרע איז די ערגסטע מידה און די | **Gossip is the worst habit and**
גרעסטע צרה | **causes the most trouble**
| *Loshn hore iz di ergste mide un di*
| *greste tsore* NS

רעד ניט אין די אויגן קיין חניפֿה און טו | **Don't flatter people to their faces or**
ניט אונטער די אויגן קיין רציחה | **revile them behind their backs**
| *Red nit in di oygn keyn khanife un tu*
| *nit unter di oygn keyn retsikhe* NS

טראָג ניט קיין טובֿות אין די הײַזער | **Don't carry favors into other**
| **people's houses**
| *Trog nit keyn toyves in di hayzer* AC

ווען מען קומט זיך צונויף דברט מען | **When people meet, they jabber**
| *Ven men kumt zikh tsunoyf dabert*
| *men* AC

ווער עס טראָגט צו מיר טראָגט אויך | **Whoever brings to me also carries**
אַוועק פֿון מיר | **away from me**
| *Ver es trogt tsu mir trogt oykh avek fun*
| *mir* IB

זאָג ניט אַלץ וואָס דו גלייבסט, גלייב ניט | **Don't tell everything you know,**
אַלץ וואָס דו הערסט | **don't believe everything you hear**
| *Zog nit alts vos du gleybst, gleyb nit*
| *alts vos du herst* AC

GREED

אַז מען לאָזט אַ חזיר אױפֿן באַנק וויל | **Give a pig a chair and he wants to**
ער אױפֿן טיש | **climb onto the table**
| *Az men lozt a khazer oyfn bank vil er*
| *oyfn tish*

די אויגן זײַנען גרעסער פֿון מויל (מאָגן)

The eyes are bigger than the mouth (stomach)
Di oygn zaynen greser fun moyl (mogn) AC

מען קען ניט פֿאַרקױפֿן די קו און בלײַבן מיט מילך אױך

You can't sell the cow and keep the milk, too
Men ken nit farkoyfn di ku un blaybn mit milkh oykh AC

ווען דער מענטש וואָלט געקאָנט האָבן אַ העלפֿט וואָס ער פֿאַרלאַנגט וואָלט ער זיך טאָפּלט פֿאַרגרעסערט די צרות

If a person could have half he desired, he would double his troubles
Ven der mentsh volt gekont hobn a helft vos er farlangt volt er zikh toplt fargresert di tsores AC

GROWTH

דרײַ זאַכן וואַקסן איבערנאַכט – רווחים, דירה-געלט און מיידן

Three things grow overnight— profits, rent-money, and girls
Dray zakhn vaksn ibernakht— revokhim, dire-gelt un meydn NS

פֿון צוקומעניש טוט דער קאָפּ ניט וויי

From acquisitions you don't get a headache
Fun tsukumenish tut der kop nit vey AC

נאָך איז בײַם גלח אין אַרבל

More is up the priest's sleeve
Nokh iz baym galekh in arbl NS

GUESTS

אַ גאַסט איז ווי אַ רעגן, אַז ער דויערט צו לאַנג ווערט ער אַ לאַסט

A guest is like rain, if he lingers he becomes a pain
A gast iz vi a regn, az er doyert tsu lang vert er a last NS

אַז דער אורח הוסט פֿעלט אים אַ לעפֿל	**When the guest coughs it's because he needs a spoon** *Az der oyrekh hust felt im a lefl* IB
דאָרט וווּ מען האָט דיך ליב גיי וייניק, וווּ מען האָט דיק פֿײַנט גיי גאָר ניט	**Where you're liked, go seldom; where you're disliked, don't go at all** *Dort vu men hot dikh libt gey veynik,* *vu men hot dikh faynt gey gor nit* AC
ער איז אַרײַן ווי אַ יוון אין סוכה	**He entered like a soldier into the succah** [Like a bull in a china shop] *Er iz arayn vi a yovn in suke* NS
גוטע געסט קומען אומגעבעטן	**Welcome guests come uninvited** *Gute gest kumen umgebetn* IB
מען זאָל תמיד בעטן אויף גוטע געסט	**Always pray for good guests** *Men zol tomed beth oyf gute gest* IB
מיט מיטגעבראַכטן ברויט איז מען אומעטום אַ גוטער אורח	**A guest who brings bread is welcome everywhere** *Mit mitgebrakhtn broyt iz men umetum* *a guter oyrekh* IB
וואָס קלענער דער עולם אַלץ גרעסער די שׂמחה	**The smaller the gathering the more festive the celebration** [More food and drink to go around] *Vos klener der oylem alts greser di* *simkhe* IB
זונטיק אַ גאַסט, מאָנטיק אַ לאַסט, דינסטיק ניט פֿריש, מיטוואָך געמאַכט פֿיס	**Sunday a guest; Monday a pest; Tuesday not fresh; Wednesday get lost!** *Zuntik a gast, montik a last, dinstik nit* *frish, mitvokh gemakht fis!* AC

HAPPINESS

עס איז שבת איבער דער גאַנצער וועלט! | It's Shabbes the whole world over!
Es iz shabes iber der gantser velt! IB

געזונט און פרנסה איז די בעסטע בקשה | Health and earnings are the best yearnings
Gezunt un parnose iz di beste bakoshe NS

ניט יעדעס האַרץ וואָס לאַכט איז פֿרײלעך | Not every heart that laughs is joyful
Nit yedes harts vos lakht iz freylekh AC

ווען פֿרײען זיך חדר ייִנגלעך? ווען דער רבי זיצט שבֿעה | When do schoolboys rejoice? When the rabbi sits shiveh
[Because they don't have to go to kheyder]
Ven freyen zikh kheyder yinglekh? ven der rebe zitst shive AC

HASTE

אַן אָרעמאַן און אַ קראַנקער זײַנען
שטענדיק תּיכּף

**A pauper and a sick person never
have enough time**

*An oreman un a kranker zaynen
shtendik teykef* IB

ער לויפֿט ווי נאָך דער באָבעס ירושה

**He pursues it as though it were his
grandmother's legacy**

Er loyft vi nokh der bobe's yerushe IF

עס טויג ניט תּיכּף און באַלד ווען מען
מוז שרײַען גוואַלד

**Nothing quickly comes about just
because we rail and shout**

*Es toyg nit teykef un bald ven men muz
shrayen gvald* NS

פֿון אײַלעניש קומט קיין גוטס ניט
אַרויס

No good comes from hurrying

*Fun aylenish kumt keyn guts nit
aroys* P

שבת שטעך האַלטן ניט

Shabbes stitches don't hold

[Said of a tailor rushing to complete
a garment before the onset of
Shabbes]

Shabes shtekh haltn nit IB

HEALTH

אַז אַ מענטש איז געזונט מיינט ער אַז
עס קומט אים

**If a person is healthy, he thinks it's
his due**

*Az a mentsh iz gezunt meynt er as es
kumt im* AC

אַז מען פֿאַרלאָזט זיך קריגט מען אַ פּאַרך

**If you neglect to look after yourself,
you get scabies**

*Az men farlozt zikh krigt men a
parekh* AC

גאָט זאָל געבן געזונט – דאָס לעבן קען
מען זיך אַליין נעמען

**God give us health! We can always
manage to take our own lives**
*Got zol gebn gezunt—dos lebn ken
men zikh aleyn nemen* AC

מען זאָל נאָר האָבן כּוח צו זינדיקן!

**May one always have strength
enough to sin!**
*Men zol nor hobn koyekh tsu
zindikn!* AC

HEARING

אַז אַ טויבער הערט אַ גראַגער מאַכט ער
אַ ברכה איבער אַ דונער

**When a deaf person hears a rattle,
he recites the blessing over thunder**
*Az a toyber hert a grager makht er a
brokhe iber a duner* AC

איבער דעם האָט גאָט געגעבן דעם
מענטשן צוויי אויערן און איין מויל כּדי
ער זאָל מער הערן און ווייניקער רעדן

**God gave mankind two ears, but
only one mouth so that he would
hear more and talk less**
*Iber dem hot got gegebn dem mentshn
tsvey oyern un eyn moyl, kedey er zol
mer hern un veyniker redn* NS

קיינער איז ניט אַזוי טויב ווי דער וואָס
וויל ניט הערן

**None so deaf as those who will not
hear**
*Keyner iz nit azoy toyb vi der vos vil nit
hern* P

וואָס אַ טויבער דערהערט ניט, דאָס
טראַכט ער זיך אויס

**What a deaf person doesn't hear, he
imagines**
*Vos a toyber derhert nit, dos trakht er
zikh oys* NS

HEART

אַ האַרץ איז אַ שלאָס, מען דאַרף דעם
ריכטיקן שליסל

A heart is a lock, you need the right key
A harts iz a shlos, men darf dem rikhtikn shlisl NS

אַ שווער האַרץ רעדט אַ סך

A heavy heart talks a lot
A shver harts ret a sakh NS

אַז דאָס האַרץ איז פֿול גייען די אויגן
איבער

When the heart is full, the eyes overflow
Az dos harts iz ful geyen di oygn iber IB

אַז אויף דעם האַרצן איז ביטער העלפֿט
ניט אין מויל קיין צוקער

When the heart turns sour, sugar loses its power
Az oyf dem hartsn iz biter helft nit in moyl keyn tsiker NS

דאָס האַרץ זעט בעסער פֿון אויג

The heart sees better than the eye
Dos harts zet beser fun oyg AC

יעדעס האַרץ האָט סודות

Every heart has its secrets
Yedes harts hot soydes AC

יעדער האַרץ האָט זײַן שמערץ

Every heart has its smart
Yeder herts hot zayn shmerts NS

HEAVEN AND HELL

אפֿילו אין גן-עדן איז נישט גוט צו זײַן
אַליין

Even in paradise it's not good to be alone
Afile in ganeydn iz nisht gut tsu zayn aleyn AC

דעם גן-עדן און דעם גהינום קען מען
האָבן אויף דער וועלט

Both heaven and hell can be had in this world
Dem ganeydn un dem gehenem ken men hobn oyf der velt NS

פֿאַר דרײַ האָט גאָט אָנגעגרייט אַ
באַזונדערן גן-עדן: פֿאַר רבנים, נאמנים
און מלמדים, נאָר עס שטייט נאָך עד
היום ליידיק

God has prepared a special paradise for three kinds of people: rabbis, the faithful, and teachers; however, to this day it's empty
Far dray hot got ongegreyt a bazundern ganeydn: far rebonim, nemonim un melamdim, nor es shteyt nokh ad hayom leydik NS

HEREDITY

אַז דער טאַטע איז אַ פֿורמאַן פֿאַרשטייט
דער זון ווי אײַנצושפּאַנען

If the father is a coachman, the son will know about harnessing
Az der tate iz a furman farshteyt der zun vi ayntsushpanen NS

אַז דער טאַטע איז אַ לץ איז דער זון אַ
פּאָדליעץ

If the father is a clown, the son is a buffoon
Az der tate iz a lets iz der zun a podlets NS

דער טאַטע אַ וואָלף, דער זון אַ הונט

If the father is a wolf, the son is a dog
Der tate a volf, der zun a hunt NS

משוגענע גענדז, משוגענע גריוון

Crazy geese, crazy cracklings
[That is, offspring]
Meshugene genz, meshugene grivn AC

HINDSIGHT

אחר-המעשׂה איז יעדערער אַ חכם

Afterwards, everyone is smart
*Akher-hamayse iz yederer a
khokhem* AC

אַז מען בריט זיך אויפֿן הייסן בלאָזט מען
אויפֿן קאַלטן

**Scalded by the hot, one blows on
the cold**
*Az men brit zikh oyfn heysn blozt men
oyfn kaltn* P

אַז מען גנבֿעט אַוועק דאָס פֿערד
פֿאַרשליסט מען ערשט די שטאַל

**The stable door is locked only after
the horse is stolen**
*Az men ganvet avek dos ferd farshlist
men ersht di shtal* NS

חכמה דערנאָך איז אַ גוטער בראָך

Smart too late is a disastrous state
Khokhme dernokh iz a guter brokh AC

שאַרפֿע אידעען קומען ווי די
פֿײַערלעשער – צו שפּעט

**Clever ideas come like firemen—
too late**
*Sharfe ideyen kumen vi di
fayerlesher—tsu shpet* NS

HOLIDAYS

אַז עס קומט פּורים פֿאַרגעסט מען אַלע
יסורים

**When Purim begins, we forget our
troubles and sins**
*Az es kumt purim fargest men ale
yesurim* AC

אַז מען האָט אויף פּורים יסורים איז
אויף פּסח חושך

**If Purim brings troubles, then
Passover will bring gloom**
*Az men hot oyf purim yesurim iz oyf
peysekh khoyshekh* IB

ערב יום-כיפור ווערן אלע גנבים פֿרום

On the eve of Yom Kippur all thieves become pious
Erev yomkiper vern ale ganovim frum AC

עס איז שבת איבער די גאַנצע וועלט

It's Shabbes the whole world over
Es iz shabes iber di gantse velt IB

פורים איז ניט קיין יום-טובֿ און קדחת איז ניט קיין קרענק

If Purim is no holiday, then convulsions is no disease
Purim iz nit keyn yontev un kadokhes iz nit keyn krenk P

פורים נאָך דער סעודה איז קיין ייד ניט הונגעריק

Purim after the feast no Jew is hungry
Purim nokh der sude iz keyn yid nit hungerik IB

HONESTY

אַז מען זאָגט דעם אמת פֿאַרשפּאָרט מען צו שווערן

Tell the truth and you won't need to swear
Az men zogt dem emes farshport men tsu shvern IB

איין גנבֿ גלייבט ניט דעם צווייטן

One thief doesn't believe another
Eyn ganef gleybt nit dem tsveytn NS

אויף זײַנע רייד קען מען ניט בויען קיין בנין

You can't erect a building on his word
Oyf zayne reyd ken men nit boyen keyn binyen AC

זאַלץ און ברויט זאָלסטו עסן און דעם אמת ניט פֿאַרגעסן

Of bread and salt partake, but the truth don't forsake
Zalts un broyt zolstu esn un dem emes nit fargesn NS

HONOR

אַ מענטש איז אומעטום אַ מענטש

An honorable person behaves well everywhere
A mentsh iz umetum a mentsh P

אַ נגיד האַסט כּבֿוד װי אַ קאַץ האַסט סמעטענע

A rich man hates esteem like a cat hates cream
A noged hast koved vi a kats hast smetene NS

אַז מען זאָגט דעם אמת פֿאַרשפּאָרט מען צו שװערן

If you tell the truth, you don't have to swear
Az men zogt dem emes farshport men tsu shvern IB

דער כּבֿוד איז פֿון דעם װאָס גיט אים און ניט פֿון דעם װאָס קריגט אים

Honor is measured by him who gives it and not by him who receives it
Der koved iz fun dem vos git im un nit fun dem vos krigt im NS

ערע איז פֿיל טײַערער װי געלט

Honor is more precious than money
Ere iz fil tayerer vi gelt NS

פֿאַר אומכּבֿוד אַנטלױף אָבער יאָג זיך ניט נאָך כּבֿוד

Run from an insult but don't chase honor
Far umkoved antloyf ober yog zikh nit nokh koved NS

האַלט דיר דעם כּבֿוד און זיץ אין דער הײם

Hang on to your dignity and stay home
Halt dir dem koved un zits in der heym AC

157

כּבֿוד איז ווי אַ שאָטן, וואָס מער מען
לויפֿט אים נאָך אַלץ ווײַטער אַנטלויפֿט
ער

**Honor is like a shadow; the more
you chase it, the more it escapes
you**

*Koved iz vi a shotn, vos mer men loyft
im nokh alts vayter antloyft er* NS

לויף ניט נאָך דעם כּבֿוד וועט ער אַליין
צו דיר קומען

**Don't chase after honor, and it will
come by itself**

*Loyf nit nokh dem koved vet er aleyn
tsu dir kumen* AC

אויף דער מצבֿה זײַנען אַלע ייִדן שיין

**According to the gravestones, all
Jews were honorable**

*Oyf der matseyve zaynen ale yidn
sheyn* NS

צו פֿיל כּבֿוד איז אַ האַלבע שאַנד

Too much honor is half disgrace

Tsu fil koved iz a halbe shand IB

ווו איך זיץ איז דער מזרח וואַנט

Wherever I sit is the eastern wall
[The seat of honor]

Vu ikh zits iz der mizrekh vant P

HOPE

אַז מען האָט בטחון גיט מען אויס
טעכטער

**With faith, you'll marry off your
daughters**

*Az men hot bitokhn git men oys
tekhter* AC

אַז מען האָט בטחון קומט מען אַלץ
אַדורך

**With faith you can overcome
anything**

*Az men hot bitokhn kumt men alts
adurkh* AC

אַז ס'איז דאָ ביינער וועט זײַן פֿלייש אויך

As long as there are bones, there'll also be meat
Az s'iz do beyner vet zayn fleysh oykh AC

דער מענטש טוט האָפֿן ביז ער ווערט אַנטשלאָפֿן

A person's hope will keep until he enters his final sleep
Der mentsh tut hofn biz er vert antshlofn NS

די גרוב איז שוין אָפֿן און דער מענטש טוט נאָך האָפֿן

Even though the grave is prepared, hope is unimpaired
Di grub iz shoyn ofn un der mentsh tut nokh hofn NS

פֿון האָפֿן ווערט מען ניט זאָט

Hope alone doesn't satisfy
Fun hofn vert men nit zat AC

גוט צו האָפֿן, שווער צו וואַרטן

It's good to hope, hard to wait
Gut tsu hofn, shver tsu vartn NS

מען וואַרט אויף אַ מלאך און עס קומט אַ גלח

One expects an angel at the very least, but all one gets is the priest
Men vart oyf a malekh un es kumt a galekh IB

אויף גאָט דאַרף מען האָפֿן און אַליין אויך ניט שלאָפֿן

Faith in God keep, but don't fall asleep
Oyf got darf men hofn un aleyn oykh nit shlofn NS

וואָס גרעסער דער דלות, אַלץ גרעסער די האָפֿענונג

The greater the poverty, the greater the hope
Vos greser der dales, alts greser di hofnung NS

HUNGER

אַ ניכטערער מאָגן קען קיין גוטס ניט
זאָגן

An empty stomach is not a good
advisor
*A nikhterer mogn ken keyn guts nit
zogn* NS

אַז מען האָט ניט קיין ברויט איז ערגער
ווי דער טויט

If you have no bread, it's worse
than being dead
*Az men hot nit keyn broyt iz erger vi
der toyt* IB

אַז מען לייגט זיך אומגעגעסן צײלט מען
די סטאָלאָוואַניעס

Go to bed hungry and you'll count
the rafters
[To forget]
*Az men leygt zikh umgegesn tseylt men
di stolovanyes* NS

ביסט הונגעריק? לעק זאַלץ וועט דיר
דאָרשטן

You're hungry? Lick salt and you'll
be thirsty instead
*Bist hungerik? lek zalts vet dir
darshtn* NS

"דבש וחלב תחת לשונו" – און אין דער
היים נישטאָ קיין פּוטער אויף ברויט

"Honey and milk on his tongue"—
but at home there's no butter for
bread
*"Dvash v'khalev tokhes l'shoyne"—un
in der heym nishto keyn puter oyf
broyt* IB

פֿאַר אַ הונגעריקן בײַכל איז קירבעס
אויך אַ מאכל

To a hungry belly, a pumpkin is
also a delicacy
*Far a hungerikn baykhl iz kirbes oykh
a maykhl* NS

פֿון על חטא ווערט מען ניט פֿעט

From fasting you don't gain weight
Fun al khet vert men nit fet NS

פֿון תּהילים זאָגן טוט דער בױך ניט װײ From psalm-saying the belly won't
אָבער זאַט װערן קען מען ניט ache, but it won't be satisfied either
Fun tilim zogn tut der boykh nit vey
ober zat vern ken men nit NS

הונגער קען ניט קײן געבאָט Hunger recognizes no law
Hunger ken nit keyn gebot P

ליפעלעך אפֿילו ראָזינקע בעטן עסן Lips, however rosy, must be fed
Lipelekh afile rozinke betn esn AC

אױף אַ ניכטערן מאָגן קען מען קײן זאַך An empty stomach can't tolerate
ניט פֿאַרטראָגן anything
Oyf a nikhtern mogn ken men keyn
zakh nit fartrogn NS

פֿאַר אַ הונגעריקן איז דאָס זױערע זיס To the hungry, the sour tastes sweet
Far a hungerikn iz dos zoyere zis AC

װען זינגט אַ ייִד? װען ער איז הונגעריק When does a Jew sing? When he's
hungry
[That is, to forget]
Ven zingt a yid? ven er iz hungerik IB

װאָס נוצט כּבֿוד אַז מען האָט ניט צו What use is honor when there's not
עסן? enough to eat?
Vos nutst koved az men hot nit tsu
esn? AC

HYPOCRISY

דער גױ איז טרײף אָבער די שיקסע איז The Goy is treyf, but the non-Jewish
כּשר girl is kosher
Der goy iz treyf ober di shikse iz
kosher AC

דער חזיר איז טרייף אָבער דער מקח איז
כשר

The pig is treyf but the price is kosher
Der khazer iz treyf ober der mekekh iz kosher IB

דער שמשׂ קלאַפּט 'אין שול אַרייַן' און
אַליין לייגט ער זיך שלאָפֿן

The sexton calls: "to the synagogue!" But he himself goes to sleep
Der shames kapt: 'in shul arayn' un aleyn leygt er zikh shlofn NS

ער גלייבט ניט אין גאָט און בעט זייַן
גענאָד

He doesn't believe in God yet he seeks His mercy
Er gleybt nit in got un bet zayn genod AC

ער מיינט ניט די דרשה נאָר די בקשה

Not the sermon is he after, but the fee that comes thereafter
Er meynt nit di droshe nor di bakoshe NS

ער מיינט ניט די חרסות נאָר די ארבע
כוסות

Not of the charoseth does he think, but of the four cups of wine he'll drink
[Refers to the Passover Seder]
Er meynt nit di kharoyses nor di arbe koyses NS

ערבֿ יום-כיפּור װערן אַלע גנבֿים פֿרום

On the eve of Yom Kippur, all thieves become pious
Erev yomkiper vern ale ganovim frum AC

קוש מיך ניט און זייַ ניט מייַן מחותן

Don't kiss me and don't become my in-law
Kush mikh nit un zay nit mayn mekhutn AC

צו ליגן מיט אַ שיקסע איז ניט טרייף, צו
הייראַטן מיט אַ שיקסע איז ניט כּשר

**To lie with a Gentile girl is not
forbidden, but to marry one is not
kosher**
*Tsu lign mit a shikse iz nit treyf, tsu
hayratn mit a shikse iz nit kosher* AC

טו מיר ניט אָן קיין מענטעלע און גיב
מיר ניט קיין הענטעלע

**Don't dress me grand and don't give
me the back of your hand**
*Tu mir nit on keyn mentele un gib mir
nit keyn hentele* NS

ווער עס האָט אַ שם פֿאַר אַ פֿריען
אויפֿשטייער דער מעג ביז זייגער צוועלף
אין בעט ליגן

**He who is known as an early riser
may lie in bed until noon**
*Ver es hot a shem far a fri'en oyfshteyer
der meg biz zeyger tsvelf in bet lign* NS

וואָס העכער ער רעדט פֿון זייַן כּבֿוד אַלץ
שנעלער ציילט מען די לעפֿל

**The louder he talks of his honor,
the faster we count the cutlery**
*Vos hekher er ret fun zayn koved alts
shneler tseylt men di lefl* AC

יעדער מענטש קען פֿאַרטראָגן זייַן
אייגענעם פֿאָרץ

**Every person can tolerate his own
fart**
*Yeder mentsh ken fartrogn zayn
eygenem forts* AC

יונגערהייט אַ זונה, אויף דער עלטער אַ
גבאיטע

**When young, a whore; when old, a
model of propriety**
*Yungerheyt a zoyne, oyf der elter a
gabete* AC

זייַ מיר ניט קיין פֿייַגעלע און האָב אויף
מיר ניט קיין רחמנות

**Don't be a little bird, and don't take
pity on me**
[Don't pelt me with droppings]
*Zay mir nit keyn feygele un hob oyf mir
nit keyn rakhmones* AC

IGNORANCE

אַ גוי בלײַבט אַ גוי   **A Goy remains a Goy**
A goy glaybt a goy   P

אַ שלעכטע ראָד סקריפעט אַמערגסטנס   **A faulty wheel makes the most noise**
A shlekhte rod skripet amergstns   NS

אַן עם-הארץ דאַרף הויך ניט דאַוועגען   **An ignoramus doesn't need to pray aloud**
An amorets darf hoykh nit davenen   NS

אַן אָקס האָט אַ לאַנגע צונג און קען קיין שופֿר ניט בלאָזן   **An ox has a long tongue but can't blow the shofar**
An oks hot a lange tsung un ken keyn shoyfer nit blozn   NS

אַז דער חזן קען קיין עבֿרי ניט הייסט ער אַ 'קענטאָר'   **If the hazzan doesn't know Hebrew he's called a "cantor"**
Az der khazn ken keyn ivre nit heyst er a 'kentor'   AC

אַז מען איז מכבד אַן עם-הארץ מיט
הגבה זאָגט ער אַז ער איז הייזעריק

**Honor an ignoramus with the
raising of the Torah, and he'll
decline saying he's hoarse**
*Az men iz mekhabed an amorets mit
hagbe zogt er az er iz heyzerik* AC

אַז מען קלאַפּט אין טיש רופֿט זיך אָפּ די
שער

**When you thump the table, the
scissors jump**
*Az men klapt in tish ruft zikh op di
sher* IB

אַז מען וואַרפֿט אַ שטעקן אין דער וואַנט
בלייבט ער אַלץ שטעקן

**Throw a stick against the wall, it
still remains a stick**
*Az men varft a shtekn in der vant
blaybt er alts shtekn* IB

אַז מען ווייסט ניט זאָל מען זיך
אַוועקזעצן אין אַ זייט און שווייגן

**If you don't know, stand aside and
keep quiet**
*Az men veyst nit zol men zikh
avekzetsn in a zayt un shvaygn* AC

אַז מען זעצט אַריין אַ גאָנדז אין האָבער
שטאַרבט זי פֿון הונגער

**Let a goose loose in the oats and it
starves from hunger**
*Az men zetst arayn a ganz in hober
shtarbt zi fun hunger* NS

דער חמור טראָגט ספֿרים אָבער העלפֿן
העלפֿט עס ניט

**The ass carries books but it doesn't
help**
*Der khamer trogt sforim ober helfn
helft es nit* AC

דער וואָס קען ניט קיין עבֿרי איז אַן
עם-הארץ, דער וואָס קען ניט קיין יידיש
איז אַ גוי

**If you know no Hebrew, you're an
ignoramus; if you know no Yiddish,
you're a Goy**
*Der vos ken nit keyn ivre iz an
amorets, der vos ken nit keyn yidish iz
a goy* IB

די הון הערט דעם האָנס דרשה און זוכט
זיך אַ קערנדל פּראָסע

The hen hears the rooster's sermon
but continues to peck for a kernel
*Di hun hert dem hons droshe un zukht
zikh a kerndl prose* IB

ער איז אַ דאָקטער – ער קען אַ קרענק!

He's some doctor—all he knows is
ailments!
Er iz a dokter—er ken a krenk! P

ער איז אויסגעגאַנגען אַלע
קלאַסן – באָרוועס!

He graduated every class—barefoot!
*Er iz oysgegangen ale klasn—
borves!* NS

ער שרײַבט נח מיט זיבן גרײַזן!

He spells Noah with seven mistakes!
[Noah is written with two letters in
Hebrew]
Er shraybt noyekh mit zibn grayzn! IB

איינער רעדט רוסיש ווי אַ ייִד, אַן
אַנדערער רעדט ייִדיש ווי אַ גוי

One person speaks Russian like a
Jew, another speaks Yiddish like a
Goy
*Eyner ret rusish vi a yid, an anderer ret
yidish vi a goy* NS

"כתר" האָט ער פֿאַרגעסן און "נעריצך"
האָט ער זיך ניט אויסגעלערנט

The old prayer he forgot, and the
new one he still hasn't learned
*"Keyser" hot er fargesn un "naritsekho"
hot er zikh nit oysgelernt* AC

מען לערנט זיך ביז זיבעציק און מען
שטאַרבט אַ נאַר

You study until seventy and die a
fool anyway
*Men lernt zikh biz zibetsik un men
shtarbt a nar* NS

אויף וואָס דאַרף אַ מענטש האָבן
אויערן? דאָס היטל זאָל ניט אַראָפּפֿאַלן
איבער די אויגן

Why does a person need ears? So
his cap won't fall into his eyes
*Oyf vos darf a mentsh hobn oyern? dos
hitl zol nit aropfaln iber di oygn* AC

166

וועַן אַ פֿערד וואָלט געוווּסט ווי קליין
דער מענטש איז – וואָלט עס אים דורס
געוועַן

If a horse knew how small man is—
it would trample him
*Ven a ferd volt gevust vi kleyn der
mentsh iz—volt es im doyres geven* NS

וועַן איין בלינדער פֿירט דעם אַנדערן
פֿאַלן ביידע אין גרוב אַריַין

When the blind lead the blind, they
all fall into the ditch
*Ven eyn blinder firt dem andern faln
beyde in grub arayn* IB

וויפֿל משה רבינוס זײַנען דאָ אויף דער
וועלט? דרײַ: משה דער שוסטער,
אבֿרהמל דער שנײַדער און איך, מאָטקע

How many Moses Our Teacher are
there in this world? Three: Moses
the shoemaker, Avreml the tailor
and me, Motke!
*Vifl moyshe rabeynus zaynen do oyf
der velt? dray: moyshe der shuster,
avreml der shnayder un ikh, motke!* IB

וואָס געפֿעלט אַ פֿערד? האָבער

What appeals to a horse? Oats
Vos gefelt a ferd? hober NS

וואָס ווייניקער אַלץ געזינטער

The less you know, the healthier
Vos veyniker alts gezinter AC

זיבן יאָר איז די בעל-הביתטע אין שטוב
און ווייסט נאָך אַלץ ניט אַז די קאַץ איז
אָן אַן עק

A housewife for seven years and
she still doesn't know that the cat
has no tail!
*Zibn yor iz di balebuste in shtub un
veyst nokh alts nit az di kats iz on an
ek!* NS

ILLNESS

אַ קראַנקן פֿרעגט מען, אַ געזונטן גיט
מען

Inquire of the sick, feed the healthy
unasked
*A krankn fregt men a gezuntn git
men* P

167

אַמאָל איז די רפֿואה ערגער פֿאַר דער מכה	**Sometimes the cure is worse than the disease** *Amol iz di refu'e erger far der make* P
אַראָפ דער קאָפ, אַראָפ דער ווייטיק!	**Off with the head, off with the headache!** *Arop der kop, arop der veytik!* NS
אַז עס בײַסט קראַצט מען זיך	**If it itches, scratch** *Az es bayst kratst men zikh* NS
דעם קראַנקן אַרט אפֿילו אַ פֿליג אויף דער וואַנט	**A sick person is bothered even by a fly on the wall** *Dem krankn art afile a flig oyf der vant* AC
דרײַ מענטשן מוזן האָבן שמירה: אַ חתן, אַ כלה און אַ חולה	**Three people need to be guarded: a bride, a groom, and a sick person** *Dray mentshn muzn hobn shmire: a khosn, a kale un a khoyle* NS
איינער ווערט קראַנק פֿון איבערעסן, דער צווייטער ווערט קראַנק פֿון ניט דערעסן	**One person gets sick from overeating, another from not enough to eat** *Eyner vert krank fun iberesn, der tsveyter vert krank fun nit deresn* IB
איינער ווייסט ניט דעם אַנדערנס קרענק	**No one can know another's ailment** *Eyner veyst nit dem anderns krenk* P
גאָט זאָל אָפּהיטן פֿון ווײַסע ירמולקעס!	**God protect us from white skullcaps!** [White skull caps were often worn by sick people to ward off the Angel of Death] *Got zol op'hitn fun vayse yarmulkes!* IB

ווען תהילים זאָל זײַן אַ רפֿואה וואָלט
מען עס פֿאַרקויפֿט אין אַפטייק

**If psalms could cure, they'd sell
them at the drugstore**
*Ven tilim zol zayn a refu'e volt men es
farkoyft in apteyk* NS

INCOMPETENCE

אַ גרויסער אויוון – אַ קלײנער חלה!

A big oven—a small challah!
A groyser oyvn—a kleyner khale! P

אַ שלעמיאל פֿאַלט אויף שטרוי און
צעקלאַפֿט זיך די נאָז

**A shlemiel falls on straw and
bruises his nose**
*A shlemi'el falt oyf shtroy un tseklapt
zikh di noz* NS

אַ שלימזל: גייט ער טאַנצן צערײַסן זיך
בײַ די כלי-זמרים די סטרונעס

**When a shlimazl goes dancing, the
musicians' strings break**
*A shlimazl: geyt er tantsn tseraysn zikh
bay di klezmorim di strunes* NS

אַ שלימזל קומט אויך אַמאָל צו ניץ

**Even a shlimazl sometimes comes
in handy**
A shlimazl kumt oykh amol tsu nits AC

ביסט אַ חזן? זינג זשע, ביסט אַ גלח?
קלינג זשע

**If you're a cantor, sing; if you're a
priest, ring the bells**
*Bist a khazn? zing zhe, bist a galekh?
kling zhe* IB

דער טאַטע האָט גענומען די מאַמע און
איך מוז נעמען אַ פֿרעמדע כלה!

**My father married my mother, but
I must marry a strange female!**
*Der tate hot genumen di mame un ikh
muz nemen a fremde kale!* AC

ער האָט געהערט קלינגען און קען ניט
נאָכזינגען

**He hears the ringing but can't
follow the singing**
*Er hot gehert klingen un ken nit
nokhzingen* IF

ער איז אַ מבֿין ווי אַ קאַץ אויף הייוון	**He's an expert like a cat knows about yeast** *Er iz a meyvn vi a kats oyf heyvn* AC
די ליכטיקע וועלט איז פֿון שלימזל פֿאַרשטעלט	**The world so bright is hidden from the fool's sight** *Di likhtike velt iz fun shlimazl farshtelt* NS
ער איז ווי אַ גוט קעלבל, ער נעמט אָן בײַ יעדער קו	**He's a willing calf, he sucks up to any cow** *Er iz vi a gut kelbl, er nemt on bay yeder ku* IF
ער קען זיך נאָך אויסרײַבן אויף אַ שמאַטע!	**He could yet wear himself out into a rag!** *Er ken zikh nokh oysraybn oyf a shmate!* IB
ער נעמט אַ מעסער און גייט זיך הענגען	**He takes a knife to hang himself** *Er nemt a meser un geyt zikh hengen!* NS
ער שנײַצט די נאָז און שמירט זיך דאָס פנים!	**He blows his nose and smears it all over his face!** *Er shnaytst di noz un shmirt zikh dos ponim!* IF
ער שטעלט צוזאַמען צוויי ווענט און עס לאָזט זיך אויס אַ בוידעם!	**He brings two walls together and the attic caves in!** *Er shtelt tsuzamen tsvey vent un es lozt zikh oys a boydem!* IF
קו געשאָרן, באָק געמאָלקן!	**Sheared the cows, milked the steers!** *Ku geshorn, bok gemolkn!* NS

מען שיקט אים צום רב, גייט ער צו דער
רביצין!

Send him to the rabbi, he goes to the rabbi's wife instead!
Men shikt im tsum rov geyt er tsu der rebetsin! AC

אויך מיר אַ קונץ צו זײַן אַ בעקער – מען
נעמט אַ טייגל און מען מאַכט אַ בייגל!

Baking—some skill! You take some dough and you make a bagel
Oykh mir a kunts tsu zayn a beker— men nemt a teygl un men makht a beygl! NS

אָך און ווי צו אים וועמענס ווײַב
טראָגט די הויזן!

Woe to him whose wife wears the pants!
Okh un vey tsu im vemens vayb trogt di hoyzn! IB

שלימזל, ווהין גייסטו? צום אָרעמאַן

Shlimazl, where are you going? To the pauper
Shlimazl, vuhin geystu? tsum oreman IB

ווען אַ שלימזל האָט אַ ווײַב לייגט זי זיך
אין קומפּעט ערב פּסח

When a shlimazl has a wife, she delivers the baby on the eve of Passover
[She won't be able to prepare the Seder]
Ven a shlimazl hot a vayb leygt zi zikh in kimpet erev peysekh NS

ווען חסידים וואַנדערן, רעגנט

When Hassidim go wandering, it rains
[Derogatory comment by an opponent of Hassidism]
Ven khsidim vandern, regnt NS

171

ווו ער וועט זײַן רב וועט אָפּברענען די קהילה	**Wherever he will become the rabbi, the community will burn down** *Vu er vet zayn rov vet opbrenen di kehile* NS
זאָל איך ווערן אַ היטל מאַכער וואָלטן אַלע קינדער געבוירן געוואָרן אָן קעפּ	**If I became a cap maker, all children would be born without heads** *Zol ikh vern a hitl makher voltn ale kinder geboyn gevorn on kep* AC

INDIVIDUALITY

אַז איך וועל זײַן ווי ער, ווער וועט זײַן ווי איך?	**If I will be like him, who will be like me?** *Az ikh vel zayn vi er, ver vet zayn vi ikh?* AC
איטלעכער גייט מיט זײַן ווייטיק	**Each one bears his own pain** *Itlekher geyt mit zayn veytik* NS
מײַן נשמה איז ניט קיין ראָזשינקע!	**My soul is no mere raisin!** *Mayn neshome iz nit keyn rozhinke!* AC
יעדער מענטש איז אַ גאַנצער עולם-קטן	**Every person is a whole world in miniature** *Yeder mentsh iz a gantser oylem- kotn* AC

INEVITABILITY

אַז די ערשטע שורה איז קרום טויג דער גאַנצער בריוו אויף כפרות	**When the first line is faulty, the entire letter is worthless** *Az di ershte shure iz krum toyg der gantser briv oyf kapores* IB

דער ייִד האָט נאָר געלט צו פֿאַרלירן און
צײַט קראַנק צו זײַן

**A Jew has money only to lose, and
time only to be sick**
*Der yid hot nor gelt tsu farlirn un tsayt
krank tsu zayn* NS

גזרות ברענגען צו עבֿרות

Regulations lead to violations
Gezeyres brengen tsu aveyres NS

צרות, העלץ און האָר וואַקסן אַ גאַנץ
יאָר

**Troubles, trees, and hair grow
throughout the year**
*Tsores, holts un hor vaksn a gants
yor* NS

ווער עס וואַרפֿט אויף יענעם שטיינער
קריגט צוריק אין די אייגענע ביינער

**If at others you throw stones, expect
them back at your own bones**
*Ver es varft oyf yenem shteyner krigt
tsurik in di eygene beyner* NS

וווּ מען זייט אים ניט דאָרט וואַקסט ער

**Where you don't plant him, he
sprouts**
Vu men zeyt im nit dort vakst er NS

INFORMATION

אַ וועלט שלאָפֿט ניט

The whole world isn't asleep
A velt shloft nit P

גוטע בשׂורות הערט מען פֿון דער
ווײַטנס

Good news travels from afar
Gute p'sures hert men fun der vaytns P

שיק דײַנע אויערן אין די טויערן

Send your ear out to hear
Shik dayne oyern in di toyern NS

וואָס הערט מען אין ים? מען כאַפּט פֿיש

**What's new at sea? They're
catching fish**
*Vos hert men in yam? men khapt
fish* NS

173

INSULT

אַ גוטער געהערט אויפֿן גוטן אָרט

A good person belongs in a good place
[That is, the cemetery]
A guter gehert oyfn gutn ort AC

אַ מיוחת קושט אין תחת

The upper class can kiss my ass!
A meyukhes kusht in tokhes! WZ

די מאַמע איז אַ צדיקעת און די טאָכטער איז אויך אַ זונה

The mother is a saintly one, and the daughter is also a tainted one
[Play on words]
Di mame iz a tsedeykes un di tokhter iz oykh a zoyne AC

פֿאַר אומכבֿוד אַנטלויף אָבער יאָג זיך ניט נאָך כבֿוד

Flee from an insult, but don't chase after honor
Far umkoved antloyf ober yog zikh nit nokh koved NS

גיי פֿאַרדריי דיר דײַן אייגן קאָפּ וועסטו מיינען אַז ס'איז מײַנער!

Go set your own head spinning and you'll think it's mine!
Gey fardrey dir dayn eygn kop vestu meynen az s'iz mayner! P

גיי קוש אַ בער אונטערן פֿאַרטאָך!

Go kiss a bear under his apron!
[Kiss my ass]
Gey kush a ber untern fartakh! NS

מען מוז אַראָפּשלינגען

One must swallow it
Men muz aropshlingen IF

ניט גענוג וואָס מען ווערט אָן דאָס געלט רופֿט נאָך יענער נאַר אויך!

Not enough the money was forfeited; you have to endure being called a fool, too!
Nit genug vos men vert on dos gelt, ruft nokh yener nar oykh! AC

JEWS

אַ פּריץ האָט אין זין פֿערד און הינט, אַ
יִיד האָט אין זין ווײַב און קינד

The gentry worry about horse and dog; Jews worry about wife and child
A porets hot in zin ferd un hint, a yid hot in zin vayb un kind IB

אַ יִיד אַז ער צעברעאכט אַ פֿוס זאָגט ער:
אַ גליק וואָס איך האָב דעם אַנדערן ניט
צעברעאָכן, צעברעכט ער בײַדע זאָגט ער:
אַ גליק וואָס איך האָב דעם קאַרק ניט
צעברעאָכן

When a Jew breaks a leg, he says: "It's lucky I didn't break both legs"; when he breaks both legs, he says: "It's lucky I didn't break my neck"
A yid az er tsebrakht a fus zogt er: a glik vos ikh hob dem andern nit tsebrokhn; tsebrekht er beyde, zogt er: a glik vos ikh hob dem kark nit tsebrokhn IB

אַ יִיד וואָס ער איז איז ער, קיין נאַר איז
ער ניט

A Jew, whatever he is, he's no fool
A yid, vos er iz iz er, keyn nar iz er nit AC

אַ יִידישע נשמה קען מען ניט אָפּשאַצן

A Jewish soul is without measure
A yidishe neshome ken men nit op'shatsn P

175

אַלע ייִדן האָבן אײן שכל

All Jews have the same outlook
Ale yidn hobn eyn seykhl NS

אַלע ייִדן זײַנען אײן משפחה

All Jew belongs to one family
Ale yidn zaynen eyn mishpokhe NS

"אתה בחרתנו מכל העמים" – און פֿאַרן
שייגעץ האָסטו מורא?

**"Thou didst choose us from among
the nations"—and You're afraid of
the Gentile boys?**
*"Ata bokhartanu m'kol ha'amim"—un
farn sheygets hostu moyre?* NS

אַזױ איז שױן בײַ אונדז ייִדן אַ מינהג:
טאָמער איז שױן בײַ אונדז אַמאָל אַ סדר
פֿרעגט מען: מה נשתנה?

**That's the custom among us Jews. If
once in a long while we do have a
festive meal, we ask: "Why is this
night different?"**
[Refers to the Passover Seder]
*Azoy iz shoyn bay undz yidn a minheg:
tomer iz shoyn bay undz amol a seyder
fregt men: manishtane?* NS

בעסער אין גױיִשע הענט אײדער אין
ייִדישע מײַלער

**Better in Gentile hands than in
Jewish mouths**
*Beser in goyishe hent eyder in yidishe
mayler* IB

דעם ייִדן מיטן וואַנדער שטעקן געפֿינט
מען אין אַלע עקן

**The Wandering Jew is found all
over the world**
*Dem yidn mitn vander shtekn gefint
men in ale ekn* NS

דעם ייִדן מײַדט קײן אומגליק ניט אױס

A Jew can't avoid misfortune
Dem yidn mayt keyn umglik nit oys NS

דעם ייִדנס שימחה איז מיט אַ ביסל
שרעק

**A Jew's celebration is fraught with
trepidation**
Dem yidns simkhe iz mit a bisl shrek AC

דער ייד ענטפֿערט תמיד פֿאַרקערט: A Jew always answers the opposite:
זאָגט מען אים שלום-עליכם ענטפֿערט greet him with sholem aleichem
ער עליכם-שלום and he will reply: aleichem-sholem
[Peace to you, to you peace—
customary reply to a traditional
greeting]
*Der yid entfert tomed farkert: zogt men
im sholem-aleykhem entfert er
aleykhem-sholem* IB

דער ייד איז פֿון כסדר אָן אַן איש A Jew is forever warlike—always
מלחמה – שטענדיק שלאָגט ער זיך מיט fighting with his conscience
דער דעה *Der yid iz fun keseyder on an ish
milkhome—shtendik shlogt er zikh mit
der deye* NS

דרײַ ייִדישע תענוגים: אַ פֿריילעכער Three Jewish delights: a cheerful
בית-עולם, אַ וואַרעמע מיקווה און אַ cemetery, a warm ritual bath, and a
ליכטיקע לבֿנה bright moon
*Dray yidishe tanogim: a freylekher
besoylem, a vareme mikve un a likhtike
levone* NS

איינער רעדט רוסיש ווי אַ ייד, אַן One person speaks Russian like a
אַנדערער רעדט ייִדיש ווי אַ גוי Jew, another speaks Yiddish like a
Goy
*Eyner ret rusish vi a yid, an anderer ret
yidish vi a goy* NS

פֿון ייִדישע רייד קען מען זיך ניט Ten washings cannot cleanse one of
אָפּוואַשן אפֿילו אין צען וואַסערן Jewish talk
*Fun yidishe reyd ken men zikh nit
opvashn afile in tsen vasern* NS

גנבֿעט אַ גוי העַנגט מען דעם גנבֿ, גנבֿעט If a Goy steals, the thief is hanged;
אַ ייד, העַנגט מען דעם ייד if a Jew steals, the Jew is hanged
*Ganvet a goy, hengt men dem ganef;
ganvet a yid, hengt men dem yid* NS

לעבן זאָל מען צווישן גויים, שטאַרבן
זאָל מען צווישן יידן

Live among Goyim, die among Jews
Lebn zol men tsvishn goyim, shtarbn zol men tsvishn yidn NS

מיט אַ יידן איז גוט קוגל צו עסן אָבער
ניט פֿון איין טעלער

It's good to eat pudding with a Jew, but not from the same plate
Mit a yidn iz gut kugl tsu esn ober nit fun eyn teler IB

מיט אַ יידן איז גוט אין שול צו גיין אָבער
ניט אַהיים

It's good to go to the synagogue with fellow Jews, but not to return home with them
Mit a yidn iz gut in shul tsu geyn ober nit aheym AC

טאָמער איז ביַי אונדז יידן אַמאָל אַ סדר,
טוט מען אָן אַ העמד איבער דער
קאַפּאָטע, מען טרינקט וויַין און מען
פֿאַרביַיסט מיט כריין

If a Jew has a seder once in a while, he dons a smock over his clothes, drinks wine, and eats bitter herbs
[Refers to Passover Seder]
Tomer iz bay unz yidn amol a seyder, tut men on a hemd iber der kapote, men trinkt vayn un men farbayst mit khreyn NS

ווען האָט אַ ייד אַ גוטן טאָג? אויפֿן
צווייטן טאָג נאָך קדחת

When does a Jew have a good day? The day after fever breaks
Ven hot a yid a gutn tog? oyfn tsveytn tog nokh kadokhes NS

ווען זינגט אַ ייד? ווען ער איז הונגעריק

When does a Jew sing? When he's hungry
Ven zingt a yid? ven er iz hungerik IB

178

ווער עס האָט ניט קיין בושה אין פּנים
און קיין רחמנות אין האַרץ דער קומט
ניט אַרויס פֿון ייִדן

**Whoever has not tasted humiliation
and feels no pity, doesn't descend
from Jews**
*Ver es hot nit keyn bushe in ponim un
keyn rakhmones in harts der kumt nit
aroys fun yidn* IB

ווי עס פֿאַלט אַ שטיין טרעפֿט ער דעם
ייִדן

**No matter how the stone falls, it
finds a Jew**
Vi es falt a shteyn treft er dem yidn NS

וואָס העלפֿט דעם ייִדנס יללות אַז מען
בלײַבט סײַ ווי אין גלות

**What can wailing attain if in exile
we remain?**
*Vos helft dem yidns yayles az men
blaybt say vi in goles?* AC

וואָס ירשענען ייִדן? צרות און מערידן

**What do Jews inherit? Troubles and
hemorrhoids**
*Vos yarshenen yidn? tsores un
meridn* IB

יעדער ייִד האָט זײַן שולחן-ערוך

**Every Jew observes his own Code of
Laws**
Yeder yid hot zayn shulkhn-orekh NS

ייִדישע עשירות קומט מיטן ווינט און
גייט אַוועק מיטן רויך

**Jewish wealth comes with the wind
and goes with the smoke**
*Yidishe ashires kumt mitn vint un geyt
avek mitn roykh* NS

ייִדן זײַנען גרויסע פֿילאַנטראָפּן: פֿאַר אַ
'גוט מאָרגן' גיבן זיי אַ 'גוט יאָר'

**Jews are very generous: wish them
"good morning" and they'll answer
"good year"**
*Yidn zaynen groyse filantropn: far a
'gut-morgn' gibn zey a 'gut-yor'* IB

ייִדישע קעפּלעך: קלאָגן און וויינען און
עסן ווידער קרעפּלעך

Jewish heads: they weep and wail
and eat dumplings without fail
*Yidishe keplekh: klogn un veynen un
esn vider kreplekh* NS

זײַ אַ ייִד אין דער היים און אַ מענטש אין
גאַס

Be a Jew at home and like everyone
else outside
*Zay a yid in der heym un a mentsh in
gas* IF

JUSTICE

אַז ביידע בעלי-דינים זײַנען גערעכט איז
שלעכט

When both litigants are right, it's a
sorry sight
*Az beyde baley-dinim zaynen gerekht
iz shlekht* NS

אַז דו האָסט ניט קיין יושר גיי דאַוונען
מינחה

If you don't have a sense of justice,
you might as well say your prayers
*Az du host nit keyn yoysher gey
davenen minkhe* AC

בײַם מישפּט מוז מען ביידע צדדים
אויסהערן

In a lawsuit both sides must be
heard
*Baym mishpet muz men beyde
tsadodim oys'hern* IB

דער דרך היושר איז אַלע מאָל כשר

The just way is always the right
way
*Der derekh hayoysher iz ale mol
kosher* P

איינער בויט און אַן אַנדערער וווינט

One person builds the house,
another lives in it
Eyner boyt un an anderer voynt AC

אײנער נײט, דער צװײטער גײט

One person sews and on another it shows
Eyner neyt, der tsveyter geyt AC

גנבֿעט אַ גוי העונגט מען דעם גנבֿ, גנבֿעט
אַ ייִד העונגט מען דעם ייִד

If a Goy steals, the thief is hanged; if a Jew steals, the Jew is hanged
Ganvet a goy, hengt men dem ganef; ganvet a yid, hengt men dem yid AC

"כּי ישר ה'" — דעם נגיד גיסטו עסן און
דעם קבצן גיסטו אַפּעטיט?

"How just is the Lord"—the rich You give food and the poor only appetite?
"Ki yasher adoyshem"—dem noged gistu esn un dem kaptsn gistu apetit? AC

מיט קהל איז זיך שלעכט צו מישפּטן

It's not good to fight with the community
[Go fight City Hall!]
Mit ko'ol iz zikh shlekht tsu mishpetn IB

יושר װערט דערמאָנט אפֿילו בײַ גנבֿים
װען זײ טײלן זיך

Justice is invoked even among thieves when they divide the spoils
Yoysher vert dermont afile bay ganovim ven zey teyln zikh AC

KINDNESS

גוטס געדענקט מען, שלעכטס פֿילט מען **Kindness is remembered, meanness is felt**
Guts gedenkt men, shlekhts filt men IB

גוטסקייט איז בעסער ווי פֿרומקייט **Kindness is better than piety**
Gutskeyt iz beser vi frumkeyt IB

ניט דער שטעקן העלפֿט נאָר דאָס גוטע וואָרט **It's not the stick that helps, but the kind word**
Nit der shtekn helft nor dos gute vort NS

KINSHIP

אַ משומד אין דער משפחה קומט אויך אַמאָל צו ניץ **An apostate in the family sometimes proves useful**
A meshumed in der mishpokhe kumt oykh amol tsu nits AC

אַז מען לעבט מיט אַ טייוול ווערט מען אַליין אַ טייוול **Live with a devil and you become a devil**
Az men lebt mit a tayvl vert men aleyn a tayvl NS

182

בינד מיך אויף אַלע פֿיר נאָר וואַרף מיך
צווישן אייגענע

Bind me hand and foot, but throw me among my own
Bind mikh oyf ale fir nor varf mikh tsvishn eygene IB

בלוט איז ניט קיין וואַסער

Blood is not water
Blut iz nit keyn vaser IB

אייגנס איז ליב

One's own is beloved
Eygns iz lib P

פֿון אַן אייגענעם האָט מען דאָס גענאָר

Familiarity breeds contempt
Fun an eygenem hot men dos genar P

איטלעכע משפחה האָט זיך איר גסרחה

Every family has its own stench
Itlekhe mishpokhe hot zikh ir gasrokhe NS

מײַן פֿערדס בײַטש־שטעקעלע איז
געווען בײַ זײַן זיינדס וואָגן אַ פֿלעקעלע

My little horsewhip was no more than a spot on his grandfather's wagon
Mayn ferds baytsh-shtekele iz geven bay zayn zeydns vogn a flekele IB

מען קען זיך קלײַבן פֿרײַנד אָבער ניט
קיין משפחה

You can choose your friends but not your relatives
Men ken zikh klaybn fraynd ober nit keyn mishpokhe AC

ווער שעמט זיך מיט זײַן משפחה אויף
דעם איז קיין ברכה

Who is ashamed of his kin no blessings will win
Ver shemt zikh mit zayn mishpokhe oyf dem iz keyn brokhe NS

וווּ עס איז דאָ אַן אָרעמאַן איז ער
מײַנער אַ קרוֹב

Wherever there's a pauper, he's my relative
Vu es iz do an oreman iz er mayner a korev AC

זײַן האָן האָט געקרייט אויף מײַן דאַך

His rooster crowed on my roof
[Satirical comment on a
questionable relationship]
Zayn hon hot gekreyt oyf mayn dakh   AC

KNOWLEDGE

אַ סך מענטשן זעען אָבער וייניק פֿון זיי
פֿאַרשטייןן

Many see, but few understand
*A sakh memtshn zen nor veynik fun
zey farshteyn*   AC

אַז דער הונט האָט געכאַפּט דעם בייגל
זאָל ער שוין כאַפּן דעם סידור אויך

**Since the dog grabbed the bagel, let
him grab the prayerbook, too**
[Containing the commandment:
Thou shalt not steal]
*Az der hunt hot gekhapt dem beygl zol
er shoyn khapn dem sider oykh*   NS

דער רבֿ זאָל וויסן, וואָלט ער זיך דעם
קאַפֿטן צעריסן

**If the rabbi was aware, his clothes
he'd tear**
*Der rov zol visn volt er zikh dem kaftn
tserisn*   IF

די פּען שיסט ערגער ווי אַ פֿײַל

The pen is deadlier than an arrow
Di pen shist erger vi a fay!   NS

לײַכטער צען לענדער איידער איין
מענטש צו דערקענען

**Ten countries are sooner understood
than one person**
*Laykhter tsen lender eyder eyn mentsh
tsu derkenen*   NS

ווילסטו ניט וויסן, גלייב; ווילסטו ניט
גלייבן, ווייס!

**If you don't want to know, believe;
if you don't want to believe, know!**
*Vilstu nit visn, gleyb; vilstu nit gleybn,
veys!*   AC

זײַ אַלט ווי אַ קו און לערן זיך צו!

Be old as a cow but learn how!
Zay alt vi a ku un lern zikh tsu!   AC

184

LAUGHTER AND TEARS

אַ געלעכטער הערט מען ווײַטער ווי אַ
געוויין

**Laughter is heard farther than
weeping**
*A gelekhter hert men vayter vi a
geveyn* NS

איינער לאַכט פֿון צרות און אַ צווײטער
ווינט פֿון שׂימחות

**One person laughs from sorrow
while another weeps from joy**
*Eyner lakht fun tsores un a tsveyter
veynt fun simkhes* NS

ווען מען לאַכט זעען אַלע, ווען מען
ווינט זעט קיינער ניט

**Laugh and the whole world laughs
with you; weep and you weep alone**
*Ven men lakht zen ale, ven men veynt
zet keyner nit* NS

LAZINESS

אַ פֿוילער שלאָפֿט זיצנדיק און אַרבעט
ליגנדיק

**A sluggard sleeps sitting up and
works lying down**
*A foyler shloft zitsndik un arbet
ligndik* AC

185

אַלע שלומפּערדיקע ווײַבער ווערן פרײַטיק נאָך מיטאָג די גרעסטע פֿאַרדינערינס

Slovenly women become the greatest hustlers on Friday afternoon
[That is, when everything winds down for Shabbes]
Ale shlumperdike vayber vern fraytik nokh mitog di greste fardinerins AC

אַז מען האָט אַ סך צו טאָן לייגט מען זיך שלאָפֿן

If you have a lot to do, go to sleep
Az men hot a sakh tsu ton leygt men zikh shlofn P

אַז מען איז פֿויל האָט מען ניט אין מויל

If you do nothing, you'll eat nothing
Az men iz foyl hot men nit in moyl IB

דאָס גאַנצע יאָר איז זי ליידיק געזעסן און ערבֿ יום־כיפור האָט זי אַ זאָק אָנגעהויבן

The whole year she sat idle, and on the eve of Yom Kippur she began knitting a sock!
Dos gantse yor iz zi leydik gezesn un erev yomkiper hot zi a zok ongehoybn! IB

דער ליידיקגייער האָט קיין צײַט ניט

The idler never has time
Der leydikgeyer hot keyn tsayt nit NS

פֿון מעשׂיות דערציילן קאָכט מען קיין וועטשערע ניט

From storytelling the meal won't get cooked
Fun mayses dertseyln kokht men keyn vetshere nit IB

גאָט שיקט ניט פֿון אויבן אַז מען ליגט אויפֿן אויוון

God won't send from on high if on the oven you lie
Got shikt nit fun oybn az men ligt oyfn oyvn NS

מיטן אָחור בויט מען ניט דעם בית־המיקדש

You don't build the Holy Temple sitting on your rear
Mitn akhur boyt men nit dem beysamigdesh NS

LEARNING

אַ קינד אין בויך זעט אויך
A child in the womb can also learn
A kind in boykh zet oykh AC

אַ פען איז גוט — אַז מען קען
Its good to have a pen—if you know how and when
A pen iz gut—az men ken AC

אַ יונג ביימעלע בייגט זיך, אַן אַלטער בוים ברעכט זיך
A young tree bends, an old one breaks
A yung beymele beygt zikh, an alter boym brekht zikh IB

אַזוי ווי מען וויגט איַין אַזוי וויגט מען אויס
The way you raise your children, that's how they'll grow
Azoy vi men vigt ayn azoy vigt men oys P

פֿאַראַן מענטשן וואָס לערנען אַזוי פֿיל זיי האָבן קיין ציַיט ניט צו וויסן
Some people study so much they don't have time to know
Faran mentshn vos lernen azoy fil zey hobn keyn tsayt nit tsu visn AC

פרובירן גייט איבער שטודירן
To examine is more important than to study
Prubim geyt iber shtudirn AC

שריַיען העלפֿט ניט אָבער אַ שטעקן העלפֿט
Scolding won't help, but the stick will
Shrayen helft nit ober a shtekn helft NS

וויל נאָר וועסטו זיַין אַ ווילנער
Will it, and you can become a great scholar
[Play on words: vilner refers to the great sage, the Gaon of Vilna]
Vil nor vestu zayn a vilner NS

187

LIFE

אַלץ נעמט אַן עק אַפֿילו "כי הנה
כחומר"

**Everything comes to an end, even
"I am nothing but dust"**
*Alts nemt an ek afile "ki hiney
kekhomer"* NS

אַז דאָס לעבן איז זיס איז די וועלט
הפֿקר

**If life is sweet, then the world is
abandoned**
Az dos lebn iz zis iz di velt hefker IB

אַז מען עסט טשאָלנט ביז הונדערט און
צוואַנציק לעבט מען לאַנג

**If you eat cholent for 120 years,
you'll live long**
*Az men est tsholnt biz hundert un
tsvantsik lebt men lang* P

אַז מען וויל לאַנג און גליקלעך לעבן זאָל
מען אָטעמען דורכן נאָז און האַלטן דאָס
מויל צו

**For a long and happy life, breathe
through your nose and keep your
mouth shut**
*Az men vil lang un gliklekh lebn zol
men otemen durkhn noz un haltn dos
moyl tsu* AC

דאָס לעבן איז אַ בלאָטער אויף אַ
געשוויר און אַ מכה נאָך דערצו

**Life is a blister on top of an abscess,
and a boil on top of that**
*Dos lebn iz a bloter oyf a geshvir un a
make nokh dertsu* NS

דאָס לעבן איז אַ חלום פֿאַרן חכם, אַ
שפיל פֿאַרן נאַר, אַ קאָמעדיע פֿאַרן נגיד
און אַ טראַגעדיע פֿאַר די אָרעמעלײַט

**Life is a dream for the wise, a game
for the fool, a comedy for the rich,
and a tragedy for the poor**
*Dos lebn iz a kholem farn khokhem, a
shpil farn nar, a komedye farn noged
un a tragedye far di oremelayt* NS

דאָס לעבן איז די גרעסטע מציאה – מען
קריגט עס אומזיסט

Life is the greatest bargain—you get it free
Dos lebn iz di greste metsi'e—men krigt es umzist AC

דאָס לעבן איז װי אַ
קינדערהעמדל – קורץ און באַש

Life is like a child's undershirt—short and soiled
Dos lebn iz vi a kinderhemdl—kurts un bash NS

דאָס מיאוסטע לעבן איז בעסער װי דער
שענסטער טויט

The ugliest life is better than the fanciest death
Dos mi'este lebn iz beser vi der shenster toyt NS

עס איז ביטער װי גאַל און אָן גאַל קען
מען ניט לעבן

It's bitter as bile and without bile you can't live
Es iz biter vi gal un on gal ken men nit lebn NS

געלעבט װי אַ האַר, געשטאָרבן װי אַ
נאַר

Lived like a lord, died like a fool
Gelebt vi a har, geshtorbn vi a nar NS

"הכּל הבל" – און געהבלט מוז דאָך
װערן

"All is vanity"—yet one can't help being vain
"Hakol hevel"—un gehevlt muz dokh vern NS

כּל-זמן עס רירט זיך אָן אבֿר קלערט מען
ניט פֿון קבֿר

As long as one limb stirs, thoughts of the grave are deferred
Kolzman es rirt zikh an eyver klert men nit fun keyver NS

מען װײנט אויף "מי יחיה" װי אויף "מי
ימות"

"Who will live" causes a much weeping as "who will die"
Men veynt oyf "mi yikhye" vi oyf "mi yamut" AC

אויסברוקירט מיט צרות איז דער וועג
צום בית-הקבֿרות

Sorrows pave the way to the grave
Oysbrukirt mit tsores iz der veg tsum
beysakvores NS

ווי לאַנג די אויגן זיינען אָפֿן ווילט זיך
איינשלינגען אַ וועלט

As long as one's eyes are open, one
wants to swallow up the world
Vi lang di oygn zaynen ofn vilt zikh
aynshlingen a velt IB

LIQUOR

אַ שיכּור קען זיך צעטאַנצן ביי אַ לוויה
ווי ביי אַ שׂימחה

A drunkard can as easily dance at a
funeral as at a wedding
A shiker ken zikh tsetantsn bay a
levaye vi bay a simkhe AC

אַ טרונק בראָנפֿן וואַרעמט אין ווינטער
און קילט אין זומער

A drink of brandy warms in winter
and cools in summer
A trunk bronfn varemt in vinter un kilt
in zumer IB

אַז איך נעם אַ טרונק בראָנפֿן ווער איך
אַן אַנדער מענטש און דער אַנדערער
וויל אויך אַ טרונק בראָנפֿן

When I take a drink of brandy, I
become another person, and that
other person also wants a drink
Az ikh nem a trunk bronfn ver ikh an
ander mentsh un der anderer vil oykh
a trunk bronfn AC

ביים גלעזל געפֿינט מען אַ סך גוטע
פֿריינד

Over a glass you find many good
friends
Baym glezl gefint men a sakh gute
fraynd IB

ביז צו דער קרעטשמע דאַרף מען אויך אַ
טרונק בראָנפֿן

On the way to the tavern you also
need a drink
Biz tsu der kretshme darf men oykh a
trunk bronfn AC

ברָאנפֿן קען פֿארדרייען דעם קאָפ אָבער
צרות נעמען אים אין גאַנצן אראָפּ

Liquor can muddle the head, but troubles will lop it off instead
Bronfn key fardreyen dem kop ober tsores nemen im in gantsn arop NS

ברָאנפֿן וויינט ארויס פֿון שיכּור

Brandy weeps out of the drunkard
Bronfn veynt aroys fun shiker NS

דער רבי ווערט רויטער און דאָס פֿלעשל
ווערט בלאַסער

The rabbi becomes ruddier and the bottle becomes paler
Der rebe vert royter un dos fleshl vert blaser IB

דעם רבנס עסן און דעם פֿערדס טרינקען
קען מען אויסהאַלטן אָבער דעם רבנס
טרינקען און דעם פֿערדס עסן איז
אוממעגלעך

The rabbi's eating and the horse's drinking we can afford, but the rabbi's drinking and the horse's eating is impossible
Dem rebns esn un dem ferds trinken ken men oys'haltn ober dem rebns trinken un dem ferds esn is um'meglekh IB

די מלאָכה האָט ליב צו מאַכן אַ ברכה

A blessing over liquor makes the work go quicker
Di melokhe hot lib tsu makhn a brokhe NS

ער איז אזוי שיכּור אַז ער ווייסט ניט
ווען מען לייגט זיך שלאָפֿן און ווען מען
שטייט אויף

He's so drunk he no longer knows when to go to sleep and when to get up
Er iz azoy shiker az er veyst nit ven men leygt zikh shlofn un ven men shteyt oyf AC

פֿאַראַן מער אַלטע שיכּורים ווי אַלטע
דאָקטוירים

There are more old drunks than old doctors
Faran mer alte shikurim vi alte doktoyrim P

191

פֿון שיכּור און פֿון שענקער שמעקט מען בראָנפֿן

Both the drunkard and the bartender reek of brandy
Fun shiker un fun shenker shmekt men bronfn NS

איטלעכער בעט אויף אַ שטיק ברויט און מיינט אויף אַ טרונק בראָנפֿן

Everyone prays for a piece of bread, but really means a shot of brandy
Itlekher bet oyf a shtik broyt un meynt oyf a trunk bronfn IB

לעבן אַ מת איז גוט אַ טרונק בראָנפֿן, אויף אַ ברית אַ שטיקל לעקעך און אויף אַ חתונה – ביידע

Alongside the corpse, it's good to have a drink; at a bris, it's good to have some cake, and at a wedding— it's good to have both
Lebn a mes iz gut a trunk bronfn, oyf a bris a shtikl lekekh un oyf a khasene— beyde AC

"אדם יסודו מעפֿור וסופֿו לעפֿור" – בינה לבֿינה, איז גוט אַ טרונק בראָנפֿן

"Man springs from dust and his end is dust"—in between, it's good to have a drink
"Odem yesoydoy meyofor vesoyfo leyofor"—beyne l'veyne, iz gut a trunk bronfn IB

רבינו של עולם, איך בעט דיר נאָר "לחם לאכל ובגד ללבֿש" – אַ טרונק וועל איך מיר שוין אַליין באַזאָרגן

Master of the Universe, I ask you only for "bread to eat and clothes to wear"—a drink I'll manage on my own
Reboyne-shel-oylem, ikh bet dir nor "lekhem lakhol v'beged lilvash"—a trunk vel ikh mir shoyn aleyn bazorgn AC

טינקען הייסט ניט טרינקען

Dipping isn't drinking
Tinken heyst nit trinken AC

וואָס אַ שיכּור האָט פֿאַרלוירן אַ
ניכטערער האָט געפֿונען

What a drunkard loses, the sober finds
Vos a shiker hot farloyrn a nikhterer hot gefunen IB

LIVELIHOOD

אַ מלאָכה איז אַ מלוכה

A craft is a kingdom
A melokhe iz a melukhe IB

אַ סך מלאָכות און ווייניק ברכות

Many occupations, few celebrations
A sakh melokhes un veynik brokhes NS

אַלץ דרייט זיך אַרום ברויט און טויט

Everything revolves around being dead or fed
Alts dreyt zikh arum broyt un toyt AC

אַז ביי אַ בעל-עגלה פֿאַלט אַ פֿערד
ווערט ער אַ מלמד

When his horse dies, the wagoner becomes a teacher
Az bay a balegole falt a ferd vert er a melamed NS

אַז אין דרויסן איז אַ בלאָטע פֿרייען זיך
די שוסטערס

When the streets are muddy, shoemakers rejoice
Az in droysn iz a blote freyen zikh di shusters NS

אַז מען האָט אין האנט די מלאָכה קומט
שוין אָן די מזל-ברכה

With a trade in hand, luck will be grand
Az men hot in hant di melokhe kumt shoyn on di mazl-brokhe IB

193

אַז מ'צײלט ספֿירה קומט אױף די
כּלי-זמרים אַ פּגירה

**During the counting of the days
between Passover and Shevuoth,
the musicians look like cadavers**
[Traditionally, few festivities are
celebrated during this period]
*Az m'tseylt sfire kumt oyf di klezmorim
a p'gire* IB

דער דלות פֿאַרשװינדט װען עס אַרבעטן
די הענט

**Poverty disappears when the hands
are occupied**
*Der dales farshvint ven es arbetn di
hent* NS

די קאַן פֿון בלעכער איז פֿול מיט לעכער

The tinsmith's can is full of holes
Di kan fun blekher iz ful mit lekher NS

עס שלאָגן זיך אַלע פֿאַרן שטיקעלע חלה

All fight for a bite
*Es shlogn zikh ale farn shtikele
khale* NS

געבענטשט איז דער גראָשן װאָס איז
מיט שװײס באַגאָסן

**That penny is blessed that with
sweat is dressed**
*Gebentsht iz der groshn vos iz mit
shveys bagosn* NS

קענסט שױן האַלטן די נאָדל מעגסטו בײַ
זיך זײַן אַ גדול

**If a needle you can tote, you're a
person of note**
*Kenst shoyn haltn di nodl megstu bay
zikh zayn a godl* NS

מען זאָל זיך קענען אױסקױפֿן פֿון טױט
װאָלטן די אָרעמעלײַט שײן פּרנסה
געהאַט

**If we could hire substitutes to die
for us, the poor would make a nice
living**
*Men zol zikh kenen oyskoyfn fun toyt
voltn di oremelayt sheyn parnose
gehat* NS

מיט שער-און-אַייַזן קען מען אַ סך
באַווייַזן

Much can be done with scissors and an iron
Mit sher-un-ayzn ken men a sakh bavayzn NS

מיט וואָס איינער האַנדלט דאָס שלעפט
זיך אים נאָך

Whatever you deal with leaves telltale signs
Mit vos eyner handlt dos shlept zikh im nokh NS

פרנסה היילט אַלע מכּות

Livelihood heals all ills
Parnose heylt ale makes P

רבי-לעבן, וואָס טוט מען ניט פֿאַר
פרנסה וועגן?

Rabbi, hear! Why is livelihood so dear?
Rebe-lebn, vos tut men nit far parnose vegn? AC

ווען דער קירשנער האָט ניט קיין אַרבעט
איז אים אויך קאַלט

When the furrier is out of work, he too is cold
Ven der kirshner hot nit keyn arbet iz im oykh kalt NS

זאָל זיך אַזוי מאַכן אַ קליידעלע ווי עס
מאַכט זיך אַ מיידעלע

If only the dress could be received as quickly as the daughter is conceived
Zol zikh azoy makhn a kleydele vi es makht zikh a meydele NS

LOGIC

אַ ציג מאַכט מען ניט פֿאַר קיין גערטנער

You don't make a gardener out of a goat
A tsig makht men nit far keyn gertner IB

די קאַץ זאָל לייגן אייער וואָלט זי געווען
אַ הון

If the cat laid eggs, she'd be a hen
Di kats zol leygn eyer volt zi geven a hun IB

וועמ די באָבע וואָלט געהאַט אַ באָרד | If grandma had a beard (balls)
(בצים) וואָלט זי געדאַוונט פֿאַרן עמוד | she'd be praying from the pulpit
Ven di bobe volt gehat a bord (beytsim)
volt zi gedavnt farn omed AC

וווּ וואַסער איז געלאָפֿן דאָרט וועט עס | Where water ran it will continue to
וויַיטער לויפֿן | run
Vu vaser iz gelofn dort vet es vayter
loyfn NS

וווּ הינט בילן דאָרט וווינען מענטשן | Where dogs bark, people live
Vu hint biln dort voynen mentshn NS

זינט איך לעב בין איך נישט געשטאָרבן | As long as I live, I haven't died yet
Zint ikh leb bin ikh nisht geshtorbn IF

LONELINESS

אַליין קען מען עסן נאָר ניט אַרבעטן | One can eat alone but not work
alone
Aleyn ken men esn nor nit arbetn NS

עס לאַכט זיך אַליין, עס וויינט זיך אַליין | One laughs alone, one weeps alone
Es lakht zikh aleyn, es veynt zikh
aleyn IB

אײדער געמיין בעסער אַליין | Better lonely than lowly
Eyder gemeyn beser aleyn NS

קיצל זיך אַליין און לאַך אַליין | Tickle yourself and laugh all by
yourself
Kitsel zikh aleyn un laugh aleyn AC

196

LOVE

אַ טראָפֿן ליבע ברענגט אַמאָל אַ ים מיט
טרערן

**A drop of love sometimes brings an
ocean of tears**
*A tropn libe brengt amol a yam mit
trern* AC

אַז אַ זכר האָט ליב אַ נקבֿה איז עס בדרך
הטבֿע

**When he falls in love with a she,
it's as it should be**
*Az a zokher hot lib a nekeyve iz es
b'derekh hateyve* NS

אַז מען האָט ליב די וויַיב האָט מען ליב
די גאַנצע משפּחה

**If you love your wife, you love the
whole family**
*Az men hot lib di vayb hot men lib di
gantse mishpokhe* IB

ער גייט איר נאָך ווי אַ קו דאָס קאַלב

**He follows her around like the calf
follows the cow**
Er geyt ir nokh vi a ku dos kalb IB

פֿאַר אַ ביסעלע ליבע באַצאָלט מען מיטן
גאַנצן לעבן

**For a bit of love you pay your whole
life**
*Far a bisele libe batsolt men mitn
gantsn lebn* AC

האָב ליב דעם צווייטן און לאָז זיך ניט
נאַרן פֿון דעם ערשטן

**Love the latter, but don't be deceived
by the former**
*Hob lib dem tsveytn un loz zikh nit
narn fun dem ershtn* AC

איך מיט דיר זיַינען ווי אַנדערע
צוויי — איך אָן דיר בין ווי אַ בוידעם אָן
היי

**You and I are a pair any day;
without you I'm like a loft without
hay**
*Ikh mit dir zaynen vi andere tsvey—
ikh on dir bin vi a boydem on hey* IB

קלײנע מײדלעך צערײַסן די שערצן, **Little girls tear things apart, big**
גרױסע מײדלעך צערײַסן די הערצן **girls break your heart**
Kleyne meydlekh tseraysn di shertsn,
groyse meydlekh tseraysn di hertsn NS

לײַכטע ליבעס, שווערע שאָדנס **Easy loves, heavy damages**
Laykhte libes, shvere shodns NS

מערסטנס האָבן מענטשן זיך ליב פֿון **Mostly, people love each other from**
דערווײַטנס **a distance**
Merstns hobn mentshn zikh lib fun
dervaytns P

ווען די ליבע פֿאַקט דעם מענטשן **When love grabs hold of someone,**
העלפֿט ניט קײן דאַוװענען העלפֿט ניט **neither praying nor reciting**
קײן בענטשן **blessings help**
Ven di libe pakt dem mentshn helft nit
keyn davenen helft nit keyn bentshn IF

זײ האָבן זיך בײדע ליב: ער זיך און זי זיך **They are both in love: he with**
himself and she with herself
Zey hobn zikh beyde lib: er zikh un zi
zikh P

LUCK

אַז די הצלחה שפּילט גילט ערשט די **If luck plays a part, cleverness**
חכמה **succeeds**
Az di hatslokhe shpilt gilt ersht di
khokhme NS

אַז דאָס מזל גײט וווינט מען נאָענט צו **With luck you'll live close to the**
דער חתונה און ווײַט פֿון דער שרפֿה **wedding and far from the inferno**
Az dos mazl geyt voynt men no'ent tsu
der khasene un vayt fun der sreyfe NS

אַז אליהו הנבֿיא איז דער בעל־עגלה
פֿאָרט מען ווײַט

**With Elijah the Prophet as the
driver, you can travel far**
[According to folklore, Elijah the
Prophet is a heavenly emissary sent
to earth to combat social injustice]
*Az elyenove iz der balegole fort men
vayt* IB

אַז מען וואַרפֿט אַ גליקלעכן אין ים
קומט ער צוריק מיט אַ פֿיש אין מויל

**Throw a lucky person into the sea
and he returns with a fish in his
mouth**
*Az men varft a gliklekhn in yam kumt
er tsurik mit a fish in moyl* NS

דאָס מזל מאַכט קלוג ווײַל דאָס מזל
מאַכט רײַך

**Luck makes you smart because it
makes you rich**
*Dos mazl makht klug vayl dos mazl
makht raykh* NS

דאָס מזל האָט האַזל

Luck provides shelter
Dos mazl hot hazl NS

פֿון גליק צום אומגליק איז אַ
שפּאַן – פֿון אומגליק צו גליק איז אַ
שטיק וועג

**From fortune to misfortune is a
leap; from misfortune to good
fortune is a long way**
*Fun glik tsum umglik iz a shpan—fun
umglik tsu glik iz a shtik veg* NS

האָסט ברויט מיט פּוטער איז דאָס מזל
אַ גוטער

**If bread and butter is your food,
you have it good**
*Host broyt mit puter is dos mazl a
guter* NS

מען דאַרף האָבן מזל צו ירשענען שׂכל

You need luck to inherit brains
*Men darf hobn mazl tsu yarshenen
seykhl* P

נדן און ירושה ברענגט ניט קיין ברכה

Dowry and inheritance don't guarantee good luck
Nadn un yerushe brengt nit keyn brokhe IB

אָן מזל וואָס טויג יאָרן?

Without luck, what use are years?
On mazl vos toyg yorn? NS

צום גליק באַדאַרף מען קיין חכמה ניט

You don't have to be smart to be lucky
Tsum glik badarf men keyn khokhme nit IB

וואָלטן מיר אזוי פֿיל מזל געהאַט צו זעען אַלץ וואָס מיר הערן

If only we were lucky enough to see all that we hear
Voltn mir azoy fil mazl gehat tsu zen alts vos mir hern AC

וואָס ניצט מזל אָן ברכה?

What use is luck without blessings?
Vos nitst mazl on brokhe? IB

LUNACY

אַ משוגענער שלאָגט נאָר יענעם ניט זיך

A lunatic only beats up others, not himself
A meshugener shlogt nor yenem nit zikh IB

אַז מען זאָגט: משוגע, גלייב

If everyone says "crazy," better believe it!
Az men zogt: meshuge, gleyb NS

די גאנצע וועלט איז ניט משוגע

The entire world isn't crazy
Di gantse velt iz nit meshuge P

200

ער איז גאַנץ נאָרמאַל, ווע011 ער עסט
שיקסעס און טאַנצט מיט חזירים ...

He is entirely normal, but if he ate
Gentile girls and danced with
pigs...
[Then there would be reason to
doubt his sanity]
*Er iz gants normal, ven er est shikses
un tantst mit khazeyrim...* AC

איטלעכע שטאָט האָט איר משוגענעם

Every town has its own lunatic
Itlekhe shtot hot it meshugenem IB

יעדער גאָון האָט זיַין שגעון

Every genius has his own quirk
Yeder go'en hot zayn shigo'en IB

זיַין גאַנץ לעבן הענגט אויף אַ האָר און
ער קריכט נאָר יענעם אויפֿן קאָפּ

His whole life hangs by a hair, and
all he wants to do is to get into
other people's hair
*Zayn gants lebn hengt oyf a hor un er
krikht nor yenem oyfn kop* LMF

MAJORITY

אַ רבים פֿירט שטענדיק אויס   **Majority always rules**
A rabim firt shtendik oys   NS

אַז די וועלט זאָגט זאָל מען גלייבן   **If everyone says it's so, believe it**
Az di velt zogt zol men gleybn   P

אַז מען זאָגט משוגע-גלייב   **If everyone says "crazy"—you'd
better believe it**
Az men zogt meshuge—gleyb   P

MARRIAGE

אַ גנבֿ און אַ שיכּור מעגן זיך משדך זײַן   **A thief and a drunkard may marry
off their children to each other**
*A ganef un a shiker megn zikh
meshadekh zayn*   NS

אַ חזן דאַרף זײַן אַ באַוויַיבטער ער זאָל
קענען דאַוונען מיט אַ צעבראָכן האַרץ   **A cantor should be married so that
he can pray with a broken heart**
*A khazn darf zayn a bavaybter er zol
kenen davenen mit a tsebrokhn
harts*   NS

א ספֿר-תּורה זאָל מען פֿאַרזעצן און אַ
מײדל זאָל מען חתונה מאַכן

Even pawn the Torah scroll, but marry off your daughter
A sefer toyre zol men farzetsn un a meydl zol men khasene makhn IB

אַ טאָפּ װי מיאוס געפֿינט זיך איר
שטערצל

A pot, however ugly, finds its lid
A top vi mi'es gefint zikh ir shtertsl AC

אַ יונגע פֿרוי און אַן אַלטער װײַן – פֿון
בײדע פֿאַרלירט מען דעם שׂכל

A young woman and an old wine—both make you lose your senses
A yunge froy un an alter vayn—fun beyde farlirt men dem seykhl NS

אַן אָקס מיט אַ פֿערד שפּאַנט מען ניט
אײַן אין אײן װאָגן

You don't hitch an ox and a horse to the same wagon
An oks mit a ferd shpant men nit ayn in eyn vogn IB

אַז אַן אַלטער מאַן נעמט אַ יונגע װײַב
װערט ער יונג און זי אַלט

When an old man marries a young wife, he gets young and she old
Az an alter man nemt a yunge vayb vert er yung un zi alt NS

אַז מען באַגראָבט לעבעדיקערהייט קען
מען קיין תּחית-המתים ניט אויפֿשטיין

If you get buried alive, you can't be resurrected
Az men bagrobt lebedikerheyt ken men keyn tkhi'es hameysim nit oyfshteyn AC

אַז מען האָט חתונה מיטן שװער שלאָפֿט
מען מיטן בער

If you wed your father-in-law, you bed a bear
Az men hot khasene mitn shver shloft men mitn ber NS

אַז מען טאַנצט אויף אַלע חתונות װײנט
מען נאָך אַלע מתים

If you dance at every wedding, you weep after every corpse
Az men tantst oyf ale khasenes veynt men nokh ale meysim NS

אַז מען וויל וויסן וואָס מען איז ווערט
זאָל מען זיך לאָזן רעדן שידוכים

If you want to know what you're worth, start talking about marrying off children

Az men vil visn vos men iz vert zol men zikh lozn redn shidukhim NS

בײַ טאָג צום גט, בײַ נאַכט צום בעט

By day they fight, to bed at night

Bay tog tsum get, bay nakht tsum bet IB

דער ערשטער מאַן וואָלט קיין ווײַב ניט
גענומען ווען מען וואַרפֿט ניט אָן אויף
אים אַ שלאָף

Adam would never have taken a wife if he wouldn't have been put to sleep first

Der ershter man volt keyn vayb nit genumen ven men varft nit on oyf im a shlof AC

די ערשטע ווײַב איז פֿון גאָט, די צווייטע
פֿון מענטשן

The first wife is sent by God, the second one by people

Di ershte vayb iz fun got, di tsveyte fun mentshn NS

דאָס לעבן איז אַ זיסער חלום – און
חתונה האָבן איז דער וועק-זייגער

Life is a sweet dream—but marriage is the alarm clock

Dos lebn iz a ziser kholem—un khasene hobn iz der vek-zeyger NS

עס איז ניטאָ קיין ייִדישער קלויסטער

There are no Jewish churches

Es iz nito keyn yidisher kloyster NS

פֿרי אויפֿשטעטין און פֿרי חתונה האָבן
שאַט ניט

Early rising and early marriage do no harm

Fri oyfshteyn un fri khasene hobn shat nit NS

פֿון צוויי שלעכטע קלײַב אויס דעם
קלענסטן, פֿון צוויי פֿרויען – די דריטע

From two evils, pick the least; from two women—pick a third

Fun tsvey shlekhte klayb oys dem klentstn, fun tsvey froyen—di drite AC

אין דער שיסל ליגט דער שלום-בית

Domestic bliss is found in the dish
In der shisl ligt der sholem-bayes NS

חתונה האָבן דויערט אַ שעה און צרות
האָט מען אַ גאַנץ לעבן

The wedding lasts only an hour, but troubles last a whole life
Khasene hobn doyert a sho un tsores hot men a gants lebn NS

מען ליגט אַזוי לאַנג אויף איין קישן ביז
וואַנען מען באַקומט איין געוויסן

Lie long enough on one cushion and you end up with the same disposition
Men ligt azoy lang oyf eyn kishn biz vanen men bakumt eyn gevisn AC

מער חסרון – מער נדן

More flaws—more dowry
Mer khisorn—mer nadn NS

נדן און קעסט געדויערן איבער די פֿרעסט

Dowry and board over the winter are stored
Nadn un kest gedoyern iber di frest NS

ניט קיין מזומנים איז אויס מחותנים!

No money to pay, no wedding day!
Nit keyn mezumonim iz oys mekhutonim! IB

אָנצוווערן נדן און ירושה איז ניט קיין
בושה

Forfeiting dowry and inheritance is nothing to be ashamed of
Ontsuvern nadn un yerushe iz nit keyn bushe IB

ווייבער זײַנען געבילדעט און קענען
צוויי שפּראַכן – איינע פֿאַר דער חתונה
און איינע נאָך דער חתונה

Women are educated and know two languages—one before the wedding and one afterwards
Vayber zaynen gebildet un kenen tsvey shprakhn—eyne far der khasene un eyne nokh der khasene NS

205

וווּ ליבשאַפֿט איז קיין ענגשאַפֿט

Where there's affection there's no constriction
Vu libshaft iz keyn engshaft NS

BRIDES AND GROOMS

אַ רײַכע כּלה איז ווי אַ שמאַלץ גרוב – דאָס שמאַלץ רינט איבער און דער גרוב בלײַבט איבער

A wealthy bride is like a greasepit— the fat overflows but the pit remains
A raykhe kale iz vi a shmaltsgrub—dos shmalts rint iber un di grub blaybt iber NS

אַלע כּלות זײַנען שיין, אַלע מתים זײַנען פֿרום

All brides are beautiful, all corpses are pious
Ale kales zaynen sheyn, ale meysim zaynen frum IB

אַז דער חתן איז דער באַגערטער דאַרף די כּלה ניט קיין ווערטער

When the groom is desired, no words are required
Az der khosn iz der bagerter darf di kale nit keyn verter NS

אַז עס זײַנען ניטאָ קיין אַנדערע מעלות איז אַ זומערשפּרינקעלע אויך אַ מעלה

If there are no other virtues, then a freckle is also a virtue
Az es zaynen nito keyn andere mayles iz a zumershprinkele oykh a mayle NS

עס ביינער וועסטו האָבן אַ ווײַסן חתן

Chew on bones and you'll get a handsome husband
Es beyner vestu hobn a vaysn khosn NS

חתן-כּלה האָבן גלעזערנע אויגן

Bride and groom have glass eyes
Khosn kale hobn glezerne oygn IB

מיט וואָס שמעקט אַ חתן נאָך דער חתונה? מיט דער נאָז

With what does a bridegroom smell after the wedding? With his nose
Mit vos shmekt a khosn nokh der khasene? mit der noz AC

206

אויף אַלע כּלות רוט די שכינה

On every bride rests The Divine Presence
Oyf ale kales rut di shkhine NS

ווען די כּלה איז אויף דער צײַט קוקן די מחותּנים אין דער זײַט

When the bride is in the family way, the in-laws look away
Ven di kale iz oyf der tsayt kukn di mekhutonim in der zayt NS

ווען חתן-כּלה קושן זיך מעגן די שדכנים גיין אַהיים

When the bridal pair kiss, the matchmakers can go home
Ven khosn-kale kushn zikh megn di shadkhonim geyn aheym IB

יאָ אַ שידוך? – דאָס מת לעבט אָבער דאָך!

It's really a match?—But the corpse is still living!
Yo a shidekh?—dos mes lebt ober dokh! NS

COURTSHIP

בעסער די תּנאים צערײַסן איידער די כּתובה

Better to tear up the engagement contract than the marriage contract
Beser di tno'im tseraysn eyder di k'sube IB

איטלעכער שידוך וואָס מען טוט איז גוט, נאָך אַ יאָר ווערט מען געוואָר

Every match is a catch; after a year, it becomes clear
Itlekher shidekh vos men tut iz gut, nokh a yor vert men gevor NS

ווען אַ תּלמיד-חכם גייט מקדש זײַן אַ ווײַב זאָל ער פֿירן מיט זיך אַן עם-האָרץ

When a scholar goes looking for a wife, he should take along an ignoramus as advisor
Ven a talmed-khokhem geyt mekadesh zayn a vayb zol er firn mit zikh an amorets NS

אַ גליקלעך פֿאָרפֿאָלק – אַ טויבער מאַן
און אַ בלינדע ווײַב

A happy couple—a deaf man and a blind wife
A gliklekh porfolk—a toyber man un a blinde vayb AC

אַ מאַן איז ווי אַן ענגער שוך – כאָטש
עס דריקט דאָך מוז אַ ווײַב אים טראָגן

A husband is like a tight shoe—even though it pinches, a wife must endure it
A man iz vi an enger shukh—khotsh es drikt dokh muz a vayb im trogn NS

אַ רעגן טרײַבט אַרײַן אין שטוב און אַ
בייזע ווײַב טרײַבט אַרויס

Rain chases you into the house, and a shrewish wife drives you out
A regn trayb arayn in shtub un a beyze vayb traybt aroys NS

אַ שלעכטע ווײַב איז אַ וואונד אויפֿן לײַב

A shrewish wife is like a wound on the body
A shlekhte vayb iz a vund oyfn layb IB

אַ צווייטע ווײַב איז ווי אַ הילצערנע פֿוס

A second wife is like a wooden leg
A tsveyte vayb iz vi a hiltserne fus NS

אַ ציג אַנטלויפֿט, אַ האָן ווערט פֿאַרפֿאַלן
און אַ מאַן קומט צוריק

A goat runs away, a rooster gets lost, but a husband returns
A tsig antloyft, a hon vert farfaln un a man kumt tsurik AC

אַ ווײַב אַ שלאַק פֿאַרטרײַבט אפֿילו דעם
מלאך-המוות

A shrewish wife will drive off even the Angel of Death
A vayb a shlak fartraybt afile dem malekhamoves NS

אַ ווייב איז גוט צום לייב אָבער ניט צו דער נשמה	**A wife is good for the body but not for the soul** *A vayb iz gut tsum layb ober nit tsu der neshome* IB
אַ ווייבעלע איז אַ טייבעלע און אַ טייוועלע	**The little woman can be a little dove or a little devil** *A vaybele iz a taybele un a tayvele* NS
אַ וויאַזשאָר טאָר ניט נעמען אַ שיין ווייב	**A traveling salesman should not take a pretty wife** *A voyazhor tor nit nemen a sheyn vayb* NS
אַן אלמנה איז אַ סכּנה, אַ גרושה איז אַ בושה, אַ בתולה איז אַ גדולה	**A widow is dangerous, a divorcee is a scandal, but a virgin is a delight** *An almone iz a sakone, a grushe iz a bushe, a p'sule iz a g'dule* IB
אַז אַ בחור נעמט אַן אלמנה פֿאַר איר ברויט האָט ער פֿון איר דעם טויט	**When a bachelor marries a widow for her bread, he'll get troubles instead** *Az a bokher nemt an almone far ir broyt hot er fun ir dem toyt* NS
אַז דער רבֿ גייט אין שטריימל גייט די רביצין אין ספּאָדיק	**When the rabbi dons his holiday hat, his wife puts on the higher fur hat** *Az der rov geyt in shtrayml geyt di rebetsin in spodik* IB
אַז דאָס ווייב איז אַ ילדות איז דער מאַן אַ יאָלד	**If the wife is childish, the husband is simple-minded** *Az dos vayb iz a yoldes iz der man a yold* SK

אַז גאָט וויל שטראָפֿן אַן אפיקורס גיט
ער אים אַ פֿרומע ווײַב

**When God wants to punish an
unbeliever, He gives him a pious
wife**
*Az got vil shtrofn an apikoyres git er im
a frume vayb* IF

אַז מען איז גוט צו לײַט צו מען איז שלעכט
צו דער ווײַב

Good to all, bad to one's own wife
*Az men iz gut tsu layt iz men shlekht
tsu der vayb* IB

בעסער צען משומדים איידער איין
שלעכט ווײַב

**Better ten apostates than one
shrewish wife**
*Beser tsen meshumdim eyder eyn
shlekht vayb* IB

ביסטו ערלעך מיט דײַן ווײַב האָסטו אַ
געזונט לײַב

**If you're faithful to your wife, you'll
have a healthy body**
*Bistu erlekh mit dayn vayb hostu a
gezunt layb* NS

דער רוח נעמט אַלץ צו – נאָר אַ שלעכט
ווײַב נעמט ער ניט צו

**The devil takes everything—only a
shrewish wife he won't take back**
*Der ru'ekh nemt alts tsu—nor a shlekht
vayb nemt er nit tsu* NS

דאָס ערשטע ווײַב איז פֿון גאָט, דאָס
צווייטע פֿון מענטשן און דאָס דריטע פֿון
דעם רוח

**The first wife is from God, the
second from people, and the third
is from the Devil**
*Dos ershte vayb iz fun got, dos tsveyte
iz fun mentshn un dos drite fun dem
ru'ekh* IB

דאָס ערשטע ווײַב שלעפּט דעם וואָגן,
דאָס צווייטע רײַט אויפֿן זאָטל

**The first wife pulls the wagon, the
second wife sits in the saddle**
*Dos ershte vayb shlept dem vogn, dos
tsveyte rayt oyfn zotl* NS

ער האָט פֿײַנט דאָס ווײַב און האָט אַ סך
קינדער

He detests his wife, yet has a lot of
children
*Er hot faynt dos vayb un hot a sakh
kinder* NS

ער רײַט אויף דער קאָטשערע און זי רײַט
אויפֿן פֿאַרטאָך

He rides the coach and she rides
the apron
*Er rayt oyf der kotshere un zi rayt oyfn
fartakh* NS

אײן שלעכטע ווײַב איז נאָר דאָ אויף
דער וועלט און יעדערער מיינט אַז דאָס
איז זײַנע

There's only one shrewish wife in
the entire world, and every
husband is convinced she's his
*Eyn shlekhte vayb iz nor do oyf der velt
un yederer meynt az dos iz zayne* AC

פֿון אַ קאַץ אַ קראַץ און פֿון אַ ווײַב אַ
קללה

From a cat a scratch, and from a
wife a curse
*Fun a kats a krats un fun a vayb a
klole* NS

פֿון אַן אַלטן בחור ווערט אַ
יונגער-מאַנטשיק

An old bachelor becomes a
youngish husband
*Fun an altn bokher vert a yunger-
mantshik* IB

האָסט זיך אונטערגענומען אַ מאַן צו
זײַן, ברענג זשע ברויט אין שטוב אַרײַן

You've undertaken a husband's
care, so bring the bread for us to
share
*Host zikh untergenumen a man tsu
zayn, breng zhe broyt in shtub
arayn* NS

איטלעכער אָדם האָט זײַן חווה

Every Adam has his Eve
Itlekher odem hot zayn khave AC

מאַנס געטרײַקייט – הונטס געטרײַקייט

Husband's loyalty—dog's loyalty
Mans getraykeyt—hunts getraykeyt NS

מאַן און װײַב זײַנען אײן לײַב

Husband and wife are one flesh
Man un vayb zaynen eyn layb NS

מיט אַ שלעכטן מאַן אױף אַ יריד איז װי
מיט אַ קלײן קינד אױף אַ חתונה

A difficult husband at a fair is like being with a small child at a wedding
Mit a shlekhtn man oyf a yarid iz vi mit a kleyn kind oyf a khasene AC

ניט פֿון אַ שײנער צורהקע װערט אַ גוטע
װײַב

A pretty face alone doesn't make for a good wife
Nit fun a sheyner tsurke vert a gute vayb NS

״והוא ימשל בך״ — און װאָס זי װיל טוט
זי דאָך

"And he shall rule over you"—but what she wants she does anyway
"Vehu yimshel bokh"—un vos zi vil tut zi dokh IB

װען די מײדל איז אײדל איז די װײַבל אַ
טײַבל

If the girl is refined, the wife will be a dove
Ven di meydl iz eydl iz di vaybl a taybl NS

װען די װײַב טראָגט די הױזן װאַשט דער
מאַן די ספּאָדניצע

When the wife wears the pants, the husband washes the skirt
Ven di vayb trogt di hoyzn vasht der man di spodnitse NS

װען די װײַב װיל אַז דער מאַן זאָל זײַן
אין שטוב רעדט זי װײניקער און גיסט
װאַסער מער

When the wife wants her husband to stay home, she talks less and cleans more
Ven di vayb vil az der man zol zayn in shtub ret zi veyniker un gist vaser mer! NS

וווער עס האָט קיין ווײַב ניט דער איז A man without a wife isn't a decent
קיין מענטש ניט human being
*Ver es hot keyn vayb nit der iz keyn
mentsh nit* NS

ווו דאָס ווײַב רעגירט ווערט מען Where women rule, life is cruel
איבערגעפֿירט *Vu dos vayb regirt vert men ibergefirt* IB

יענעמס ווײַב איז ווי אַ ספֿר-תּורה, עס Someone else's wife is like a Torah
איז אַ מיצווה אַ קוש צו טאָן scroll: it's a good deed to give it a
kiss
*Yenems vayb iz vi a seyfer-toyre, es iz a
mitsve a kush tsu ton* AC

זיי לעבן ווי די טויבן און רײַסן זיך ווי די They live like doves and fight like
קעץ cats
*Zey lebn vi di toybn un raysn zikh vi di
kets* IB

זיך אַליין ווי מען וויל, אַ ווײַב אַ קינד Do as you like, but keep your wife
מוז מען מאַכן pregnant
*Zikh aleyn vi men vil, a vayb a kind
muz men makhn* IB

MASSES

אַז די וועלט זאָגט זאָל מען גלייבן If everyone says it's so, believe it
Az di velt zogt zol men gleybn AC

עס איז ביטער און שלעכט ווען דער The result can be terror when the
רבים איז אומגערעכט masses are in error
*Es iz biter un shlekht ven der rabim iz
umgerekht* NS

מיט אַ רבים טאָר מען ניט אָנהייבן Don't start up with the masses
Mit a rabim tor men nit onheybn NS

MEASURE

אַ ביסל און אַ ביסל ווערט אַ פֿולע שיסל

A little and a little makes for a lot in the pot
A bisl un a bisl vert a fule shisl NS

אַרײַן איז די טיר ברייט און אַרויס איז זי שמאָל

Entrances are wide, exits narrow
Arayn iz di tir breyt un aroys iz zi shmol IB

בעסער צוויי בהמות איידער איין ציג

Better two cows than one goat
Beser tsvey beheymes eyder eyn tsig NS

דער ערשטער געווינער איז דער לעצטער פֿאַרשפּילער

The first winner is the last loser
Der ershter geviner iz der letster farshpiler NS

עס איז ברייטער ווי לענגער

It's wider than longer
Es iz breyter vi lenger NS

עס קען ניט ווערן צען אַז קיין איינס איז ניטאָ

You can't have ten if there isn't one to begin with
Es ken nit vern tsen az keyn eyns iz nito NS

פֿון נישט ווערט נישט

From nothing you get nothing
Fun nisht vert nisht NS

גענייט און געאַרבעט, געקאָכט און געבאַקן איז קיין מאָל ניט צו פֿיל

There's never enough of sewing and making, cooking and baking
Geneyt un ge'arbet, gekokht un gebakn iz keyn mol nit tsu fil NS

אין צווייען איז שטאַרקער און אין דרײַען האַלט

Double is stronger, and triple keeps
In tsveyen iz shtarker un in drayen halt NS

ניקס איז גוט צו די אויגן   **"Nothing" is good only for the eyes**
Niks iz gut tsu di oygn IB

וואָס צו איז איבעריק   **Too much is superfluous**
Vos tsu iz iberik NS

MIRACLES

בײַ אײַך איז אַ נס וואָס גאָט טוט דעם   **To you, it's a miracle if God does**
רבינס ווילן, בײַ אונדז איז אַ נס אַז דער   **what your rabbi wants; to us, it's a**
רבי טוט גאָטס ווילן   **miracle if the rabbi does what God**
wants
Bay aykh iz a nes vos got tut dem rebns
viln, bay undz iz a nes as der rebe tut
gots viln NS

האָף אויף נסים און פֿאַרלאָז זיך ניט   **Hope for miracles but don't rely on**
אויף אַ נס   **them**
Hof oyf nisim un farloz zikh nit oyf a
nes NS

ניט יעדן מעת-לעת טרעפֿט זיך אַ נס   **Not every day brings a miracle**
your way
Nit yedn mesles treft zikh a nes NS

נאָר נאַראָנים פֿאַרלאָזן זיך אויף נסים   **Only fools rely on miracles**
Nor naronim farlozn zikh oyf nisim NS

MISERLINESS

אַ קאַרגער צאָלט טײַערער און אַ פֿוילער   **The miser pays more and the**
גייט מער   **sluggard walks farther**
A karger tsolt tayerer un a foyler geyt
mer NS

אַז אַ קאַרגער צעהוליעט זיך איז אַ
פֿרעמד קערבל ביַי אים בלאָטע

When a miser goes on a spree, other people's money is free

Az a karger tsehulyet zikh iz a fremd kerbl bay im blote NS

אַז אַ קאַרגער ווערט שוין מילד עסט ער
באָרשט און פֿאַרבײַסט מיט לעקעך

When a miser becomes extravagant, he sips borsht and takes a bit of cake

Az a karger vert shoyn mild est er borsht un farbayst mit lekekh NS

ער איז רײַך ווי קרח און נעמט נישט קיין
אורח

With the riches of Korakh he's blessed, yet he won't accept a single guest

Er iz raykh vi korekh un nemt nisht keyn oyrekh LMF

עס איז אַ מיצווה אַ חזיר אַ האָר
אַרויסצוריַיסן

It's a good deal to pull a bristle out of a pig

Es iz a mitsve a khazer a hor aroysturaysn IB

קאַרגע לײַט דינען די עבֿודה-זרה

Misers are idol worshippers

Karge layt dinen di avoyde-zore NS

וואָס רײַכער מען ווערט אַלץ קאַרגער
ווערט מען

The richer one becomes, the more miserly

Vos raykher men vert alts karger vert men IB

MISFORTUNE

פֿון גליק צום אומגליק איז אַ שפֿאַן, פֿון
אומגליק צו גליק איז אַ שטיקל וועג

From luck to misfortune is a leap; from misfortune to good luck is a long way

Fun glik tsum umglik iz a shpan, fun umglik tsu glik iz a shtikl veg NS

216

נאָך דעם אָרעמאַן שלעפּט זיך דער
שלימזל

Misfortune dogs the pauper
*Nokh dem oreman shlept zikh der
shlimazl* NS

אומגליק בינדט צונויף

Misfortune binds together
Umglik bint tsunoyf NS

MONEY

אַ דאַנק קען מען אין קעשענע ניט לייגן

**You can't put a "thank you" into
into your pocket**
A dank ken men in keshene nit leygn P

אַ כּפרה געלט! – אַבי כּבֿוד איז גרויס

**To hell with money!—as long as
there's lots of honors**
A kapore gelt!—abi koved iz groys NS

אַ נאָענטער גראָשן איז בעסער ווי אַ
ווײַטער קערבל

**A penny at hand is worth more
than a distant dollar**
*A no'enter groshn iz beser vi a vayter
kerbl* NS

אַ שטענדיקער גראָשן איז בעסער ווי אַ
זעלטענער רובל

**Better a steady dime than a rare
dollar**
*A shtendiker groshn iz beser vi a
zeltener rubl* NS

אַלע פֿלעקן קען מען אַרויסנעמען מיט אַ
ביסל גאָלד

**All spots can be removed with a
little gold**
*Ale flekn ken men aroysnemen mit a
bisl gold* NS

אַן אָקס פֿאַר אַ גראשן – אַז דער גראָשן
איז ניטאָ?

**An ox for a penny—but if you don't
have the penny?**
*An oks far a groshn—az der groshn iz
nito?* NS

217

אז מען האָט אַ גאָלד הענטל האָט מען דאָס לעבערל פֿון ענטל

If you have a golden touch, you'll eat goose liver and such
Az men hot a gold hentl hot men dos leberl fun entl NS

אַז מען האָט געלט איז מען קלוג און שײן און מ'קען גוט זינגען אויך

If you have money you're wise, you're handsome, and you can sing well too
Az men hot gelt iz men klug un sheyn un m'ken gut zingen oykh AC

אַז מען האָט ניט קײן קלינגער איז מען אַלײן װי אַ פֿינגער

If you have no money to jingle, you'll remain single
Az men hot nit ken klinger iz men aleyn vi a finger NS

אַז מען שפּאָרט ניט דעם גראָשן האָט מען ניט דעם רובל

If you don't save the pennies, you won't have the dollar
Az men shport nit dem groshn hot men nit dem rubl IB

דער סוד פֿון דעם רובל ליגט אין דעם גראָשן

The secret of the dollar lies in the penny
Der sod fun dem rubl ligt in dem groshn NS

דאָס קערבל איז ניט קײן ממזר

A coin is not a bastard
Das kerbl iz nit keyn mamzer IB

עס שטימען די צינגער װען דו האָסט אין קעשענע קלינגער

The tongues won't wag when you have cash in the bag
Es shtimen di tsinger ven du host in keshene klinger NS

פֿאַר געלט באַקומט מען אַלץ נאָר קײן שׂכל ניט

Money buys everything except brains
Far gelt bakumt men alts nor keyn seykhl nit NS

גועלט ברע011גט צו גאווה און גאווה צו
זינד

Money leads to arrogance, and
arrogance to sin
*Gelt brengt tsu gayve un gayve tsu
zind* NS

גועלט איז בלאָטע אָבער ס׳איז גוט צו
האָבן פֿולע קעשענעס

Money is mud, but it's good to have
full pockets
*Gelt iz blote ober s'iz gut tsu hobn fule
keshenes* NS

גועלט איז קײַלעכדיק — אַמאָל איז עס
דאָ, אַמאָל דאָרט

Money is round and it rolls—
sometimes here, sometimes there
*Gelt iz kaylekhdik—amol iz es do,
amol dort* AC

גועלטעלע באַלײַכט ווי זון מײַן
וועלטעלע

A little money makes my world
sunny
*Geltele balaykht vi zun mayn
veltele* NS

גאָלד איז אַן עבֿודה-זרה אָבער אַז עס
איז ניטאָ איז אַ גרויסע צרה

Gold is idol worship, but without it,
it's big trouble
*Gold iz an avoyde-zore ober az es iz
nito iz a groyse tsore* IB

אין שלעכטע צײַטן איז אַ פּעני אויך
גועלט

In bad times, even a penny is money
*In shlekhte tsaytn iz a peni oykh
gelt* AC

כּבֿוד און גועלט רעגירן די וועלט

Honor and dough make the world
go
Koved un gelt regirn di velt NS

מיט גועלט קען מען אַלץ טאָן

With money you can do anything
Mit gelt ken men alts ton IB

אָן מעות איז תּמיד אַ טעות

Without cash it's always a hash
On mo'es iz tomed a to'es IB

אויף מצות און תכריכים מוז זײַן

For matzahs and shrouds money is always found
Oyf matses un takhrikhim muz zayn IB

ריבי-פֿיש, געלט אויפֿן טיש!

Money on the table!
[put up or shut up!]
Ribi-fish, gelt oyfn tish! IB

תכלית (תחת) אויפֿן טיש!

Substance (ass) on the table!
Takhles (tokhes) oyfn tish! AC

צוליב געלט איז געוואָרן מיאוס די וועלט

Because of money the world became ugly
Tsulib gelt iz gevorn mi'es di velt NS

צוזאָגן און ליב האָבן קאָסט קיין געלט ניט

Promises and love don't cost money
Tsuzogn un lib hobn kost keyn gelt nit NS

ווען עס וואַקסט דער טײַסטער וואַקסן די באַדערפֿענישן

As the wallet grows, so do the needs
Ven es vakst der tayster vaksn di baderfenishn NS

ווער עס האָט געלט האָט די גאַנצע וועלט

With money in your purse, you have the universe
Ver es hot gelt hot di gantse velt NS

וואָס ביליק איז טײַער

What looks cheap ends up being expensive
Vos bilik iz tayer AC

NECESSITY

אַז עס זײַנען ניטאָ קײן אַנדערע מעלות
איז אַ זומערשפרינקעלע אויך אַ מעלה

**If there are no other virtues, a
freckle is also a virtue**
*Az es zaynen nito keyn andere mayles
iz a zumershprinkele oykh a mayle* NS

אַז מען דאַרף דעם גנבֿ נעמט מען אים
פֿון דער תליה אַראָפ

**If the thief is needed badly enough,
he's even taken off the gallows**
*Az men darf dem ganef nemt men im
fun der tli'e arop* P

אַז מען קען ניט אַרויף מוז מען
אַרונטער, אַז מען קען ניט אַריבער – מוז
מען אַריבער

**If you can't go over, go under; if you
can't cross over—you must anyway**
*Az men ken nit aroyf muz men arunter,
az men ken nit ariber—muz men
ariber* NS

די נויט שאַרפֿט דעם שׂכל

Necessity sharpens the brain
Di noyt sharft dem seykhl NS

פֿאַר דעם טײַוולס וועגן פֿעלט ניט

For the devil's sake, one finds
Far dem tayvls vegn felt nit AC

פֿאָר נויט טוט מען אָן דער שבת אין דער וואָכן

If necessary, you make Shabbes in the middle of the week
Far noyt tut men on der shabes in der vokhn IB

כּל־זמן די בהמה לאָזט זיך מעלקן פֿירט מען איר ניט צום שוחט

As long as the cow allows herself to be milked, she's not led to the slaughter
Kolzman di beheyme lozt zikh melkn firt men ir nit tsum shoykhet NS

ווען מען נויטיקט זיך אין אַ וואַרעמען אויוון קוקט מען ניט אויף זײַן אויסזען

When you need a warm oven, you don't quibble over its appearance
Ven men noytikt zikh in a varemen oyvn kukt men nit oyf zayn oyszen AC

Old and New

דאָס איז דאָך פֿון מלך סוביעצקעס יאָרן!

That's left over from King
Sobietski's times!
*Dos iz dokh fun meylekh subyetskes
yorn!* IF

מיט אַן אויסגעשטשערבעטן מעסער
שנײַדט זיך ניט בעסער

A worn-out knife doesn't cut any
better
*Mit an oysgeshtsherbetn meser shnayt
zikh nit beser* NS

צו יעדן נײַעם ליד קען מען צופאַסן אַן
אַלטן ניגון

To every new song you can match
an old melody
*Tsu yedn nayem lid ken men tsupasn
an altn nign* AC

Ownership

עס איז גוט צו זײַן אַ בעל-הבית אַז עס
איז דאָ מיט וואָס

It's good to be an owner if you've
got something worth owning
*Es iz gut tsu zayn a balebos az es iz do
mit vos* AC

223

אויף פֿרעמדע ערד בויט מען ניט **You don't build on someone else's land**
Oyf fremde erd boyt men nit AC

אויף פֿרעמדע קבֿרים וויינט מען זיך ניט אויס **One doesn't weep at the graves of strangers**
Oyf fremde kvorim veynt men zikh nit oys IB

יעדער וואָרעם האָט זײַן לאָך **Every worm has its hole**
Yeder vorem hot zayn lokh NS

224

PAIN

קיינער זאָגט ניט 'איי' אז ס'טוט ניט ווי **No one will complain if he's not in pain**
Keyner zogt nit 'ey' az s'tut nit vey IB

מען זאָגט ניט 'אָך' אַז ס'גיט ניט קיין שטאָך **No one will complain if he isn't in pain**
Men zogt nit 'okh' az s'git nit keyn shtokh NS

ווו מען לייגט אַ קראָנקן טוט אים אַלץ ווי **No matter where you place the sick person, he's still in pain**
Vu men leygt a krankn tut im alts vey AC

PARENTS

בעסער אויף דער וועלט ניט צו לעבן איידער אָנקומען צו אַ קינד **Better not to live than to become dependent upon one's child**
Beser oyf der velt nit tsu lebn eyder onkumen tsu a kind NS

225

עלטערן קענען אַלץ געבן נאָר קיין מזל
קענען זיי ניט געבן

Parents can provide everything except luck
Eltern kenen alts gebn nor keyn mazl kenen zey nit gebn IB

לעבן אַ שווערן וואָגן איז לייכט צו פֿוס
צו גיין

Alongside a loaded wagon it's easy to walk
Lebn a shvern vogn iz laykht tsu fus tsu geyn IB

מאַמעס טרערן און טאַטעס שמיץ
קומען אין לעבן שטאַרק צו ניץ

A mother's tears, a father's cuff, in this life prove useful enough
Mames trern un tates shmits kumen in lebn shtark tsu nits NS

טאַטע-מאַמע דאַרפֿן אַ קינד ניט לויבן
ווייל קיינער וועט זיי ניט גלויבן

Parents shouldn't praise their own children; no one will believe them
Tate-mame darfn a kind nit loybn vayl keyner vet zey nit gloybn NS

צער-בנים איז ערגער פֿון צער-לחם

Worry over children is worse than worry over bread
Tsar-bonim iz erger fun tsar-lekhem NS

ווער עס האָט קינדער אין די וויגן זאָל
זיך מיט דער וועלט ניט קריגן

If in cradles your childen sleep, away from quarrels you should keep
Ver es hot kinder in di vign zol zikh mit der velt nit krign P

FATHERS

אַז דער טאַטע איז אַ לץ איז דער זון אַ
פּאָדליעץ

If the father is a clown, the son is a buffoon
Az der tate iz a lets iz der zun a podlets NS

226

אַז מען האָט אַ טאַטן אַ הונט מעג מען
אים באַהאַנדלען ווי אַ הונט

If your father behaves like a dog, you may treat him like a dog
Az men hot a tatn a hunt meg men im bahandlen vi a hunt AC

דער פֿאָטער איז געטרײַ ווען די מוטער
שטייט דערבײַ

Father is true as long as mother is in view
Der foter iz getray ven di muter shteyt derbay NS

איין טאַטע קען צען קינדער אויסהאַלטן,
צען קינדער אייַן טאַטן איז שווער

One father can support ten children; ten children have a hard time supporting one father
Eyn tate ken tsen kinder oys'haltn, tsen kinder eyn tatn iz shver AC

IN-LAWS

אַ שוויגער און אַ שנור אין איין הויז
זײַנען ווי צוויי קעץ אין איין זאַק

A mother-in-law and a daughter-in-law in the same house are like two cats in one sack
A shviger un a shnur in eyn hoyz zaynen vi tsvey kets in eyn zak NS

MOTHERS

אַ מאַמע איז אַ פּאָקרישקע: זי דעקט צו
די קינדערס חסרונות און דעם מאַנס
ביזיונות

A mother is like a pot-lid: she covers up her children's flaws and her husband's humiliations
A mame iz a pokrishke: zi dekt tsu di kinders khasroynes un dem mans bizyoynes NS

אַ שלעכטע מאַמע איז ניטאָ

There's no such thing as a bad mother
A shlekhte mame iz nito AC

227

אַ שלעכטע מאַמע און אַ גוטער טויט איז ניטאָ	There's no such thing as a bad mother or a good death *A shlekhte mame un a guter toyt iz nito* NS
די מאַמע איז אַ קנעכט, דער טאַטע איז שטענדיק גערעכט	Mother is a slavish sight, father is always right *Di mame iz a k'nekht, der tate iz shtendik gerekht* AC
די מאַמע ווייסט אַמבעסטן צי דאָס קינד גערֹאָט אַרײַן אין טאַטן	Mother knows best whether the child takes after its father *Di mame veyst ambestn tsi dos kind gerot arayn in tatn* NS
עס איז ניטאָ קיין געטרײַעס ווי אַ מוטער	There is none so devoted as a mother *Es iz nito keyn getrayes vi a muter* NS
פֿון אַ שלעכטער מוטער איז דער זון ניט קיין גוטער	From a bad mother don't expect a good son *Fun a shlekhter muter iz der zun nit keyn guter* NS
וואָס אַ קינד זאָל ניט דערײדן וועט די מוטער אים פֿאַרשטיין	What a child babbles, its mother will understand *Vos a kind zol nit dereydn vet di muter im farshteyn* NS

STEPMOTHERS

אַ שטיף-מוטער גיט דעם שטיף-קינד דאָס ערשטע פֿון דער טיי און דאָס לעצטע פֿון דער קאַווע	A stepmother gives her stepchild the first of the tea and the last of the coffee *A shtif-muter git dem shtif-kind dos ershte fun der tey un dos letste fun der kave* NS

אַ שטיף-מוטער איז אַ שטאָך-מוטער   **A stepmother is a stab-mother**
A shtif-muter iz a shtokh-muter IF

PARTNERSHIP

אַ קאַץ און אַ ראַץ מאַכן שלום איבער   **A cat and a rat make peace over the**
דער פּגירה   **carcass**
A kats un a rats makhn sholem iber der
pgire AC

איר זײַט טאַקע אַ קרוב מיט מיר אָבער   **You may be a relative of mine, but**
ניט מיט מײַן יויך   **you're no partner to my soup!**
Ir zayt take a korev mit mir ober nit mit
mayn yoykh! AC

שותפֿות איז גוט נאָר מיט דער ווײַב   **Partnership is good only with one's**
wife
Shutfes iz gut nor mit der vayb NS

PAYMENT

אַבי מען נעמט אָפּ קבֿורה-געלט, מעג זיך   **As long as you get the burial fees,**
דער מת אַליין באַגראָבן   **the corpse can go bury itself!**
Abi men nemt op kvure-gelt, meg zikh
der mes aleyn bagrobn! NS

אַלץ הייסט רבי-געלט!   **Everything involves payment to the**
rabbi
[Chalk it up to experience]
Alts heyst rebe-gelt! P

ברית, בר מיצווה, חתונה,   **Circumcision, bar mitsvah, wedding,**
קבֿורה-געלט – באַלד נתנין   **burial—all too soon to be paid for**
Bris, barmitsve, khasene, kvure-gelt—
bald nosenen NS

די רעכענונג איז דאָ אָבער די געלט איז
נישטאָ!

The reckoning is here but not the money!

Di rekhenung iz do ober di gelt iz nishto! LMF

PEACE

אַ שלעכטער שלום איז אַלץ בעסער ווי
אַ גוטער קריג

A bad peace is still better than a good war

A shlekhter sholem iz alts beser vi a guter krig NS

פֿאַר שלום וועגן מעג מען אפֿילו אַ ליגן
זאָגן אָבער שלום טאָר קיין ליגן ניט זאָגן

For the sake of peace one may even tell a lie, but Sholem himself should never lie

[Sholem is also a man's name meaning peace]

Far sholem vegn meg men afile a lign zogn ober sholem tor keyn lign nit zogn NS

ווו שלום דאָרט איז ברכה

Where there's peace, there's blessing

Vu sholem dort iz brokhe NS

PEDIGREE

אַ גרויסער ייִחוס! שוסטער בן שוסטער

A noble pedigree! Shoemaker, son of shoemakers

A groyser yikhes! shuster ben shuster AC

אַמאָל איז דער משרת מער יחסן ווי דער
פּריץ

Sometimes the servant is nobler than the master

Amol iz der meshores mer yakhsn vi der porets NS

בײַ פֿערד קוקט מען אויף די צײן, בײַ
מענטשן אויפֿן שׂכל

Horses are examined by their teeth,
people by their intelligence
*Bay ferd kukt men oyf di tseyn, bay
mentshn oyfn seykhl* NS

דער וואָס באַרימט זיך מיט זײַן ייִחוס
איז גלײַך צו אַ בולבע – די בעסטע טייל
ליגט אין דר׳ערד

He who boasts of his ancestry is
comparable to a potato—the best
part lies underground
*Der vos barimt zikh mit zayn yikhes iz
glaykh tsu a bulbe—di beste teyl ligt in
dr'erd* AC

ער שטאַמט פֿון אַ גרויסן ייִחוס! ער איז
דעם אַלטן גנבֿס אַן אוראייניקל

He comes of a noble line! He's the
venerable thief's great-grandson
*Er shtamt fun a groysn yikhes! er iz
dem altn ganefs an ureynikl* AC

געוואָרן איז נישט געבוירן

Became so is not the same as born
so
Gevorn iz nisht geboyrn NS

פּנחס בן אליעזר בן אהרן הכהן – אַז ער
האָט ניט קיין געלט איז ער פֿאָרט אַ
פּאַרך

Even if he's Pinkhus, son of Elezar,
son of Aaron the High Priest—if he
has no money he's still an outcast
*Pinkhes ben elezer ben arn
hakoyen—az er hot nit keyn gelt iz
er fort a parekh* AC

זכות-אבֿות איז קיין קאַטאָוועס

The merit of ancestors is no joking
matter
Skhus-oves iz keyn katoves AC

וואָס פֿאַר אַ נאָמען, אַזאַ פּנים

As the esteem, so the mien
Vos far a nomen, aza ponim NS

ייחוס איז אויפֿן בית-הקבֿרות, ייחוס
עצמו איז בעסער

**Respect is found in the cemetery;
self-respect is better**

*Yikhes iz oyfn beysakvores, yikhes
atsmo iz beser* AC

PEOPLE

אַ מענטש דאַרף איבער זיך קיין ערגערס
ניט האָבן ווי אַ מענטשן

**A person needs nothing worse over
him than another person**

*A mentsh darf iber zikh keyn ergers nit
hobn vi a mentshn* AC

אַ מענטש איז ניט קיין מלאך

A human being is no angel

A mentsh iz nit keyn malekh P

אַז מען האָט נישט וואָס צו טאָן נעמט
מען זיך צו קהלישע זאַכן

**People who don't have enough to do
take up community work**

*Az men hot nisht vos tsu ton nemt men
zikh tsu ko'oleshe zakhn* AC

דער מענטש קען אַלץ פֿאַרגעסן נאָר
נישט עסן

**From memory you can delete
everything except when to eat**

*Der mentsh ken alts fargesn nor nisht
esn* NS

די וועלט איז שיין נאָר די מענטשן מאַכן
מיאוס

**The world is beautiful but people
make it ugly**

*Di velt iz sheyn nor di mentshn makhn
mi'es* IB

פֿאַר דער וועלט מוז מען יוצא זײַן ווי
פֿאַר גאָט אַליין

**It's just as important to please
people as to please God**

*Far der velt muz men yoytse zayn vi far
got aleyn* NS

איטלעכער האָט דערהערט ווי יענער
האָט געגעסן קנאָבל

Everyone suspects that someone else ate garlic
Itlekher hot derhert vi yener hot gegesn k'nobl IB

ווען דער מזל זעצט אים אויף אַ שטול
זעצן אים מענטשן נאָך העכער

When luck places someone on a stool, people place him even higher
Ven der mazl zetst im oyf a shtul zetsn im mentshn nokh hekher NS

וואָס איינער האָט אין זיך וואַרפֿט ער
פֿון זיך

What's in a person will out
Vos eyner hot in zikh varft er fun zikh NS

יעדער מענטש איז אַ גאַנצער עולם-קטן

Every person is a whole world in miniature
Yeder mentsh iz a gantser oylem-kotn AC

PIETY

אַ ייִד אַ למדן קען קיין חסיד ניט זײַן

A knowledgeable Jew can't be a blind believer
A yid a lamdn ken keyn khosed nit zayn IB

אַן אויפֿגעקלערטער אין אַ קליין שטעטל
עסט שנויץ מיט ברויט

An enlightened person in a small town eats pork with his bread
An oyfgeklerter in a kleyn shtetl est shnoyts mit broyt IB

אַז מען אַנטלויפֿט פֿון אַ ברענענדיק הויז
שטעלט מען זיך ניט אָפּ קושן די מזוזה

When you flee a burning house, you don't stop to kiss the mezzuzah
Az men antloyft fun a brenendik hoyz shtelt men zikh nit op kushn di mezuze AC

דער רבי האַלט ניט פֿון קיין קאָרטן, ער
האַלט בעסער פֿון קוויטלעך

The rabbi doesn't approve of playing cards, he prefers praying cards
Der rebe halt nit fun keyn kortn, er halt beser fun kvitlekh AC

איך בין אַ פֿרומער, נישט קיין קרומער

I may be pious, but I'm not biased
Ikh bin a frumer, nisht keyn krumer AC

PITY

כאָטש שוואַרץ אַבי אַ גוט האַרץ

Even black as long as one is merciful
Khotsh shvarts abi a gut harts NS

אויף אַ שלאַנג טאָר מען קיין רחמנות
ניט האָבן

Don't take pity on a snake
Oyf a shlang tor men keyn rakhmones nit hobn IB

טראָג ניט קיין טובֿות אין די הײַזער

Don't carry favors into other peoples houses
Trog nit keyn toyves in di hayzer AC

ווער עס האָט ניט קיין בושה אין פנים
און קיין רחמנות אין האַרץ דער קומט
ניט אַרויס פֿון ייִדן

Whoever hasn't tasted humiliation or felt pity doesn't come from Jews
Ver es hot nit keyn bushe in ponem un keyn rakhmones in harts der kumt nit aroys fun yidn NS

POVERTY

אַ גאַנץ יאָר באָרוועס און תּישעה-באָבֿ
אין זאָקן

A whole year barefoot and Tisheh-b'Av in stocking feet
A gants yor borves un tishebov in zokn IB

א רוסישער פּאָדריאַטשיק גייט אין
קאַלאָשן און האָט ניט קיין גראָשן

**A Russian contractor has overshoes
to wear but no money to spare**

*A rusisher podri'atshik geyt in kaloshn
un hot nit keyn groshn* NS

אַן אָרעמאַן האָט אַ בייז שלימזל

A pauper has rotten luck

An oreman hot a beyz shlimazl IB

אַן אָרעמאַן האָט קיין מורא ניט פֿאַר
קיין גנבֿה

**A pauper is not afraid of being
robbed**

*An oreman hot keyn moyre nit far keyn
ganeyve* IB

אַן אָרעמאַן איז ווי אַ לעכערדיקער זאַק

A pauper is like a torn sack

An oreman iz vi a lekherdiker zak IB

אַן אָרעמאַן קוויקט זיך מיט חלשות

A pauper revels in his own nausea

An oreman kvikt zikh mit khaloshes IB

אַן אָרעמאַן וויל אויך לעבן

A pauper also wants to live

An oreman vil oykh lebn AC

אַז אַן אָרעמאַן מאַכט חתונה קריגט דער
הונט קדחת

**When the pauper makes a wedding,
all the dog gets is the shivers**

*Az an oreman makht khasene krigt der
hunt kadokhes* NS

אַז עס רעגנט מיט גאָלד שטייט דער
אָרעמאַן אונטערן דאַך

**When it rains gold, the pauper
stands under the roof**

*Az es regnt mit gold shteyt der oreman
untern dakh* AC

אַז מען האָט ניט קיין וועש פֿאַרשפּאָרט
מען וועשגעלט צו צאָלן

**If you have no linen, you save on
laundry bills**

*Az men hot nit keyn vesh farshport
men veshgelt tsu tsoln* IB

בײַ אַן אבֿיון אַ צװילינג איז װי אַ פֿינפֿטער ראָד צום װאָגן	**To a pauper, twins are like a fifth wheel on the wagon** *Bay an evyon a tsviling iz vi a finfter rod tsum vogn* IB
בײַם פּריץ מערן זיך די רינדער, בײַם אָרעמאַן מערן זיך די קינדער	**For the landowner, cattle multiply; for the pauper, children multiply** *Baym porets mern zikh di rinder, baym oreman mern zikh di kinder* IB
ביז דער פֿעטער װערט מאָגער גייט דער מאָגערער צו גרונט	**Before the fat person grows thin, the thin one wastes away** *Biz der feter vert moger geyt der mogerer tsu grunt* NS
דער דלות פֿאַרשטעלט די חכמה	**Poverty conceals wisdom** *Der dales farshtelt di khokhme* MS
דער דלות האָט אַ גראָבן קאָפּ	**Poverty has a thick head** *Der dales hot a grobn kop* MS
דער דלות מעג אַלעס	**Poverty dares** [The poor have nothing to lose] *Der dales meg ales* IB
דער נגיד עסט ניט קיין רענדלעך און דער אָרעמאַן עסט ניט קיין שטיינדלעך	**The rich can't eat golden coins, and the poor can't eat stones** *Der noged est nit keyn rendlekh un der oreman est nit keyn shteyndlekh* AC
דער אָרעמאַן האָט װייניק פֿײַנט, דער רײַכער האָט װייניק פֿרײַנד	**The poor have few enemies, the rich have few friends** *Der oreman hot veynik faynt, der raykher hot veynik fraynd* NS
דער אָרעמאַן טראַכט, דער נגיד לאַכט	**The poor contemplate, the rich celebrate** *Der oreman trakht, der noged lakht* AC

דער שווערסטער עול איז אַ ליידיקע
קעשענע

The heaviest burden is an empty pocket
Der shverster ol iz a leydike keshene MS

די שיך פֿון אָרעמאַנס קינד וואַקסן מיטן
פֿיסל

The shoes on a pauper's child grow with its feet
Di shikh fun oremans kind vaksn mitn fisl NS

ער האָט אַזוי פֿיל געלט ווי אַ ייד האָט
חזירים

He has as much money as a Jew has pigs
Er hot azoy fil gelt vi a yid hot khazeyrim AC

ער מיינט אַז ער איז רײַך: ער פֿאַרמאָגט
אַ גאַנץ קעפּל קרויט

He thinks he's rich: he owns a whole head of cabbage!
Er meynt az er iz raykh: er farmogt a gants kepl kroyt! AC

עס איז נאָך אַ שטיקל גליק וואָס
אָרעמעלײַט שטאַרבן

It's a piece of good luck that the poor die
Es iz nokh a shtikl glik vos oremelayt shtarbn NS

עס קומט מקבל פנים זײַן אַן
אָרעמאַן – אַ קאַלטער ווינט און בייזע
הינט

Who greets a pauper? A cold wind and angry dogs
Es kumt m'kabel ponim zayn an oreman—a kalter vint un beyze hint NS

פֿאַר אַן אָרעמאַן איז אַ 'שוואַרץ יאָר'
אויך גענוג

To a pauper, "go to the devil" is good enough
Far an oreman iz a 'shvarts yor' oykh genug IB

פֿאַרוואָס פֿײַפֿט דער דלות? ווייל ער
האָט נאָר אַ דודע

Why does poverty whistle? Because it only has a whistle
Farvos fayft der dales? vayl er hot nor a dude MS

פֿאַרוואָס קלאַפֿט דער דלות? ווייל ער
גייט נאָר אין קלאָמפּעס

Why does poverty clump? Because it only has wooden shoes
Farvos klapt der dales? vayl er geyt nor in klompes MS

גאָט היט דעם אָרעמאַן – ער פֿאַרהיט
אים פֿון טײַערער עבֿירות

God protects the pauper—He protects him from expensive sins
Got hit dem oreman—er farhit im fun tayere aveyres NS

איטלעכער אָרעמאַן ווייסט פֿון זײַן
עשירות

Every pauper knows his own wealth
Itlekher oreman veyst fun zayn ashires IB

מיט אַ באַרשט און מיט אַ נאָדל
באַהאַלט מען דעם דלות

With needles and brush poverty can be concealed
Mit a barsht un mit a nodl bahalt men dem dales MS

מיט אַ פֿוילן שטעקן קען מען ניט
אַרויסטרײַבן דעם דלות

With a lazy stick you can't drive out poverty
Mit a foyln shtekn ken men nit aroystraybn dem dales NS

אָרעם איז ניט קיין שאַנדע אַבי ניט
סמאַרקאַטע

Poverty is no disgrace as long as there's no snivelling
Orem iz nit keyn shande abi nit smarkate AC

אָרעמעלײַט שטאַרבן, נגידים בלײַבן

The poor die, the rich remain
Oremelayt shtarbn, negidim blaybn IF

אָרעמעלײַט זײַנען שטענדיק ברייט

The penniless are always generous
Oremelayt zaynen shtendik brayt AC

238

צוויי חתונות אין איין טאָג איז דעם
בעטלערס יאָמער און קלאָג

**Two weddings in one day puts the
beggars in a despairing way**
*Tsvey khasenes in eyn tog iz dem
betlers yomer un klog* NS

צוויי מאָל אַ יאָר איז שלעכט דעם
אָרעמאַן: זומער און ווינטער

**Twice a year the poor are badly off:
summer and winter**
*Tsvey mol a yor iz shlekht dem oreman:
zumer un vinter* NS

ווען עס פֿעלט פּוטער צו ברויט איז עס
נאָך ניט קיין נויט

**When you lack butter for your
bread, it's not yet true poverty**
*Ven es felt puter tsu broyt iz es nokh nit
keyn noyt* NS

ווען פֿרייט זיך אָן אָרעמאַן? ווען ער
פֿאַרלירט און געפֿינט

**When does the pauper rejoice?
When he loes something and finds
it again**
*Ven freyt zikh an oreman? ven er farlirt
un gefint* IB

וווּ דער דלות קלעפּט זיך אָן קען מען
אים אַזוי לײַכט ניט פּטור ווערן

**Where poverty fastens itself, it's no
easy matter to get rid of**
*Vu der dales klebt zikh on ken men im
azoy laykht nit poter vern* MS

זינגען זינגט דער אָרעמאַן, דער רײַכער
הערט זיך נאָר צו

**The pauper does the singing; the
rich only listen**
*Zingen zingt der oreman, der raykher
hert zikh nor tsu* NS

PRAYER

די תּפֿילה גייט אַרויף און די ברכה גייט
אַראָפּ

Prayers go up, blessings come down
*Di tfile geyt aroyf un di brokhe geyt
arop* NS

גאָט, אויב דו העלפֿסט מיר ניט וועל איך
בעטן מײַן פֿעטער אין אַמעריקע

God, if You don't help me I'll appeal to my uncle in America

Got, oyb du helfst mir nit vel ikh betn mayn feter in amerike NS

גאָט זאָל אָפּהיטן פֿון אַ רויטן קאָלנער
און פֿאַר בלויע הויזן

God protect us from a red collar and blue trousers

[That is, the police]

Got zol op'hitn fun a roytn kolner un far bloye hoyzn IB

גאָט זאָל אָפּהיטן פֿון די ווײַסע
ירמולקעס

God protect us from the white skullcaps!

[White skullcaps were often worn by sickly people to ward off the Angel of Death]

Got zol op'hitn fun di vayse yarmulkes! IB

גאָט זאָל אָפּהיטן פֿון די
לשון־הרעניצעס, פֿאַר די צנועות וועט
מען זיך שוין אַליין היטן

God protect us from malicious gossips; we can protect ourselves from virtuous ones

Got zol op'hitn fun di loshn-horenitses, far di tsni'es vet men zikh shoyn aleyn hitn AC

גאָט זאָל אָפּהיטן וואָס דער מענטש קען
אַלץ פֿאַרטראָגן

May God spare us all we are capable of enduring

Got zol op'hitn vos der mentsh ken alts fartrogn NS

לייז אונדז אויס גאָט, פֿון גלות און פֿון
די בעל־עגלות

God, redeem us from exile and also from the uncouth and vile

Leyz undz oys got, fun goles un fun di balegoles MS

240

רבינו-של-עולם, העלף מיר זיך
אויפֿצוהייבן, אַרונטערפֿאַלן קען איך
אַליין

**Master of the Universe, help me to
get up; I can fall down all by myself**
*Reboyne-sheloylem, helf mir zikh
oyftsuheybn, arunterfaln ken ikh
aleyn* NS

רבינו-של-עולם, הייב מיך ניט אויף און
וואַרף מיך ניט אַראָפ

**Master of the Universe, don't raise
me up and don't cast me down**
*Reboyne-sheloylem, heyb mikh nit oyf
un varf mikh nit arop* AC

תּפֿילה אָן כּוונה איז ווי אַ גוף אָן אַ
נשמה

**A prayer without devotion is like a
body without a soul**
*Tfile on kavone iz vi a guf on a
neshome* NS

PREPARATION

אַז מען גרייט זיך אָן אין דער יוגנט האָט
מען אויף דער עלטער

**Whatever you prepare for in youth,
you have in old age**
*Az men greyt zikh on in der yugnt hot
men oyf der elter* AC

אַז מען לעבט אָן רעכנונג שטאַרבט מען
אָן ווידו

**If you live without reckoning, you
die without confession**
*Az men lebt on rekhnung shtarbt men
on vide* IF

אין דער בעסטער צייַט זאָלסטו זייַן
גרייט צו באַגעגענען צרות און לייַד

**In the best of times, prepare to meet
sorrow and despair**
*In der bester tsayt zolstu zayn greyt tsu
bagegenen tsores un layd* IB

ווען מען ווייסט אַז מען וועט פֿאַלן
וואָלט מען זיך אונטערגעלייגט אַ קישן

**If people knew they would fall,
they'd lay down a cushion**
*Ven men veyst az men vet faln volt
men zikh untergeleygt a kishn* IB

241

ווער עס גרייט ניט אן ערב שבת דער
האָט ניט אויף שבת

If you don't prepare for Shabbes, you won't have what to eat on Shabbes
Ver es greyt nit on erev shabes der hot nit oyf shabes NS

ווי מען בראָקט זיך איין די פֿערפֿל אַזוי
עסט מען זיי אויף

How you prepare the noodles is how you'll eat them
Vi men brokt zikh ayn di ferfl azoy est men zey oyf IB

וואָס מען גרייט זיך ניט אָן אויף דער
וועלט דאָס נעמט מען ניט אויף יענער
וועלט

Whatever you don't prepare in this world you don't take into the next
Vos men greyt zikh nit on oyf der velt dos nemt men nit oyf yener velt IB

PRIDE

דער וואָס וויל גאווה טרייבן מוז הונגער
ליידן

He who stands upon his pride has starvation at his side
Der vos vil gayve traybn muz hunger laydn NS

גאווה איז די מיאוסטע תאווה

Arrogance is the ugliest of passions
Gayve iz di mi'este tayve NS

מאַך זיך ניט פֿאַר קיין מויז וועט די קאַץ
דיך ניט אויפֿעסן

Don't make a mouse out of yourself and the cat won't eat you
Makh zikh nit far keyn moyz vet di kats dikh nit oyfesn AC

מיט צו פֿיל שטאָלץ ליגט מען אין
תפֿיסה

To be too proud is to be in prison
Mit tsu fil shtolts ligt men in t'fise NS

PUNISHMENT

אַ פּאַטש איז לײַכטער צו באַקומען ווי
צו געבן

It's easier to take a blow than to give it

A patsh iz laykhter tsu bakumen vi tsu gebn AC

אַז גאָט וויל שטראָפֿן אַן אפיקורס גיט
ער אים אַ פֿרום ווײַב

When God wants to punish an unbeliever, He gives him a pious wife

Az got vil shtrofn an apikoyres git er im a frum vayb IF

אַז מען שלאָגט, שלאָגט מען אויס
פּוטער

If you must beat, churn butter

Az men shlogt, shlogt men oys puter NS

אַז מ'איז פֿרײַ מיט דער צונג קריגט מען
מתנות יד

If you're too loose with your tongue, you get thrashed

Az m'iz fray mit der tsung krigt men matnes yad IB

תּפֿיסה איז אזוי ווי מיתה

Incarceration is like expiration

T'fise iz azoy vi mise NS

QUARRELS

אַ טויטער מאַכט קיין קריג ניט   **A corpse doesn't make trouble**
A toyter makht keyn krig nit NS

אַז דער מילנער שלאָגט זיך מיטן קוימען   **When the miller fights with the**
קערער ווערט דער מילנער שוואַרץ און **chimney sweep, the miller turns**
דער קוימען קערער ווײַס **black and the chimney sweep turns**
white
Az der milner shlogt zikh mitn koymen
kerer vert der milner shvarts un der
koymen kerer vays NS

אַז מען גרייט דעם טיש פֿאַרגייט דער   **A table with food ends a**
געקריג **quarrelsome mood**
Az men greyt dem tish fargeyt der
gekrig NS

אַז מען קריגט זיך מיטן רבֿ מוז מען   **If you're at odds with the rabbi,**
שלום מאַכן מיטן שענקער **make peace with the bartender**
Az men krigt zikh mitn rov muz men
sholem makhn mitn shenker NS

דער ערשטער ברוגז איז דער בעסטער
ברוגז

The first quarrel is the best quarrel
*Der ershter broyges iz der bester
broyges* NS

איין האָלץ קען ניט ברענען, איין מענטש
קען זיך ניט קריגן

**One piece of wood can't burn all by
itself; one person can't quarrel all
by himself**
*Eyn holts ken nit brenen, eyn mentsh
ken zikh nit krign* AC

פֿון אַ װאָרט װערט אַ קװאָרט

One word becomes a herd
Fun a vort vert a kvort NS

איבער אַ האָן מיט אַ הון איז חרוב
געװאָרן אַ שטאָט

**Over a chicken and a rooster the
whole town was ruined**
*Iber a hon mit a hun iz khorev gevorn
a shtot* AC

קהל קריגט זיך און דעם שמש שמײַסט
מען

**The congregation quarrels and the
sexton gets punished**
*Ko'ol krigt zikh un dem shames
shmayst men* NS

װען איין זעלנער װאָלט געװוּסט װאָס
דער אַנדערער טראַכט װאָלט קיין קריג
ניט געװען

**If one soldier knew what the other
one thought, there'd be no war**
*Ven eyn zelner volt gevust vos der
anderer trakht volt keyn krig nit
geven* AC

QUESTIONS

אַ מקשן פֿאַלט תמיד אין דער בלאָטע
אַרײַן

**A questioner always sinks into the
mud**
*A makshen falt tomed in der blote
arayn* NS

אַז מען וויל גוט בודק זײַן איז אַלעס טרייף

If you examine carefully enough, everything becomes forbidden
Az men vil gut boydek zayn iz ales treyf IB

בעסער צוויי מאָל פֿרעגן איידער איין מאָל בלאָנדזען

Better to ask once than to stray twice
Beser tsvey mol fregn eyder eyn mol blondzhen AC

אויף איטלעכן תירוץ קען מען געפֿינען אַ נײַע קשיא

To every answer you can find a new question
Oyf itlekhn terets ken men gefinen a naye kashe NS

ווער עס פֿרעגט אַ סך שאלות באַקומט אַ סך תשובֿות

If you ask too many questions, you'll get varying answers
Ver es fregt a sakh shayles bakumt a sakh tshuves NS

יעדער וואָרום האָט זײַן דאָרום

Every wherefore has its therefore
Yeder varum hot zayn darum NS

RABBIS

אַ פֿעטער רבֿ און אַ מאָגערער גלח טויגן
ביידע ניט

**A fat rabbi and a skinny priest are
both useless**

*A feter rov un a mogerer galekh toygn
beyde nit* IB

אַ רבי און אַ דאָקטער ווערן רייַך נאָר פֿון
ווייַבער

**Rabbis and doctors get rich only
from women**

*A rebe un a dokter vern raykh nor fun
vayber* NS

אַז דער תלמיד איז אַ ווילער איז דער
רבי אויך אַ ווילער

**If the pupil is apt, the rabbi is a
good teacher**

*Az der talmed iz a voyler iz der rebe
oykh a voyler* IB

בעסער מיט אַ היימישן גנבֿ איידער מיט
אַ פֿרעמדן רבֿ

**Better with a hometown thief than
with an imported rabbi**

*Beser mit a heymishn ganef eyder mit
a fremdn rov* NS

247

דער רבי איז גרויס ווען ער האָט אַ סך
קלײנע יִידעלעך

The rabbi is a giant when surrounded with small people
Der rebe iz groys ven er hot a sakh kleyne yidelekh NS

די חסידימלעך זאָלן פֿרײלעך זײַן טרינקט
דער רבינו אויס דעם ווײַן

In order for his followers to be happy, the rabbi himself drinks up all the wine
Di khsidimlekh zoln freylekh zayn trinkt der rebenyu oys dem vayn NS

פֿאַר דרײַ האָט גאָט אָנגעגרייט אַ
באַזונדערן גן-עדן, פֿאַר רבנים, נאמנים
און מלמדים, נאָר עס שטייט נאָך עד
היום, ליידיק

God has prepared a special paradise for three kinds of people: rabbis, the faithful, and teachers; however, to this day, it's empty
Far dray hot got ongegreyt a bazundern gan-eydn, far rabonim, nemonim un melamdim, nor es shteyt nokh ad hayom, leydik NS

נײַן רבנים קענען קיין מנין ניט מאַכן
אָבער צען שוסטערס יאָ

Nine rabbis can't make a minyan but ten shoemakers can
Nayn rabonim kenen keyn minyen nit makhn ober tsen shusters yo IB

ווען דער תלמיד האָט זיך געשמדט איז
דער רבי דער משומד

If the pupil converts, the rabbi is blamed
Ven der talmed hot zikh geshmat iz der rebe der meshumed NS

וווּ ער וועט זײַן רבֿ וועט אָפּברענען די
קהילה

Wherever he will become rabbi, the entire community will burn down
Vu er vet zayn rov vet opbrenen di kehile NS

REGION

אַ ליטוואַק האָט אַ געצלמטן קאָפּ

A Litvak has a crossed head
[because he lays himself out in the
length and in the breadth to prove
that he's in the right]
A litvak hot a getseylemtn kop NS

אַ ליטוואַק נעמט זיך אונטער אפֿילו אַן
אַם צו זײַן

**A Litvak will undertake to become
even a wet-nurse**
*A litvak nemt zikh unter afile an am
tsu zayn* NS

אַ ליטוואַק טוט תּשובֿה נאָך איידער ער
זינדיקט

**A Litvak repents before he even
commits the sin**
*A litvak tut tshuve nokh eyder er
zindikt* AC

אַלע חכמות קומען אַרויס פֿון
דײַטש – און אַליין בלײַבט ער אַ נאַר

**Clever things come from the
Germans—yet they themselves
remain fools**
*Ale khokhmes kumen aroys fun
daytsh—un aleyn blaybt er a nar* NS

די דײַטשן זײַנען אַ פֿײַן פֿאָלק נאָר דאָס
לשון הרגט זיי אַוועק

**The Germans are a fine people, but
their language does them in**
*Di daytshn zaynen a fayn folk nor dos
loshn harget zey avek* MS

די כעלעמער זײַנען גאָר קיין נאַראָנים
ניט, נאָר אַלע נאַרישקייטן טרעפֿן זיך בײַ
זיי

**The people of Chelm are not fools
at all; it's just that foolish things
happen to them**
*Di khelemer zaynen gor keyn naronim
nit, nor ale narishkeytn trefn zikh bay
zey* NS

גאַנץ קוטנאָ איז איין טלית

The entire town of Kutno is one prayer shawl
[It is said that the nobleman of Kutno levied a tax on every prayer shawl. The Jews of Kutno solved the problem by everyone praying under one shawl.]
Gants kutno iz eyn tales IB

אין אַמעריקע לעבט מען מען זאָל עסן,
אין רוסלאַנד עסט מען מען זאָל לעבן

In America people live to eat; in Russia people eat to live
In amerike lebt men men zol esn, in rusland est men men zol lebn NS

אין פּוילן גייען די ווײַבער אין הויזן

In Poland, women wear the pants
In poyln geyen di vayber in hoyzn NS

אין פּויזן גייען די ווײַבער אין הויזן

In Posen, women wear the pants
In poyzn geyen di vayber in hoyzn IB

איטלעכע שטאָט האָט זיך איר
משוגענעם

Every town has its own lunatic
Itlekhe shtot hot zikh ir meshugenem NS

קריגן זאָל ער דער לעמבערגער בראָך!

May the Lemberg disaster befall him!
Krign zol er der lemberger brokh! AC

צען מייל פֿון אָדעס ברענט דער גהינום

Ten miles from Odessa, hell fires burn
Tsen mayl fun odes brent der gehenem NS

וואַרשעוּוער ווײַבער האָבן האַרטע לײַבער

Warsaw women have tough hides
Varshever vayber hobn harte layber NS

ווען ניט די לוקניקער יידן וואָלטן די
שקאָצים קיין שטיינער ניט געוואָרפֿן

**If not for the Lukniker Jews, the
Gentile boys wouldn't throw stones**
*Ven nit di lukniker yidn voltn di
shkotsim keyn shteyner nit gevorfn* AC

וואָס רעדט מען אין וואַרשע? דאָס
וויַיסל ברענט

**What do they talk about in Warsaw?
The river's on fire**
[Pun on vaysl, which means the
white of an egg as well as the
Vistula river]
*Vos ret men in varshe? dos vaysl
brent* IB

וווּ אַ ליטוואַק גייט דאָרט וואַקסט ניט
קיין גראָז

**Grass won't grow where a Litvak
goes**
*Vu a litvak geyt dort vakst nit keyn
groz* NS

וווּ אדם הראשון האָט ניט געפּישט איז
קיין שטאָט נישט

If Adam didn't pee there, it's no city
*Vu odem harishon hot nit gepisht iz
keyn shtot nisht* NS

REGRET

אין דער יוגנט אַ גנבֿ, אויף דער עלטער אַ
בעל-תשובֿה

In youth a thief, in old age repentant
*In der yugnt a ganef, oyf der elter a
baltshuve* NS

חרטה איז נישט סוחריש

Regret isn't businesslike
Kharote iz nisht sokhrish AC

אויף ניט גיין און ניט פֿאָרן זאָל מען קיין
חרטה ניט האָבן

**Don't regret that you haven't
traveled**
*Oyf nit geyn un nit forn zol men keyn
kharote nit hobn* NS

נאָכן טויט העלפֿט ניט קיין תשובֿה

Repentance is useless once you're dead
Nokhn toyt helft nit keyn tshuve NS

וואָס עס איז פֿאַרפֿאַלן זאָל ניט באַנג
טאָן

What's past shouldn't be regretted
Vos es iz farfaln zol nit bang ton AC

RELATIONSHIP

אַ חתונה? ווי קומט אָבער דער הונט
דערצו?

A wedding? How did the dog get invited?
A khasene? vi kumt ober der hunt dertsu? IB

עס האָט זיך אָנגעהויבן מיט קידוש און
געענדיקט מיט קדיש

It started with a benediction and ended with mourning
Es hot zikh ongehoybn mit kidesh un ge'endikt mit kadesh AC

עס ווענדט זיך ווו דער חמור שטייט

It depends where the substance is located
[Khamer has three meanings: if in a stall, it's a donkey; if in the cellar, it's wine; and if in a pit, it's lime. Play on words]
Es vent zikh vu der khamer shteyt IB

ווי קומען די ריבן אין דעם זאָק?

How do the turnips get into the sack?
Vi kumen di ribn in dem zak? IB

ווי קומט "אתה הראית" צו דער
אַרענדע?

How does a Simchat-Torah recitation get into the lease?
Vi kumt "ato hareyso" tsu der arenda? IB

וי קומט דער קרבן צו דעם מזבח? | How did the sacrifice get to the altar?
Vi kumt der korbn tsu dem mazbeyekh? NS

וי קומט עשׂו אין דער "קריאת-שמע" אַרײַן? | How did Esau get into the daily prayers?
Vi kumt eysev in der "krishme" arayn? NS

וי קומט הודו אין מיקווה אַרײַן? | How does India get into the ritual bath?
Vi kumt hodu in mikve arayn? IB

וואָס טויג מיר נירענבערג אַז איך האָב דאָרט ניט קיין הויז? | What is the use of Nuremberg to me if I don't own a house there?
Vos toyg mir nirenberg az ikh hob dort nit keyn hoyz? IB

REMEDIES

אַז דאָס ווײַבל דאַרף שוין צו האָבן שיקט מען ערשט נאָך דער באָבען | Not until the wife is ready to deliver is the midwife sent for
Az dos vaybl darf shoyn tsu hobn shikt men ersht nokh der boben AC

די צײַט איז דער בעסטער רופֿה | Time is the best healer
Di tsayt iz der bester royfe AC

פֿאַר אַן עקשן איז קיין רפֿואה ניטאָ | There's no cure for stubbornness
Far an akshn iz keyn refu'e nito NS

טיי און תּהילים שאַטן ניט | Tea and reciting psalms can't hurt
Tey un tilim shatn nit NS

וועַן תהילים זאָלן זיַין אַ רפֿואה וואָלט   **If psalms could cure, they'd sell**
מען עס פֿאַרקויפֿט אין אפטייק   **them at the drugstore**
Ven tilim zoln zayn a refu'e volt men es
farkoyft in apteyk NS

REPETITION

אַז מען חזרט איבער צו פֿיל װי גערעכט   **If you repeat you're right too often,**
מען איז, ווערט מען אומגערעכט   **you're wrong**
Az men khazert iber tsu fil vi gerekht
men iz, vert men umgerekht AC

אייַן מאָל איז שייַן, צווייַ מאָל האָט נאָך   **Once it's nice, the second time has**
חן, דרייַ מאָל ברעכט מען שוין האַלדז   **charm, the third time gets you a**
און בייַן   **broken arm**
Eyn mol iz sheyn, tsvey mol hot nokh
kheyn, dray mol brekht men shoyn
haldz un beyn AC

ער מאָלט געמאָלן מעל   **He grinds already ground flour**
Er molt gemoln mel AC

חזיר איבער איז תריפֿה   **Repetition is a bore, and a boar**
isn't kosher
[Play on words]
Khazer iber iz treyfe AC

RESPONSIBILITY

אַז מען גיט אויס דאָס געלט אויף פוטער   **If you spend on butter you won't**
האָט מען ניט אויף ברויט   **have for bread**
Az men git oys dos gelt oyf puter hot
men nit oyf broyt NS

אַז מען לעבט אויסגערעכנט דאַרף מען
צו קיינעם ניט אָנקומען

If you live responsibly, you don't have to ask anyone for help
Az men lebt oysgerekhnt darf men tsu keynem nit onkumen NS

עס קען זיַין האַרב אויך די ריַיכסטע אַרב

The richest inheritance can become an encumbrance
Es ken zayn harb oykh di raykhste arb NS

עס וויַיסט די קאַץ וועמענס פֿלייש זי
האָט אויפֿגעגעסן

The cat knows whose meat it ate
Es veyst di kats vemens fleysh zi hot oyfgegesn NS

ווען דער תלמיד האָט זיך געשמדט איז
דער רבי דער משומד

If the pupil converts, the rabbi is blamed
Ven der talmed hot zikh geshmat iz der rebe der meshumed NS

וואָס גייט מיך אָן קראָקע אַז איך בין אין
לעמבערג?

What do I care about Cracow if I live in Lemberg?
Vos geyt mikh on kroke az ikh bin in lemberg? IF

REST

דער וואָגן רוט אין ווינטער, דער שליטן
אין זומער און דאָס פֿערד קיינמאָל ניט

The wagon rests in winter, the sled in summer, and the horse never
Der vogn rut in vinter, der shlitn in zumer un dos ferd keynmol nit NS

נאָר אין קבֿר האָט מען רו

Only in the grave is there rest
Nor in keyver hot men ru AC

שבת האָט דער רשע אין גהינום אויך רו

Even the wicked in hell have respite on Shabbes
Shabes hot der roshe in gehenem oykh ru NS

REVENGE

אַ נקמה אין דער שנור דער זון איז געשטאָרבן.

Some revenge on the daughter-in-law when the son dies!
A nekome in der shnur der zun iz geshtorbn IB

די קלענסטע נקמה פֿאָרסמט די נשמה

The smallest vengeance poisons the soul
Di klenste nekome farsamt di neshome NS

מיר קדחת אַבי יענעם צו להכעיס!

Even convulsions for me if spited they'll be!
Mir kadokhes abi yenem tsu lehakhes! SK

SECRECY

אַ סוד גייט נאָר אין הויזן   **A secret wears trousers only**
A sod geyt nor in hoyzn NS

אַז מען וואַרפֿט אַרײַן דעם סוד אין ים   **If you toss your secret into the sea,**
וואַרפֿט אים דער ים אַרויס   **the sea will cast it out**
Az men varft arayn dem sod in yam
varft im der yam aroys NS

דער מאָגן האַלט אַ סוד בעסער ווי דאָס   **The stomach keeps a secret better**
האַרץ   **than the heart**
Der mogn halt a sod beser vi dos
harts NS

דרײַ זאַכן קען מען ניט באַהאַלטן: ליבע,   **Three things can't be hidden: love,**
הוסטן און דלות   **coughing, and poverty**
Dray zakhn ken men nit bahaltn: libe,
hustn un dales NS

פֿאַרן דאָקטער און פֿאַרן בעדער זײַנען   **You can't keep secrets from the**
ניטאָ קיין סודות   **doctor or the bathhouse attendant**
Farn dokter un farn beder zaynen nito
keyn soydes NS

גיי אַרויס פֿון שטוב – מען רעדט דיר אַ
שידוך

Leave the house—they're arranging a wedding for you
Gey aroys fun shtub—men ret dir a shidekh IB

אין בויך זעט קיינער ניט

No one sees inside the stomach
In boykh zet keyner nit NS

וואָס בײַ אַ ניכטערן אויפֿן לונג איז בײַ אַ
שיכורן אויפֿן צונג

What the sober conceal, the drunk reveal
Vos bay a nikhtern oyf lung iz bay a shikern oyfn tsung IB

ווו אַ סוד, דאָרט אַ גנבֿה

Where a secret, there a theft
Vu a sod, dort a ganeyve IB

זאָג דער ווײַב אַ סוד און שנײַד איר אויס
די צונג

Tell your wife a secret and cut out her tongue
Zog der vayb a sod un shnayd ir oys di tsung NS

SEX

אַ ווײַבל מיט אַ גרויסן שלייער און האָט
ליב האַרטע אייער

A woman, even behind a veil, likes balls on a male
A vaybl mit a groysn shleyer un hot lib harte eyer WZ

אַן אשת-איש איז אַ מתּן-בסתר

A married woman is like an anonymous donation
An eyshes ish iz a matn b'seyser WZ

אַז דער קליינער וויל ניט שטיין מוז מען
זיך מיט אַ פֿינגער באַגיין

If the little one won't stand, you have to do it all by hand
Az der kleyner vil nisht shteyn muz men zikh mit a finger bageyn WZ

אַז עס וואָלט געווען אַן עבֿירה וואָלט
עס דער רבֿ ניט געטאָן, אַז עס וואָלט
געווען אַ סכּנה וואָלט עס דער דאָקטער
ניט געטאָן

**If it's a sin, the rabbi wouldn't do it;
if it's dangerous, the doctor
wouldn't do it**

*Az es volt geven an aveyre volt es der
rov nit geton, az es volt geven a sakone
volt es der dokter nit geton* NS

אַז מען שעמט זיך האָט מען קיין קינדער
ניט

**If you're bashful, you don't have
children**

*Az men shemt zikh hot men keyn
kinder nit* AC

ער האָט דעם טאַטנס טבֿע, ער שטאַרבט
נאָך אַ נקבֿה

**He has his father's ways: females
he craves**

*Er hot dem tatns teyve, er shtarbt nokh
a nekeyve* IF

איינער האָט ליב דעם רבֿ, דער אַנדערער
האָט ליב די רביצין

**One person likes the rabbi, another
likes the rabbi's wife**

*Eyner hot lib dem rov, der anderer hot
lib di rebetsin* AC

פֿון דעם מאַנס רפֿואה ווערט די ווײַב
קראַנק אין נײַן חדשים

**What cures the husband makes the
wife ill nine months later**

*Fun dem mans refu'e vert di vayb krank
in nayn khadoshim* NS

איטלעכעס טעפּל געפֿינט זיך זײַן
שטערצל, איטלעכעס פּעצל געפֿינט זיך
זײַן לעכל

**Every pot finds its lid; every prick
finds its niche**

*Itlekhes tepl gefint zikh zayn shtertsl,
itlekhes petsl gefint zikh zayn lekhl* WZ

נאָך וואָס דאַרף מען די קו קויפֿן אַז די
מילך קריגט מען בחינום?

**Why buy the cow when you get the
milk for free?**

*Nokh vos darf men di ku koyfn az di
milkh krigt men bekhinem?* AC

אָנמוטן קען מען אפילו ביַי דער רביצין
אויך

You can make suggestions even to
the rabbi's wife
*Onmutn ken men afile bay der rebetsin
oykh* IB

אונטער דער קאָלדרע איז די שוואַרצע
אַזוי גוט ווי די וויַיסע

Under the covers, the swarthy is as
good as the fair
*Unter der koldre iz di shvartse azoy gut
vi di vayse* AC

ווען עס וואָלטן געווען וויניקער חזירים
וואָלטן געווען וויניקער ממזרים

If there were fewer swine, there'd
be fewer bastards
*Ven es voltn geven veyniker khazeyrim
voltn geven veyniker mamzeyrim* NS

ווען עס וואָלטן ניט געווען קיין קינדער
וווּ וואָלטן זיך גענומען די עזות-פּנימער?

If there were no children, where
would the hypocrites come from?
*Ven es voltn nit geven keyn kinder vu
voltn zikh genumen di azes-
penimer?* NS

ייִדן זיַינען געווען צו פאַרנומען קינדער
האָבן צו זאָרגן זיך וועגן סעקס

Jews were too busy having children
to worry about sex
*Yidn zaynen geven tsu farnumen kinder
hobn tsu zorgn zikh vegn seks* AC

SIGHT

אַ בלינדער האָט אַ ליַיכטן טויט – מען
פּאַרשפּאָרט אים די אויגן צוצומאַכן

A blind person has an easy death—
it's not necessary to close his eyes
*A blinder hot a laykhtn toyt—men
farshport im di oygn tsutsumakhn* NS

אַז ס'איז ניטאָ וואָס צו זען העלפן ניט
קיין ברילן

If there's nothing worth seeing,
eyeglasses won't help
*Az s'iz nito vos tsu zen helfn nit keyn
briln* AC

די אויגן זײַנען דער שפּיגל פֿון דער נשמה

Eyes are the mirror of the soul
Di oygn zaynen der shpigl fun der neshome NS

פֿאַר אָנקוקן צאָלט מען קיין געלט ניט

Looking doesn't cost money
Far onkukn tsolt men keyn gelt nit AC

צו וואָס גלויבן אַז עס זײַנען דאָ אויגן?

Why believe if you have eyes to perceive?
Tsu vos gloybn az es zaynen do oygn? NS

ווען די אויגן זעען ניט, טוט ניט וויי דאָס האַרץ

When the eyes don't see, the heart won't ache
Ven di oygn ze'en nit tut nit vey dos harts NS

וואָס לענגער אַ בלינדער לעבט אַלץ מער זעט ער

The longer a blind person lives, the more he sees
Vos lenger a blinder lebt, alts mer zet er NS

SIGNS

אַלע סימנים זײַנען נאַראָנים

All signs are misleading
Ale simonim zaynen naronim IB

אַלע סימנים זײַנען נאַראָנים אָבער סימן דלות בלײַבט

All signs are misleading; only the sign of poverty is credible
Ale simonim zaynen naronim ober simen dales blaybt AC

אַז אַ מיידל ווערט געבוירן איז עס אַ הצלחה אין דער משפּחה

When a daughter is born, it's a good sign for the family
Az a meydl vert geboyrn iz es a hatslokhe in der mishpokhe NS

261

אַז עס דונערט איז אַ סימן פֿון אַ זול

Thunder is a sign of coming plenty
Az es dunert iz a simen fun a zol NS

אַז עס איז אַ רעגנבױגן װײַזט גאָט דעם
סימן אַז ער איז אונדז מוחל

When there's a rainbow, it's a sign that God has forgiven us
Az es iz a regnboygn vayzt got dem simen az er iz undz moykhl NS

SILENCE

אַ בהמה האָט אַ לאַנגע צונג און קען ניט
רעדן, דער מענטש האָט אַ קורצע צונג
און טאָר ניט רעדן

A cow has a long tongue and can't speak; a person has a short one and shouldn't speak
A beyeyme hot a lange tsung un ken nit redn, der mentsh hot a kurtse tsung un tor nit redn NS

אַ װאָרט איז װערט אַ גראָשן, שװײַגן
איז װערט צװײ

A word is worth a penny, silence is worth two
A vort iz vert a groshen, shvaygn iz vert tsvey NS

אַז דאָס װאָרט איז אין מויל איז מען אַ
האַר, אַז מען לאָזט עס אַרויס איז מען אַ
נאַר

A lord before you utter a word, a fool after you've been heard
Az dos vort iz in moyl iz men a har, az men lozt es aroys iz men a nar NS

אַז מען שװײַגט איז מען אַ האַלבער נאַר,
אַז מען רעדט איז מען אַ גאַנצער נאַר

Keep quiet and you're half a fool; speak up and you become a complete one
Az men shvaygt iz men a halber nar, az men ret iz men a gantser nar AC

דער װאָס שװײַגט מיינט אויך עפּעס

Silence also tells you something
Der vos shvaygt meynt oykh epes AC

דורך שוויַיגן קען מען ניט שטיַיגן

You can't climb a rung by holding your tongue
Durkh shvaygn ken men nit shtaygn NS

עס וואָס גוט און וווֹיל און האַלט די צונג אין מויל

Eat what has taste and don't speak in haste
Es vos gut un voyl un halt di tsung in moyl NS

אין אַ גוטער שעה צו רעדן, אין אַ בייזער שעה צו שוויַיגן

In good times talk, in bad times keep silent
In a guter sho tsu redn, in a beyzer sho tsu shvaygn NS

"מרבה דבֿרים, מרבה שטות" – וואָס ווינציקער מ'רעדט, געזינטער איז

"A lot of words, a lot of foolishness"—the less you talk, the healthier
"marbe dvorim, marbe shtus"—vos vintsiker m'ret, gezinter iz IB

רעדן איז שווער און שוויַיגן קען מען ניט

Speech is difficult but silence is impossible
Redn iz shver un shvaygn ken men nit P

רעדן איז זילבער, שוויַיגן איז גאָלד

Speech is silver, silence is gold
Redn iz zilber, shvaygn iz gold NS

שיין שוויַיגן איז שענער ווי שיין רעדן

Appropriate silence is finer than pretty words
Sheyn shvaygn iz shener vi sheyn redn NS

ווען דאָס פֿערד וואָלט געהאַט וואָס צו זאָגן וואָלט עס גערעדט

If the horse had anything to say, it would speak up
Ven dos ferd volt gehat vos tsu zogn volt es geret NS

SIN

א ליטוואָק טוט תשובה איידער ער
זינדיקט

A Litvak repents even before he commits the sin

A litvak tut tshuve eyder er zindikt AC

אַז מען האָט נאָר אין זין בראָנפֿן און
קורוועס גייט מען צום סוף נאַקעט און
באָרוועס

If drinking and whoring is your only care, you'll end up naked and bare

Az men hot nor in zin bronfn un kurves geyt men tsum sof naket un borves WZ

דער מענטש זינדיקט און דער האָן איז די
כפרה

The person sins and the rooster is punished

[Refers to High Holy Day ritual in which a rooster is used as a scapegoat for past sins]

Der mentsh zindikt un der hon iz di kapore AC

דאָס אויג זעט, דאָס האַרץ גלוסט און
דער גוף זינדיקט

The eyes see, the heart desires, but the body does the sinning

Dos oyg zet, dos harts glust un der guf zindikt AC

קענען תורה איז נישט קיין שטער צו
עבֿירה

Knowledge of the Torah is no deterrent to sin

Kenen toyre iz nisht keyn shter tsu aveyre AC

ווען די עבֿירה איז זיס איז ניט ביטער די
תשובה

When sinning is sweet, repentance is not bitter

Ven di aveyre iz zis iz nit biter di tshuve NS

יענעמס חטאים קומט קיינער ניט | Nobody can atone for another's
אָפּ – מען האָט אייגענע גענוג | sins—one has enough of one's own
Yenems khatoyim kumt keyner nit op—
men hot eygene genug AC

SIZE

אַ קליין שטיינדל קען אויך מאַכן אַ | A small stone can also make a big
גרויסע לאָך | hole
A kleyn shteyndl ken oykh makhn a
groyse lokh AC

עס איז לאַנג ביזן הימל און שטינקט פֿון | It stretches to the sky and the rot
שימל! | stinks as high!
Es iz lang bizn himl un shtinkt fun
shiml! NS

עס איז קורץ און דיק און איין שטיק! | It's short and obese and in one
piece!
Es iz kurts un dik un eyn shtik! NS

מיט אַ קליין ביינדל קען מען זיך אויך | You can choke even on a small
דערשטיקן | bone
Mit a kleyn beyndl ken men zikh oykh
dershtikn AC

זאָל מען אַזוי קענען מאַכן פֿון קליינע | If only we could make from small,
גרויסע ווי מען קען מאַכן פֿון גרויסע | big, as easily as we can make from
קליינע | big, small
Zol men azoy kenen makhn fun kleyne
groyse vi men ken makhn fun groyse
kleyne AC

265

SLEEP

אַז עס קומט ניט דער שלאָף איז די
ערגסטע שטראָף

A sleepless night is the worst blight
*Az es kumt nit der shlof iz di ergste
shtrof* NS

דער חלום איז אַ נאַר און שלאָף איז דער
האַר

**The dream is a fool and sleep is the
master**
*Der kholem iz a nar un shlof iz der
har* NS

דער שלאָף איז אַ גנבֿ

Sleep is a thief
Der shlof iz a ganef NS

דער שלאָף איז דער בעסטער דאָקטער

Sleep is the best doctor
Der shlof iz der bester dokter AC

אין שלאָף זינדיקט ניט דער מענטש נאָר
זײַנע חלומות

**A person doesn't sin in his sleep,
but his dreams do**
*In shlof zindikt nit der mentsh nor
zayne khaloymes* NS

קירצער געשלאָפֿן, לענגער געלעבט

**The less you sleep, the longer you'll
live**
Kirtser geshlofn, lenger gelebt NS

שלאָף גיכער, מען דאַרף האָבן דעם קישן

Sleep faster, we need the pillow!
*Shlof gikher, men darf hobn dem
kishn!* P

SPEECH

אַלע שטומע ווילן אַ סך רעדן

All mutes want to talk a lot
Ale shtume viln a sakh redn IB

אַז מען רעדט אַ סך קען מען זיך
אויסרעדן אַ נאַרישקייט

Talk too much and you end up talking foolishness
Az men ret a sakh ken men zikh oysredn a narishkeyt AC

בײַ נאַכט הערט זיך ווײַטער

News travels farther at night
Bay nakht hert zikh vayter NS

די צונג איז דעם מענטשנס גרעסטער שונא

The tongue is a person's worst enemy
Di tsung iz dem mentshns grester soyne AC

די צונג איז ניט אָנגעבונדן מיט אַ שטריקל

The tongue isn't tied down with string
Di tsung iz nit ongebundn mit a shtrikl NS

עס טוט זיך ניט אַזוי לײַכט ווי עס רעדט זיך

It's not as easily done as said
Es tut zikh nit azoy laykht vi es ret zikh AC

פֿאַר זיסע ריידעלעך צעגייען די מיידעלעך

Girls don't balk at sweet talk
Far zise reydelekh tsegeyen di meydelekh NS

פֿון אַ וואָרט ווערט ניט קיין לאָך אין קאָפּ

From talking you don't get a hole in the head
Fun a vort vert nit keyn lokh in kop AC

פֿון פֿיל ריידן קומט אַרויס לײַדן

Lots of talk in the air causes despair
Fun fil raydn kumt aroys laydn NS

גערעדט איז ניט געבילט

Talking isn't barking
Geret iz nit gebilt NS

גרינג צו זאָגן שווער צו טראָגן

Easy to state, hard to actuate
Gring tsu zogn shver tsu trogn NS

איבער דעם האָט גאָט געגעבן דעם
מענטשן צוויי אויערן און נאָר איין מויל,
כדי ער זאָל מער הערן און וויניקער
רעדן

**God gave mankind two ears but
only one mouth, so that he would
hear more and talk less**
*Iber dem hot got gegebn dem mentshn
tsvey oyern un nor eyn moyl, kedey er
zol mer hern un veyniker redn* NS

מען מישפט ניט דעם רעדנער, נאָר דער
אינהאַלט

Judge the speech, not the speaker
*Men mishpet nit dem redner, nor der
inhalt* AC

ניט אַלץ וואָס מען ווייסט מעג מען זאָגן

**Not everything one knows should
be said**
Nit alts vos men veyst meg men zogn P

אָן אַ צונג איז ווי אָן אַ גלאָק

**Without a tongue is like without a
bell**
On a tsung iz vi on a glok NS

אויף דעם שפיץ צונג ליגט די גאַנצע
וועלט

**The entire world rests on the tip of
the tongue**
*Oyf dem shpits tsung ligt di gantse
velt* NS

וואָס מען שעמט זיך צו זאָגן אויף ייִדיש
זאָגט מען אויף לשון-קודש

**What one is ashamed to say in
Yiddish, one says in the Holy
Tongue**
[Fewer people will understand the
Hebrew]
*Vos men shemt zikh tsu zogn oyf yidish
zogt men oyf loshn-koydesh* AC

STATUS

אַ פּרנס מעג זײַן גרויס ווי אַ האָן, זיצט
ער פֿאָרט אויבן אָן

An official in the community, however minor, still gets the seat of honor
A parnes meg zayn groys vi a hon, zitst er fort oybn on IB

אַ ציג איז נישט קיין בהמה און אַ
בעל-מלאכה (שנײַדער) איז נישט קיין
מענטש

A goat is not a cow, and a craftsman (tailor) is not a person of worth
A tsig iz nisht keyn beheyme un a bal-melokhe (shnayder) iz nisht keyn mentsh IF

אַז מען רײַבט זיך אַרום אַ גבֿיר רײַבט
מען זיך אויס אַ לאָך

If you rub elbows with the rich, all you'll get is a hole
Az men raybt zikh arum a gvir raybt men zikh oys a lokh IB

בײַ אַ דינסט איז נישט גוט צו דינען

It's not good to serve a servant
Bay a dinst iz nisht gut tsu dinen IB

בײַ די מחותנים זײַנען אַלע יחסונים

Compared to these in-laws, everyone else is high-class
Bay di mekhutonim zaynen ale yakhsonim AC

דאָס בעסטע פֿערד איז נאָר אַ פּאַדלע
ווען עס פגרט

The best horse is only a carcass when it dies
Dos beste ferd iz nor a padle ven es peygert NS

ער איז אַ שמש אין אַ זויערן פֿאַבריק

He is a beadle in a pickle factory
[That is, low man on the totem pole]
Er iz a shames in a zoyern fabrik AC

פֿאַר אַ זעקסער אַ האָן אין דרייט זיך
אויך אין קאָן

A rooster worth nothing also
prances in the ring
*Far a zekser a hon un dreyt zikh oykh
in kon* SK

קוק אַראָפּ וועסטו זען ווי הויך דו
שטייסט

Look down if you want to see how
tall you stand
*Kuk arop vestu zen vi hoykh du
shteyst* NS

ניט איטלעכער וואָס זיצט אויבן אָן איז
אַ פּאַן

Not all who sit at the head of the
table are aristocrats
*Nit itlekher vos zitst oybn on iz a
pan* NS

אויס כּלה, ווידער אַ מויד

No longer a bride-to-be, again an
old maid
Oys kale, vider a moyd IF

אונטערן פּאַן איז יאַן און אונטער יאַן
איז זײַן פֿערדל

Under the master is Jan, and under
Jan is his horse
*Untern pan iz yan un unter yan iz
zayn ferdl* NS

ייחוס געפֿינט מען אויפֿן בית-הקבֿרות,
ייחוס עצמו איז בעסער

Respect is found at the cemetery;
self-respect is better
*Yikhes gefint men oyfn beysakvores,
yikhes atsmo iz beser* AC

STUBBORNNESS

אַ בן-יחיד איז אַן עקשן און אַן עקשן איז
אַ משומד

A one-and-only son is stubborn,
and one who is stubborn will
become even an apostate
*A benyokhed iz an akshn un an akshn
iz a meshumed* NS

פֿאַר עקשנות וועגן גייט מען אַמאָל פֿון
גן-עדן אין גהינום אַרײַן

Stubbornness often leads you from heaven straight to hell
Far akshones vegn geyt men amol fun ganeydn in gehenem arayn NS

צוויי האַרטע שטיינער מאָלן ניט

Two hard stones won't grind
Tsvey harte shteyner moln nit NS

SUCCESS

אַז עס גייט, גייט עס דורך טיר און דורך
טויער

If it succeeds, it overcomes all obstacles
Az es geyt, geyt es durkh tir un durkh toyer AC

עס איז געראָטן אויף אַלע נאָטן

It's successful and bright in every light!
Es iz gerotn oyf ale notn! NS

ניט פֿאַרברענט און ניט פֿאַרבראָטן, נאָר
טאַקע געראָטן!

Not burnt and not roasted but truly well-toasted!
Nit farbrent un nit farbrotn, nor take gerotn! IB

אויף דער טיר פֿון דערפֿאָלג איז
אָנגעשריבן 'שטופ' און 'צי'

On the door of success is written: "push" and "pull"
Oyf der tir fun derfolg iz ongeshribn: 'shtup' un 'tsi' NS

SUITABILITY

אַ פֿערד און אַן אָקס שפּאַנט מען ניט
אײַן אין איין וואָגן

Don't hitch a horse and an ox to the same wagon
A ferd un an oks shpant men nit ayn in eyn vogn NS

271

א קאָפּ ווי אַ מיניסטער און הענט ווי אַ
שוסטער!

**A head like a senator but hands like
a shoemaker!**

*A kop vi a minister un hent vi a
shuster!* IB

אַ פרוכות אָן גלעקלעך און משררים אָן
שמעקלעך איז קיין ייִדישע שול ניט

**A Torah curtain without bells and
singers without balls is no
synagogue**
[Derisive comment on allowing
women choir singers in modern
synagogues]

*A paroykhes on gleklekh un meshor'rim
on shmeklekh iz keyn yidishe shul
nit* WZ

אַ שפּריכוואָרט איז זייער גוט ווען מען
זאָגט עס ווען עס פּאַסט

**A proverb is apt when it fits the
occasion**

*A shprikhvort iz zeyer gut ven men zogt
es ven es past* IB

אַן אָקס מיט אַ פֿערד שפּאַנט מען ניט
איין אין איין וואָגן

**You don't hitch an ox and a horse to
the same wagon**

*An oks mit a ferd shpant men nit ayn
in eyn vogn* IB

דער חזיר איז טרייף אָבער דער מקח איז
כשר

**The pig is treyf but the price is
kosher**

*Der khazer iz treyf ober der mekekh iz
kosher* IB

דרייַ זאַכן פּאַסן ניט אָבער זיי שאַטן ניט:
אַז אַן אַלטער מאַן נעמט אַ בתולה, אַ
טרונק בראָנפֿן נאָכן עסן און אַז מען
שלאָגט דאָס ווייַב

**Three things, although unsuitable,
don't hurt: an old man marrying a
virgin, taking a drink after a meal,
and beating one's wife**

*Dray zakhn pasn nit ober zey shatn
nit: az an alter man nemt a p'sule, a
trunk bronfn nokhn esn un az men
shlogt dos vayb* NS

ער איז אַרײַן װי אַ יװן אין סוכה!

He entered like a soldier into the succah!
[Like a bull in a china shop]
Er iz arayn vi a yovn in suke! NS

עס פּאַסט װי אַ חזיר אַ שטרײַמל!

It's as suitable as a fur hat on a pig!
Es past vi a khazer a shtrayml! NS

עס פּאַסט װי אַ לולבֿ מיט אַן אתרוג!

It's as compatible as a palm branch and a citron!
[Metaphor from the holiday of Succoth]
Es past vi a lulev mit an esreg! AC

אײנס מיטן דריטן איז ניט קײן מחותּן!

One with a third is absurd!
Eyns mitn dritn iz nit keyn mekhitn! IB

איטלעכעס װערטל האָט זיך זײַן ערטל

Every word has a place to be heard
Itlekhes vertl hot zikh zayn ertl IB

שבת אָן אַ קוגל איז װי אַ פֿױגל אָן פֿליגל

Shabbes without a pudding is like a bird without wings
Shabes on a kugl iz vi a foygl on fligl IB

צאָנװײטיק אין אַ װינטערנאַכט און שיבֿעה אין אַ זומערטאָג טױגן בײדע ניט

Toothache during a long winter's night and shiveh on a long summer day are both useless
Tsonveytik in a vinternakht un shive in a zumertog toygn beyde nit AC

װײַן אױף פּסח, מעל אױף שבֿועות

Wine for Passover, flour for Shevuoth
Vayn oyf peysekh, mel oyf shevu'es IB

TEACHERS

אַז בײַ אַ בעל-עגלה פֿאַלט אַ פֿערד
ווערט ער אַ מלמד

When his horse dies, the wagoneer becomes a teacher
Az bay a balegole falt a ferd vert er a melamed NS

אַז דע תלמיד איז אַ וווילער איז דער רבי
אויך אַ וווילער

If the pupil is apt, the rabbi is a good teacher
Az der talmed iz a voyler iz der rebe oykh a voyler IB

איטלעכער מלמד איז אַ שטיקל שלימזל

Every Hebrew teacher is a bit of a shlimazl
Itlekher melamed iz a shtikl shlimazl AC

ווען פֿרייען זיך חדר ייִנגלעך? ווען דער
רבי זיצט שיבעה

When do schoolboys rejoice? When the rabbi sits shiveh
[Because they don't have to go to kheyder]
Ven freyen zikh kheyder yinglekh? ven der rebe zitst shive IB

TEMPTATION

אַז דער יצר-הרע כאַפֿט אָן דעם מענטשן
העלפֿט ניט קיין תקיעת-כּף

When the evil inclination takes
over, not even a solemn handshake
will make a difference
*Az der yetser-hore khapt on dem
mentshn helft nit keyn tki'es kaf* AC

דער יצר-הרע צו באַהערשן דעם
יצר-הרע איז אַ יצר-הרע

The temptation to overcome
temptation is itself a temptation
*Der yeytser-hore tsu bahershn dem
yeytser-hore iz a yeytser-hore* AC

דער יצר-הרע האָט אַן אײַזערנעם פּיסק

Temptation has an iron jaw
[and consumes all]
*Der yeytser-hore hot an ayzernem
pisk* MS

דער יצר-הרע שלאָפֿט בײַ אַ מיידל און
איז אויף בײַ אַ ווײַבל

Temptation is asleep in a girl but
awake in a woman
*Der yeytser-hore shloft bay a meydl un
iz oyf bay a vaybl* NS

דאָרטן איז גוט וווּ מיר זײַנען ניטאָ

That place is good where we are
not
Dortn iz gut vu mir zaynen nito AC

קאָרטן האָבן אין זיך אַ מאַגנעט

Playing cards contain a magnet
Kortn hobn in zikh a magnet IB

ווען ניט די שיינע מיידלעך וואָלט מען
געהאַט דעם יצר-הרע אין דר׳ערד

If not for pretty girls, we could say
to hell with temptation
*Ven nit di sheyne meydlekh volt men
gehat dem yeytser-hore in dr'erd* AC

THEFT

אַ גנבֿ בעטלט נישט

A thief doesn't go begging
A ganef betlt nisht NS

אַ גנבֿ פֿון אַ גנבֿ איז פטור

It's no crime to steal from a thief
A ganef fun a ganef iz poter P

אַ גנבֿ האָט אַ גוטן קאָפ – ער געדענקט
ווו יענער האָט אַוועקגעלייגט

A thief has a good memory—he remembers where others hide things
A ganef hot a gutn kop—er gedenkt vu yener hot avekgeleygt AC

אַ גנבֿ האָט פֿיר אויגן

A thief has four eyes
A ganef hot fir oygn NS

אַ גנבֿ זײַן איז אַ גאַנץ גוטע פּראָפֿעסיע
ווען עס זאָל ניט אײַנשטיין בײַ קיין גנבֿ
אין די הענט

Stealing would be a very good profession if the thieves hadn't cornered the market
A ganef zayn iz a gants gute profesye ven es zol nit aynshteyn bay keyn ganef in di hent NS

אַ ייִדן דאַרף מען קיין מאָל ניט חושד
זײַן – ער איז זיכער אַ גנבֿ

It's not necessary to suspect a Jew—he probably is a thief
A yidn darf men keyn mol nit khoyshed zayn—er iz zikher a ganef NS

אַז די דינסטן קריגן זיך ווערט די
בעל-הביתטע געוווויר פֿון דער גנבֿה

When servants quarrel, the mistress learns of the theft
Az di dinstn krign zikh vert di baleboste gevoyr fun der ganeyve NS

אַז ס׳איז דאָ אַ גנבֿ אין הויז טאָר מען
ניט שמועסן פֿון הענגען

With a thief in the house, don't talk of hangings
Az s'iz do a ganef in hoyz tor men nit shmu'esn fun hengen AC

דער גנבֿ פֿאַר דער טיר איז דער בעסטער שומר

The thief at the entry is the best sentry
Der ganef far der tir iz der bester shoymer AC

דער גנבֿ האָט אַ גרינגע מלאכה און שלעכטע חלומות

A thief has easy work but bad dreams
Der ganef hot a gringe melokhe un shlekhte khaloymes NS

די הענט האָבן אים אויף די פֿיס געשטעלט

His hands put him on his feet
Di hent hobn im oyf di fis geshtelt AC

ער איז אַ צולייגער – ער לייגט צו צו זיך

He's an accumulator—he adds to what he's already got
Er iz a tseleyger—er leygt tsu tsu zikh AC

ער איז אַזאַ גנבֿ, ער האָט צוגעגנבֿעט דעם קנאַק פֿון דער בײַטש!

He's such a thief, he stole the crack of the whip!
Er iz aza ganef, er hot tsugeganvet dem k'nak fun der baytsh! AC

ער איז ניט קיין גנבֿ – נאָר די הענט זײַנען גנבֿישע

He's no thief—it's only his hands that are thievish
Er iz nit keyn ganef—nor di hent zaynen ganeyvishe AC

ערבֿ יום-כּיפּור ווערן אַלע גנבֿים פֿרום

On the eve of Yom Kippur all thieves become pious
Erev yomkiper vern ale ganovim frum AC

עס וועט פֿון אים אויסוואַקסן אַ גנבֿ אַ גאון!

He'll grow up to be a very genius of a thief!
Es vet fun im oysvaksn a ganef a go'en! AC

אייַן גנבֿ גלייבט ניט דעם צווייטן

One thief doesn't believe another
Eyn ganef gleybt nit dem tsveytn P

פֿאַרן פּעקל מאַכער איז אַ פֿינסטערע
נאַכט אַ ליכטיקע וועלט

To a crook, a dark night is a bright day
Farn pekl makher iz a finstere nakht a likhtike velt AC

גנבֿעט מייַן ברודער העט מען דעם גנבֿ

If my brother steals, it's the thief who is hanged
[No one cares to admit that one's brother is a thief]
Ganvet mayn bruder hengt men dem ganef NS

געגנבֿעט און אָפּגעגעבן הייסט געגנבֿעט

Stealing and returning is nevertheless stealing
Geganvet un opgegebn heyst geganvet NS

מער סוחרים – מער גליק, מער
גנבֿים – מער שטריק

More merchants—more hope; more thieves—more rope
Mer sokhrim—mer glik; mer ganovim—mer shtrik NS

מיט וועמען חבֿרט זיך אַ גנבֿ? מיט זייַנס
גלייַכן

Who befriends a thief? Someone just like him
Mit vemen khavert zikh a ganef? mit zayns glaykhn AC

וועלכן גנבֿ טשעפּעט מען ניט? דעם
וואָס גנבֿעט דעם אפֿיקומן

Which thief is not punished? The one who steals the afikomen
Velkhn ganef tshepet men nir? dem vos ganvet dem afikomen NS

וועון ניט דער גנבֿ וואָלט
אונטערגעגאַנגען דער גאַנצער
שלאָסערפֿאַך

If not for thieves, the locksmiths would go out of business
Ven nit der ganef volt untergegangen der gantser shloserfakh NS

וואָס עס בלײַבט איבער פֿון גנבֿ גייט
אַוועק אויף טרעפֿער

What's left over from the thief goes to the fortuneteller
Vos es blaybt iber fun ganef geyt avek oyf trefer NS

יעדער גנבֿ האָט זײַן תירוץ

Every thief has his excuse
Yeder ganef hot zayn terets NS

THREATS

איך וועל אים געבן אַז ער וועט דערזען
דעם מלאך-המוות פֿאַר די אויגן!

I'll give him so that he'll see the Angel of Death before his eyes!
Ikh vel im gebn az er vet derzen dem malekhamoves far di oygn! AC

איך וועל אים געבן אַז ער וועט דערזען
קראָקע און לעמבערג פֿאַר די אויגן!

I'll give him so that he'll see Cracow and Lemberg before his eyes!
Ikh vel im gebn az er vet derzen kroke un lemberg far di oygn! IB

איך וועל אים געבן די לאָך פֿון דעם
בייגל!

I'll give him the hole from the bagel!
Ikh vel im gebn di lokh fun dem beygl! NS

TIME

אַ זייגער איז בעסער ווי מזומן
געלט – מזומן געלט גייט אַוועק און אַ
זייגער שטעלט זיך אָפ

A clock is better than money—money goes and a clock stops
A zeyger iz beser vi mezumen gelt—mezumen gelt geyt avek un a zeyger shtelt zikh op NS

אַ זייגער וואָס שטייט איז בעסער ווי אַ
זייגער וואָס איז קאַליע, ווייל אַפֿילו אַ
זייגער וואָס שטייט באַווייזט די
ריכטיקע צייט צוויי מאָל אין טאָג

A stopped clock is better than one that is broken, because even a stopped clock shows the right time twice a day
A zeyger vos shteyt iz beser vi a zeyger vos iz kalye, vayl afile a zeyger vos shteyt bavayzt di rikhtike tsayt tsvey mol in tog NS

אַן אַלטע מויד איז זיכער מיט אַ יונגן
טויט

An old maid is sure to die young
An alte moyd iz zikher mit a yungn toyt NS

אַז מען געווינט צייט געווינט מען אַ סך

If you gain time, you gain a lot
Az men gevint tsayt gevint men a sakh NS

דער זייגער מאַכער איז אַ דאָקטער
אָבער ער דינט ניט דעם מלאך־המוות

A watchmaker is a doctor, but he doesn't serve the Angel of Death
Der zeyger makher iz a dokter ober er dint nit dem malekhamoves AC

די צייט ברענגט ווונדן און היילט ווונדן

Time brings wounds and heals wounds
Di tsayt brengt vundn un heylt vundn NS

די צייט איז טייערער ווי געלט

Time is worth more than money
Di tsayt iz tayerer vi gelt NS

כּל־זמן מען לעבט איז אַלץ קיין צייט
ניטאָ

No matter how long you live, there's never enough time
Kolzman men lebt iz alts keyn tsayt nito NS

Better bad merchandise at the right time than good merchandise at the wrong time
S'iz beser shlekhte skhoyre in a guter sho eyder gute skhoyre in a shlekhte sho IB

ס׳איז בעסער שלעכטע סחורה אין אַ
גוטער שעה איידער גוטע סחורה אין אַ
שלעכטע שעה

CHANGING TIME

The heaviest fur is light in winter; the lightest shirt is too heavy in summer
Der shverster pelts iz in vinter gring, dos gringste hemd iz in zumer shver NS

דער שווערסטער פעלץ איז אין ווינטער
גרינג, דאָס גרינגסטע העמד איז אין
זומער שווער

Time alters a pair: the mind and the hair
Di tsayt makht groy di peye un bayt di deye NS

די צייַט מאַכט גרוי די פּעה און בייַט די
דעה

What we spend on fuel in the winter we spend on foolishness in the summer
Vos es geyt avek vinter oyf heytsung geyt avek zumer oyf narishkeytn NS

וואָס עס גייט אַוועק ווינטער אויף
הייצונג גייט אַוועק זומער אויף
נאַרישקייטן

DELAYED TIME

Don't delay what should be done today
Leyg nit op oyf morgn vos du kenst haynt bazorgn NS

לייג ניט אָפּ אויף מאָרגן וואָס דו קענסט
הייַנט באַזאָרגן

Delay is not refusal
Opgeleygt iz nit opgezogt AC

אָפּגעלייגט איז ניט אָפּגעזאָגט

At the right time it's no crime
Shpilt tsu di sho iz keyn zind nito NS

שפּילט צו די שעה איז קיין זינד ניטאָ

וואָס דו האָסט היינט צו עסן, עס מאָרגן; וואָס דו האָסט מאָרגן צו טאָן, טו היינט

What food you have for today, eat tomorrow; what work you have for tomorrow, do today
Vos du host haynt tsu esn, es morgn; vos du host morgn tsu ton, tu haynt IB

PASSAGE OF TIME

די צייַט שטייט ניט, די צייַט פֿליט

Time doesn't stay, it flies away
Di tsayt shteyt nit, di tsayt flit NS

היינט דאָ, מאָרגן דאָרט

Here today, gone tomorrow
Haynt do, morgn dort AC

אין פֿריידן איז אַ יאָר אַ טאָג, אין ליידן איז אַ טאָג אַ יאָר

When happy, a year is like a day; when troubled, a day is like a year
In freydn iz a yor a tog, in laydn iz a tog a yor NS

שטרענגע האַרן רעגירן ניט לאַנג

Cruel masters don't rule for long
Shtrenge harn regirn nit lang NS

וואָלסט פֿריער אויפֿגעשטאַנען וואָלסטו ניט באַדאַרפֿט אויף זייַן אַזוי שפעט

Had you risen earlier, you wouldn't have had to stay up so late
Volst fri'er oyfgeshtanen volstu nit badarft oyf zayn azoy shpet AC

PAST TIME

אַז די צייַט איז פֿאַרבייַ איז מען פטור פֿון קרבנות

When the time is past, there's no point to the sacrifice
Az di tsayt iz farbay iz men poter fun karbones NS

דאָס וואָס איז אַוועקגעגאַנגען קומט שוין מער ניט צוריק

What is past returns no more
Dos vos iz avekgegangen kumt shoyn mer nit tsurik AC

נאָך אַמאָל היַינט איז ניטאָ   **Today will never come again**
Nokh amol haynt iz nito ᴺˢ

TORAH

בעסער לערנען חומש מיט רשי איידער   **Better to study Rashi's notes than to**
צו עסן סאָלדאַטישע קאַשע   **eat soldier's groats**
Beser lernen khumesh mit rashi eyder
tsu esn soldatishe kashe ᴬᶜ

די תורה וווינט אַמאָל אין אַ חורבע און   **The Torah sometimes dwells in a**
ביזן האַלדז איז די פּורווע   **wreck with dirt up to its neck**
Di toyre voynt amol in a khurve un
bizn haldz iz di purve ᴺˢ

אין דער תורה איז דאָ מער קללות ווי   **The Torah contains more curses**
ברכות   **than blessings**
In der toyre iz do mer kloles vi
brokhes ᴺˢ

רשי האָט אַ טבע פֿון אַ קינד – ער מאַכט   **Rashi has a childish habit—he**
אויף יעדן אָרט   **messes up everywhere**
Rashi hot a teyve fun a kind—er makht
oyf yedn ort ᴬᶜ

תורה איז די בעסטע סחורה ווען   **Torah may be the best of wares, but**
מ'האַנדלט ניט מיט איר אַזוי ווי סחורה   **don't treat it like mere merchandise**
Toyre iz di beste skhoyre ven m'handlt
nit mit ir azoy vi skhoyre ᴬᶜ

TRAVEL

אַז מען פֿאָרט אין עק האָט מען אַ וואָגן   **If on the horse's tail you sit, you'll**
מיט דרעק   **ride in a load of shit**
Az men fort in ek hot men a vogn mit
drek ᴺˢ

אַז מען וויל אָפּטאָן דעם בעל-עגלה אַ | **If you want to spite the wagon**
שפּיצל גייט מען בײַם וואָגן צו פֿוס | **driver, walk alongside the wagon**
Az men vil opton dem balegole a shpitsl geyt men baym vogn tsu fus IB

דער קורצער וועג איז גאָר דער לאַנגער | **The shortest distance turns out to be the longest**
Der kurtser veg iz gor der langer NS

דאָס שענסטע גיין איז אַז מען זיצט אין | **The nicest trip is staying home**
דער היים | *Dos shenste geyn iz az men zitst in der heym* AC

מען קען ניט וויסן ווי אַ וועג שטעלט זיך | **You can't tell beforehand how a trip will go**
Men ken nit visn vu a veg shtelt zikh NS

אויף אַן אויסגעטראָטענעם וועג | **Grass doesn't grow on a well-traveled path**
וואָקסט ניט קיין גראָז | *Oyf an oysgetrotenem veg vakst nit keyn groz* NS

אומגעקערט הייסט אויך געפֿאָרן | **Returning is also a form of travel**
Umgekert heyst oykh geforn IB

ווער עס איז אַ גאַנצער ייִד אין דער היים | **He who is a complete Jew at home**
איז נאָר אַ האַלבער ייִד ווען ער פֿאָרט | **is only half a Jew when traveling**
אויף אַ נסיעה | *Ver es iz a gantser yid in der heym iz nor a halber yid ven er fort oyf a nesi'e* AC

וווי ל איז דעם וואָס זיצט אין דער היים | **Good for them who stay at home**
Voyl iz dem vos zitst in der heym NS

ווו מען גייט פֿיל וואַקסן ניט קיין
שטיינער

Where many go, stones won't grow
[A rolling stone gathers no moss]
Vu men geyt fil vaksn nit keyn
shteyner NS

TROUBLES

אַ געשוויר איז אַ גוטע זאַך ביַי יענעם
אונטערן אָרעם

An abscess is fine under someone
else's arm
A geshvir iz a gute zakh bay yenem
untern orem NS

אַ טויטער מאַכט ניט קיין קריג

A corpse doesn't make trouble
A toyter makht nit keyn krig NS

אַ צרה קומט ניט אַליין

Troubles don't come singly
A tsore kumt nit aleyn AC

אַלע חס-ושלומס זיַינען מעגלעך

All "God forbids" are possible
Ale khas-vesholems zaynen
meglekh NS

אַז עס ווײנט זיך מיינט זיך

When there's a cry, there's a reason
why
Az es veynt zikh meynt zikh AC

אַז מען האָט אַ הויז האָט מען צוויי
דאגות – דירה-געלט טאָמער מען לעבט
און קבֿורה-געלט טאָמער מען שטאַרבט

If you have a house, you have two
worries—rent money if you live,
and burial fees if you die
Az men hot a hoyz hot men tsvey
dayges—dire-gelt tomer men lebt un
kvure-gelt tomer men shtarbt NS

אַז מען האָט אויף פּורים יסורים איז
אויף פּסח חושך

If Purim brings worries, then
Passover will bring gloom
Az men hot oyf purim yesurim iz oyf
peysekh khoyshekh IB

אַז מען טרינקט אַלע מאָל עסיק ווייסט
מען ניט אַז ס'איז דאָ אַ זיסערע זאַך

**If you always drink vinegar, you
don't know anything sweeter exists**
*Az men trinkt ale mol esik veyst men
nit az s'iz do a zisere zakh* AC

בראָנפֿן פֿאַרדרייט דעם קאָפּ, צרות
נעמען אים אין גאַנצן אַראָפּ

**Liquor befuddles the head, troubles
knock it off instead**
*Bronfn fardreyt dem kop, tsores nemen
im in gantsn arop* NS

די זאָרגן לייג אָפּ אויף מאָרגן

Put off your sorrow until tomorrow
Di zorgn leyg op oyf morgn IB

דער גרעסטער צער איז דער וועלכן מען
קען ניט אַרויסזאָגן

**The greatest sorrow is the one you
can't talk about**
*Der grester tsar iz der velkhn men ken
nit aroyszogn* AC

דער ים איז אָן אַ גרונט און יידישע צרות
אָן אַ ברעג

**The sea has no bottom and Jewish
troubles no shore**
*Der yam iz on a grunt un yidishe tsores
on a breg* AC

ער האָט שוין געפּאָקט און געמאָזלט!

He's already poxed and measled!
[He's had his share of troubles]
Er hot shoyn gepokt un gemozlt! IB

עס גייט מיר ווי אַ רשע אויף יענער
וועלט!

**I'm doing well—like the wicked in
the world to come!**
Es geyt mir vi a roshe oyf yener velt! P

עס איז מיר שטענדיק גוט: זומער איז
מיר גוט הייס, ווינטער איז מיר גוט
קאַלט, דאָס ווײַב מײַנע דערגייט מיר
גוט די יאָרן, און איך אַליין בין גוט אויף
צרות

**Things are always good with me:
summer I'm good and hot, winter
I'm good and cold, my wife nags me
good and proper, and altogether,
I'm good and miserable**
*Es iz mir shtendik gut: zumer iz mir gut
heys, vinter iz mir gut kalt, dos vayb
mayne dergeyt mir gut di yorn, un ikh
aleyn bin gut oyf tsores* AC

עס זאָל מיר אַזוי זײַן גוט בײַ מיר ווי עס
איז מיר גוט בײַ יענעם

**May things go as well for me at
home as they go for me elsewhere**
*Es zol mir azoy zayn gut bay mir vi es
iz mir gut bay yenem* IF

איינער האָט ניט אין זין, דער אַנדערער
האָט ניט פֿון ווּהין

**One person has nothing on his
mind, another no sustenance to find**
*Eyner hot nit in zin, der anderer hot nit
fun vuhin* IB

פֿון אַ שלעכטן משרת האָט דער
בעל-הבית נאָר צרות

**From a poor servant, all the master
gets is trouble**
*Fun a shlekhtn meshores hot der
balebos nor tsores* NS

פֿון צער ווערט דער ביין דאַר

Sorrow eats at the marrow
Fun tsar vert der beyn dar NS

גוטע צײַטן טראָגן אונדז, שלעכטע צײַטן
מוז מען אַריבערטראָגן

**Good times carry us, hard times
must be overcome**
*Gute tsaytn trogn undz, shlekhte tsaytn
muz men aribertrogn* AC

מאַיאָווע קדחת איז גוט פֿאַר יענעם

Maytime chills are good for others
Mayove kadokhes iz gut far yenem IB

<table>
<tr>
<td dir="rtl">מען וויינט ניט אויף "מי ימות" ווי אויף
"מי יחיה"</td>
<td>One doesn't cry as much over "who shall die" as "who shall live"
[Refers to Yom Kippur prayer]
Men veynt nit oyf "mi yamut" vi oyf "mi yikhye" IB</td>
</tr>
<tr>
<td dir="rtl">נישט אַלע צרות קומען פֿון הימל</td>
<td>Not all troubles come from heaven
Nisht ale tsores kumen fun himl AC</td>
</tr>
<tr>
<td dir="rtl">אויב מען וויל זיך פֿאַרגעסן די צרות זאָל
מען אָנטאָן אַן ענגן שוך</td>
<td>If you want to forget your troubles, put on a tight shoe
Oyb men vil zikh fargesn di tsores zol men onton an engn shukh NS</td>
</tr>
<tr>
<td dir="rtl">אויף פֿרעמדע קבֿרים וויינט מען זיך ניט
אויס</td>
<td>Don't weep at the graves of strangers
Oyf fremde kvorim veynt men zikh nit oys NS</td>
</tr>
<tr>
<td dir="rtl">צרות לייגן זיך נישט אין די קליידער נאָר
אין די ביינער</td>
<td>Troubles don't lodge in the clothes, but in the bones
Tsores leygn zikh nisht in di kleyder nor in di beyner IB</td>
</tr>
<tr>
<td dir="rtl">צרות טרײַבן אויפֿן בית-הקבֿרות</td>
<td>Misery chases to the cemetery
Tsores traybn oyfn beysakvores IB</td>
</tr>
<tr>
<td dir="rtl">צרות צעזעגן דאָס האַרץ</td>
<td>Troubles saw at the heart
Tsores tsezegn dos harts NS</td>
</tr>
<tr>
<td dir="rtl">צרות ווי האָלץ און וואָס אײַנצוהייצן
דעם אויוון איז ניטאָ</td>
<td>Troubles plentiful as twigs but nothing to heat the oven with
Tsores vi holts un vos ayntsuheytsn dem oyvn iz nito AC</td>
</tr>
</table>

צרות װיל מען ניט צונעמען, מיצװות קען
מען ניט צונעמען

Troubles no one wants to take, good
deeds no one is able to take
*Tsores vil men nit tsunemen, mitsves
ken men nit tsunemen* NS

עס — צרות זײַנען שטאַרקע טראָפּנס
טויג ניט אַ סך מיט אַמאָל

Trouble is like strong medicine—
too much at a time is harmful
*Tsores zaynen shtarke tropns—es toyg
nit a sakh mit amol* NS

װען צרות לײגן זיך ניט אױפֿן פּנים לײגן
זײ זיך אױפֿן האַרצן

When troubles don't show in the
face, they lodge in the heart
*Ven tsores leygn zikh nit oyfn ponim
leygn zey zikh oyfn hartsn* NS

װען יענער איז מיט אַ ביטערן מאָגן גײ
זיך צו אים ניט באַקלאָגן

When a person is full of care, don't
bring him your troubles to share
*Ven yener iz mit a bitern mogn gey
zikh tsu im nit baklogn* NS

װילדע גראָזן װאַקסן איבערנאַכט

Weeds grow overnight
Vilde grozn vaksn ibernakht NS

װאָס קומט אַרױס פֿון דעם זילבערנעם
בעכער אַז ער איז פֿול מיט טרערן?

What use is a silver cup if it's full of
tears?
*Vos kumt aroys fun dem zilbernem
bekher az er iz ful mit trern?* IB

װאָס מער מען קראַצט דעם פּאַרך אַלץ
מער װאַקסט ער

The more you scratch the scabs, the
more they grow
*Vos mer men kratst dem parekh alts
mer vakst er* IB

ייחוס אױפֿן בית-הקבֿרות און אין דער
הײם איז צרות

Respect on the burial ground and
misery at home is found
*Yikhes oyfn beysakvores un in er heym
iz tsores* NS

TRUTH

א האַלבער אמת זאָגט אויך עפעס

A half-truth also tells you something
A halber emes zogt oykh epes NS

א מיאוסע מויד האָט פֿײַנט דעם שפּיגל

A homely girl hates the mirror
A mi'ese moyd hot faynt dem shpigl NS

דעם אמת מעג מען זאָגן אפֿילו אַן
אייגענעם טאַטן

You can tell the truth even to your own father
Dem emes meg men zogn afile an eygenem tatn IB

דער אמת האָט אַ סך פּנימער

Truth has many faces
Der emes hot a sakh penimer NS

דער אמת איז אַ קריכער

Truth is a slowpoke
Der emes iz a krikher NS

דער אמת איז אין די אויגן, דער ליגן איז
אונטער די אויגן

Truth is in the eyes, falsehood behind them
Der emes iz in di oygn, der lign iz unter di oygn NS

דער אמת קען אַרומגיין אַ נאַקעטער,
דעם שקר מוז מען באַקליידן

Truth can walk around naked, the lie must be clothed
Der emes ken arumgeyn a naketer, dem sheker muz men bakleydn NS

דער אמת לעבט ניט, דער אמת
שטאַרבט ניט, דער אמת מאַטערט זיך

Truth is neither dead nor alive, it just struggles along
Der emes lebt nit, der emes shtarbt nit, der emes matert zikh NS

דער אמת שטאַרבט ניט אָבער עס לעבט
ווי אַן אָרעמאַן

Truth doesn't die but lives like a pauper
Der emes shtarbt nit ober es lebt vi an oreman NS

290

די ערגסטע רכילית איז דער אמת

The worst gossip is the truth
Di ergste rekhiles iz der emes NS

אמת איז אין סידור

Truth is found only in the prayerbook
Emes iz in sider AC

אמת וואַקסט פֿון דער ערד אַרויס

Truth grows right out of the earth
Emes vakst fun der erd aroys NS

פֿאַר דעם אמת שלאָגט מען

For the truth you get flogged
Far dem emes shlogt men NS

קינדער און נאַראָנים זאָגן דעם אמת

Both children and fools speak the truth
Kinder un naronim zogn dem emes IB

מיט אמת קומט מען פֿאַר גאָט

With the truth we reach God
Mit emes kumt men far got NS

אָט פֿון דאַנען שטינקט דער העכט!

Right here is where the fish stinks!
Of fun danen shtinkt der hekht! AC

ווען מען זאָגט דעם אמת דאַרף מען זיך ניט דערמאָנען

When you tell the truth, you don't have to remember
Ven men zogt dem emes darf men zikh nit dermonen AC

VALUE

א סך צו רעדן, ווייניק צו הערן | **A lot to say, little to hear**
A sakh tsu redn, veynik tsu hern NS

אז מען פֿאַלט ביי זיך פֿאַלט מען אויך ביי אַנדערע | **If you lose your self-respect, you lose the respect of others, too**
Az men falt bay zikh falt men oykh bay andere NS

דער אתרוג קאָסט דאָס גאַנצע געלט און איבערן לולב מאַכט מען די ברכה | **The citron costs the money, but the blessing is recited over the branches**
[Citron and branches refer to the holiday of Succoth]
Der esreg kost dos gantse gelt un ibern lulev makht men di brokhe IB

עס האָט אַזאַ ווערט ווי אַן אויסגעבלאָזן איי! | **It's worth as much as a blown-out egg!**
Es hot aza vert vi an oysgeblozn ey! AC

עס האָט אַזאַ ווערט ווי דרעק אויף אַ שפּענדל! | **It's worth as much as shit on a shingle!**
Es hot aza vert vi drek oyf a shpendl! NS

292

עס איז אַ זייגער פֿון זייגערלאַנד! | **It's a clock from clockland!**
[That is, worthless]
Es iz a zeyger fun zeygerland! NS

עס איז ווערט בחצי חינום! | **It's worth half of nothing!**
Es iz vert bekhetsi khinem! AC

פֿון אַ הונט קען מען אפֿילו אַ גוטן פּעלץ ניט מאַכן | **You can't even get a good hide off a dog**
Fun a hunt ken men afile a gutn pelts nit makhn NS

כּל-זמן די בהמה לאָזט זיך מעלקן פֿירט מען איר ניט צום שוחט | **As long as the cow allows herself to be milked, she's not led to the slaughter**
Kolzman di beheyme lozt zikh melkn firt men ir nit tsum shoykhet NS

ניט דער טשוואָק איז דער עיקר נאָר דער הענג לײַכטער | **It's not the nail that counts, but the chandelier**
Nit der tshvok iz der iker nor der heng laykhter IB

ניט פֿיל געטראַכט, אַבי גוט געמאַכט | **Not too much thought as long as it's well-wrought**
Nit fil getrakht, abi gut gemakht NS

WEALTH

אַ גאָלדענער שליסל עפֿנט אַלע טירן
A golden key opens all doors
A goldener shlisl efnt ale tirn IB

אַ נגידס ווייַב מעג זיך פֿאַרגינען צוויי
מאָל אין יאָר אין קימפּעט ליגן
A rich man's wife can afford to give birth twice a year
A nogeds vayb meg zikh farginen tsvey mol in yor in kimpet lign NS

אַפֿילו דער רייַכסטער זייגער האָט ניט
מער ווי זעכציק מינוט
Even the most expensive clock has no more than sixty minutes
Afile der raykhster zeyger hot nit mer vi zekhtsik minut NS

אַז אין דעם קופֿערט ליגט סאַמעט און
זייַד קען מען אין טראַנטעס גיין פֿאַר
לייַט
When velvet and silk are stored in your bags, you can parade around even in rags
Az in dem kufert ligt samet un zayd ken men in trantes geyn far layt NS

אַז מען האָט אַ גאָלדן הענטל האָט מען
דאָס לעבערל פֿון ענטל
If you've got the golden touch, you'll get duck's liver and such
Az men hot a goldn hentl hot men dos leberl fun entl NS

294

אַז מען האָט קנעכט איז מען אַ האַר און | With servants in sight, the master is
שטענדיק גערעכט | always right
Az men hot k'nekht iz men a har un
shtendik gerekht NS

אַז מען וויל וויסן וואָס מען איז ווערט | If you want to know what you're
זאָל מען זיך לאָזן רעדן שידוכים | worth, start talking about marrying
off children
Az men vil visn vos men iz vert zol
men zikh lozn redn shidukhim NS

בײַ אַ קבצן שפילט געלט קיין ראָלע ניט | To a pauper, money is no object
Bay a kaptsn shpilt gelt kayn role
nit AC

דער גבֿיר האָט דעם שׂכל אין טײַסטער | The rich man's brains are in his
wallet
Der gvir hot dem seykhl in tayster NS

דער אָרעמאַן טראַכט, דער נגיד לאַכט | The poor contemplate, the rich
celebrate
Der oreman trakht, der noged lakht AC

דער רײַכער עסט דאָס פֿלייש און דער | The rich eat meat and the poor
אָרעמאַן די ביינער | gnaw on bones
Der raykher est dos fleysh un der
oreman di beyner NS

דאָס שענסטע עפּעלע איז אין נגידס | The best apple is in the rich man's
טעפּעלע | pot
Dos shenste epele iz in nogeds
tepele NS

פֿון קושן דעם גבֿיר אין תּחת האָט מען | From kissing the asses of the rich,
קדחת | all you get is an itch
Fun kushn dem gvir in tokhes hot men
kadokhes NS

געלט האַלט זיך נאָר אין אַ גראָבן זאַק	**Money keeps only in a thick sack** [Money goes to money] *Gelt halt zikh nor in a grobn zak* NS
גענוג האָט רויטשילד	**Only Rothschild has enough** *Genug hot roytshild* AC
אין באָד דערקענט מען אויך אַ גבֿיר	**The rich man is recognized even in the bathhouse** *In bod derkent men oykh a gvir* NS
מען קען האַנדלען מיט טראַנטעס און זיך קליידן אין סאַמעט	**Even if you deal in rags, you can still dress in velvet** *Men ken handlen mit trantes un zikh kleydn in samet* NS
מיט אַ גאָלדענער קויל טרעפֿט מען שטענדיק	**A golden bullet always hits the mark** *Mit a goldener koyl treft men shtendik* AC
ניט גענוג וואָס דער נגיד איז אַ נגיד, גילט נאָך זײַן קוויטל אויך	**Not only are the rich wealthy, but their checks are good, too** *Nit genug vos der noged iz a noged, gilt nokh zayn kvitl oykh* NS
ווען דאָס מויל זאָל ניט דאַרפֿן עסן וואָלט דער קאָפּ אין גאָלד געגאַנגען	**If the mouth didn't have to eat, the head could be clothed in gold** *Ven dos moyl zol nit darfn esn volt der kop in gold gegangen* NS
ווען הונגערט אַ נגיד? ווען דער דאָקטער הייסט אים	**When does a rich man fast? When the doctor orders him to** *Ven hungert a noged? ven der dokter heyst im* NS

וויל מען זײַן אַ גבֿיר מוז מען זיך
פֿאַרשרײַבן אויף צוואַנציק יאָר אַ חזיר

If you want to be rich, you must apprentice yourself for twenty years as a swine
Vil men zayn a gvir muz men zikh farshraybn oyf tsvantsik yor a khazer NS

ייִדישע עשירות קומט מיטן ווינט און
גייט אַוועק מיטן רויך

Jewish wealth comes with the wind and departs with the smoke
Yidishe ashires kumt mitn vint un geyt avek mitn roykh NS

ייִדישע עשירות, מישטיינס
געזאָגט – פֿון תּעניתים ווערט מען רײַך

Jewish wealth, alas—from fasting you get rich
Yidishe ashires, mishteyns gezogt—fun taneysim vert men raykh NS

זינגען זינגט דער אָרעמאַן, דער נגיד
הערט זיך נאָר צו

The pauper does the singing, the rich only listen
Zingen zingt der oreman, der noged hert zikh nor tsu AC

WICKEDNESS

אַ גוטן העלפֿט אַ וואָרט, אַ שלעכטן
העלפֿט אפֿילו קיין שטעקן אויך ניט

To the decent, one word will do; to the wicked, not even the stick helps
A gutn helft a vort, a shlekhtn helft afile keyn shtekn oykh nit AC

אַ רשען העלפֿט אזוי מוסר ווי אַ טויטן
באַנקעס

To the wicked, moralizing helps like cupping a corpse
A roshen helft azoy muser vi a toytn bankes AC

דער רשע דאַרף ניט האָבן דעם טײַוול צו
הילף

The wicked don't need help from the devil
Der roshe darf nit hobn dem tayvl tsu hilf AC

297

דאָס גוטע האָט ער אויסגעקרענקט און דאָס שלעכטע איז געבליבן

The goodness he agonized out, and the wickedness remains
Dos gute hot er oysgekrenkt un dos shlekhte iz geblibn AC

ער איז אַ גוטער: אַז ער שלאָפֿט בײַסט ער ניט!

He' a good person: when he sleeps, he doesn't bite!
Er iz a guter: az er shloft bayst er nit! NS

ער נעמט אַרונטער די גאַנצע סמעטענע און לאָזט פֿאַר יענעם די זויערמילך

He skims off the cream for himself, and leaves the curdled milk for others
Er nemt arunter di gantse smetene un lozt far yenem di zoyermilkh NS

געלט גייט אַוועק און דער הונט בלײַבט אַ הונט

Money disappears but the cur remains a cur
Gelt geyt avek un der hunt blaybt a hunt NS

מיטן בעסטן הונט איז ניט קיין עסקים צו האָבן

With even the best dog there's no dealing
Mitn bestn hunt iz nit keyn asokim tsu hobn IB

אויף אַ שלאַנג טאָר מען קיין רחמנות ניט האָבן

Don't take pity on a snake
Oyf a shlang tor men keyn rakhmones nit hobn IB

טו אַ הונט גוטס בילט ער נאָך

Do a dog a favor and he still barks
Tu a hunt guts bilt er nokh NS

ווען דו האָסט אַ שטעקן טענה ניט מיט קיין הונט

When you've got the stick, don't argue with a dog
Ven du host a shtekn tayne nit mit keyn hunt AC

וועֶר עס וועט אים צוכאַפֿן בײַ נאַכט וועט אים אַוועקוואַרפֿן בײַ טאָג

Whoever nabs him at night will discard him by day

Ver es vet im tsukhapn bay nakht vet im avekvarfn bay tog AC

WIDOWHOOD

אַז מען קומט טרייסטן אַ יונגע אלמנה קוואַפּעט מען זיך ניט צו פֿאַרדינען אַ מיצווה

When one comes to comfort a young widow, one doesn't necessarily have a good deed in mind

Az men kumt treystn a yunge almone kvapet men zikh nit tsu fardinen a mitsve NS

בעסער אַ יונגע אלמנה איידער אַן אַלטע מויד

Better to be a young widow than an old maid

Beser a yunge almone eyder an alte moyd NS

ווען אַן אלמנה האָט שוין אַ גאָלדענעם דאַך איז זי פֿאָרט אַן אלמנה

Even if a widow has a golden roof, she's still only a widow

Ven an almone hot shoyn a goldenem dakh iz zi fort an almone NS

WISDOM

אַ קלוגער פֿאַרשטייט פֿון איין וואָרט צוויי

A wise person hears one word and understands two

A kluger farshteyt fun eyn vort tsvey AC

אַמאָל איז די גרעסטע חכמה ניט רעדן אַ נאַרישקייט

Sometimes, the greatest wisdom is not speaking foolishness

Amol iz di greste khokhme nit redn a narishkeyt NS

ביז זיבעציק יאָר לערנט מען שׂכל און
מען שטאַרבט אַ נאַר

**Until seventy we learn wisdom and
die fools nevertheless**
*Biz zibestik yor lernt men seykhl un
men shtarbt a nar* NS

דער שׂכל איז אַ קריכער

Wisdom creeps
Der seykhl iz a krikher NS

דער שׂכל קומט נאָך די יאָרן

Wisdom comes with age
Der seykhl kumt nokh di yorn NS

דער וואָס פֿאַרשטייט זײַן נאַרישקייט
איז אַ קלוגער

**He who understands his foolishness
is wise**
*Der vos farshteyt zayn narishkeyt iz a
kluger* AC

די ציג האָט אַ באָרד און ווערט אַלץ ניט
גערעכנט פֿאַר אַ רבֿ

**The goat may have a beard, but it's
still no rabbi**
*Di tsig hot a bord un vert alts nit
gerekhnt far a rov* AC

קלוגהייט איז בעסער ווי פֿרומהייט

Wisdom is better than piety
Klugheyt iz beser vi frumheyt NS

מען באַגריסט נאָך די קליידער, מען
באַגלייט נאָכן שׂכל

**One is greeted according to one's
dress, bade farewell according to
one's wisdom**
*Men bagrist nokh di kleyder, men
bagleyt nokhn seykhl* NS

שׂכל איז אַן איידעלע זאַך

Wisdom is a precious commodity
Seykhl iz an eydele zakh NS

וואָס טויג די חכמה אַז נאַרישקייט
גילט?

What use is wisdom if folly reigns?
*Vos toyg di khokhme az narishkeyt
gilt?* ib

WOMEN

אַ פֿרוי האָט בעסער ליב אַ ביסל מיט
פֿריידן איידער אַ סך מיט לײַדן

**Women prefer a little with levity
rather than a lot with gravity**
*A froy hot beser lib a bisl mit fraydn
eyder a sakh mit laydn* NS

אַ פֿרוי שטאַרבט צוויי מאָל – איין מאָל
ווען זי זעט אַ גרויע האָר און דאָס
צווייטע מאָל ווען זי שטאַרבט

**A woman dies twice—once when
she sees her first gray hair, and the
second time when she dies**
*A froy shtarbt tsvey mol—eyn mol ven
zi zet a groye hor un dos tsveyte mol
ven zi shtarbt* AC

אַ פֿרוי, זאָגט מען בײַ אונדז, האָט לאַנגע
האָר און אַ קורצן שׂכל

**A woman, they say, has long hair
and little sense**
*A froy, zogt men bay undz, hot lange
hor un a kurtsn seykhl* AC

אַ מיידל דאַרף זיך פּוצן פֿאַר פֿרעמדע
בחורים און אַ ווײַבל פֿאַרן אייגענעם
מאַן

**A girl should pretty herself for her
suitors, and a wife for her husband**
*A meydl darf zikh putsn far fremde
bokherim un a vaybl farn eygenem
man* NS

אַ ווײַב טויג נאָר אין בעט אַרײַן

A woman is good only in bed
A vayb toyg nor in bet arayn WZ

בשעת גאָלן די בערד קען מען ניט רעדן
דערפֿאַר וואַקסן ניט קיין בערד בײַ די
ווײַבער

**During shaving, you can't talk; that's
why beards don't grow on women**
*B'shas goln di berd ken men nit redn
derfar vaksn nit keyn berd bay di
vayber* NS

דאָס בעסטע פֿערד דאַרף האָבן אַ בײַטש
און די פֿרומסטע נקבֿה – אַ מאַן

**The best horse needs a whip, and
the chastest of women—a man**
*Dos beste ferd darf hobn a baytsh un di
frumste nekeyve—a man* NS

גאָלד פּרובירט מען מיט פּײַער – אַ פֿרוי מיט גאָלד

Gold is tested with fire—a woman with gold
Gold prubirt men mit fayer—a froy mit gold NS

משה רבינוס תורה און ווײַבערשע קינאה-שׂינאה וועלן אייביק בלײַבן

The Torah of Moses our Teacher and women's envy and hatred will always remain
Moyshe-rabeynus toyre un vaybershe kine-sine veln eybik blaybn IB

ווײַבער פֿירן צום גוטן אָדער צום בייזן – סײַ ווי פֿאַרלירט מען

Women lead to good or bad—either way, you lose
Vayber firn tsum gutn oder tsum beyzn—say vi farlirt men AC

ווײַבער האָבן נאָר איין חסרון – עס איז שלעכט אָן זיי און ביטער מיט זיי

Women have only one drawback—it's bad without them and miserable with them
Vayber hobn nor eyn khisorn—es iz shlekht on zey un biter mit zey AC

ווײַבער וועלן זיך שפּאַרן אפֿילו מיטן מלאך-המוות

Women will argue even with the Angel of Death
Vayber veln zikh shparn afile mitn malekhamoves NS

ווען בייזערן זיך ניט די ווײַבער? ווען מען נייט זייערע תכריכים

When aren't women angry? When you sew their shrouds
Ven beyzern zikh nit di vayber? ven men neyt zeyere takhrikhim NS

ווען דער טײַוול ווייסט אַז ער גייט פֿאַרלירן שיקט ער אונטער אַ פֿרוי

When the devil knows he'll lose, he sends a woman
[to do the job]
Ven der tayvl veyst az er geyt farlirn shikt er unter a froy AC

זינט גאָט האָט באַשאַפֿן די פֿרוי איז אַ
העלפֿט פֿון דער מענטשהייט אויף צרות

Since God created women, half of
humanity is in trouble
*Zint got hot bashafn di froy iz a helft
fun der mentshheyt oyf tsores* AC

WORDS

אַ גוטן העלפֿט אַ וואָרט, אַ שלעכטן
העלפֿט אפֿילו קיין שטעקן אויך ניט

To the decent, one word will do; to
the wicked, not even the stick helps
*A gutn helft a vort, a shlekhtn helft
afile keyn shtekn oykh nit* AC

אַ פּאַטש פֿאַרגייט, אַ וואָרט באַשטייט

A blow subsides, a word abides
A patsh fargeyt, a vort bashteyt NS

אַ פּען האָט צוויי שפּיצן, מען קען
דערשטעכן זיך און יענעם

A pen has two points, one to stab
yourself and one to stab others
*A pen hot tsvey shpitsn, men ken
dershtekhn zikh un yenem* NS

אַ שטאָך מאַכט אַ לאָך

A prick makes a nick
A shtokh makht a lokh AC

אַ וויץ איז נאָך ניט קיין בליץ, אַ גראַם
איז נאָך ניט קיין פֿלאַם

A joke is no lightning stroke, an
epigram is no burst of flame
*A vits iz nokh nit keyn blits, a gram iz
nokh nit keyn flam* NS

אַ וואָרט איז ווי אַ רענדל

A word is like a coin
[It can roll in any direction]
A vort iz vi a rendl NS

"איזהו גיבור?" – הכּובֿש אַ גלײַך
ווערטל

"Who's a hero?"—one who
suppresses a wisecrack
*"Eyzehu giber?"—hakoyvesh a glaykh
vertl* MS

303

פֿון אַ װאָרט װערט ניט קיין לאָך אין קאָפּ

From a word you don't get a hole in the head

Fun a vort vert nit keyn lokh in kop NS

שפּראַכן װערן דערפֿונדן כדי מענטשן זאָלן זיך ניט קענען פֿאַרשטעענדיקן

Languages are created so that people won't be able to understand one another

Shprakhn vern derfundn kedey mentshn zoln zikh nit kenen farshtendikn AC

װאָס איז געשריבן מיט דער פֿען זאָל אױסמעקן װער עס קען

What is written with the pen, let erase whoever can

Vos iz geshribn mit der pen zol oysmekn ver es ken AC

WORK

אַרבעט מיידל, װעסטו האָבן אַ קלײדל

Work, young miss, and you'll have a dress

Arbet meydl, vestu hobn a kleydl IB

דער װאָגן רוט זיך אָפּ אין װינטער, דער שליטן אין זומער – דאָס פֿערד קיינמאל ניט

The wagon rests in winter, the sled in summer, and the horse never

Der vogn rut zikh op in vinter, der shlitn in zumer un dos ferd keynmol nit NS

דינערס זײַנען געטרײַ װען זיי זײַנען נײַ

New servants are fine for a very short time

Diners zaynen getray ven zey zaynen nay NS

געבראָטענע טײַבעלעך פֿליען אַליין אױך ניט אין מױל אַרײַן

Roasted squabs don't fly into your mouth all by themselves

Gebrotene taybelekh fli'en aleyn oykh nit in moyl arayn AC

האַלטן שבת איז גרינגער ווי מאַכן שבת	**Observing Shabbes is easier than preparing it** *Haltn shabes iz gringer vi makhn shabes* AC
נישט אַזוי גיך מאַכט זיך ווי עס טראַכט זיך	**Quickly thought, not so easily wrought** *Nisht azoy gikh makht zikh vi es trakht zikh* NS
אויף מתים טאָר מען זיך ניט פֿאַרלאָזן	**Don't rely on corpses** *Oyf meysim tor men zikh nit farlozn* NS
ס׳איז בעסער צו אַרבעטן מיט אַ פּלאַן, און דער פּלאַן איז – אַז יענער זאָל אַרבעטן	**It's better to work with a plan, and the plan is—that someone else do the work** *S'iz beser tsu arbetn mit a plan, un der plan iz—az yener zol arbetn* AC
טו דאָס דײַניקע וועט גאָט טאָן דאָס זײַניקע	**You do your part and God will do his** *Tu dos daynike vet got ton dos zaynike* NS

WORLD

די גאַנצע וועלט איז אײן שטאָט	**The whole world is one town** *Di gantse velt iz eyn shtot* NS
די וועלט האָט פֿײַנט דעם מסרניק און דעם מוסרניק	**The world hates both an informer and a moralizer** *Di velt hot faynt dem masernik un dem musernik* AC

די וועלט איז פֿול מיט צרות, נאָר
יעדערער פֿילט נאָר זײַנע

The world is full of troubles, but each person feels only his own
Di velt iz ful mit tsores, nor yederer filt nor zayne NS

די וועלט איז גרויס, אירע צרות נאָך
גרעסער

The world is big, its troubles even bigger
Di velt iz groys, ire tsores nokh greser NS

די וועלט איז אַ העקעלע, איינער דאַרף
צום אַנדערן

The world is a latch: one part needs the other
Di velt iz a hekele, eyner darf tsum andern NS

פֿון יענער וועלט איז קיינער נאָך ניט
צוריקגעקומען

Nobody has yet returned from the next world
Fun yener velt iz keyner nokh nit tsurikgekumen AC

קינדער און געלט איז אַ שיינע וועלט

Children and money make the world sunny
Kinder un gelt iz a sheyne velt NS

ניט מיט שעלטן און ניט מיט לאַכן קען
מען די וועלט איבערמאַכן

Not with curses or ridicule can the world be turned around
Nit mit sheltn un nit mit lakhn ken men di velt ibermakhn NS

Glossary

Afikoman (From the Greek.) Name given to the middle of three portions of matzah on the Seder plate and eaten by all present at the conclusion of the meal. It is customary for the children to "steal" the afikoman and refuse to reveal its whereabouts until it has been ransomed by the promise of a reward.

Bagel A hard, dough-shaped roll, first boiled then baked.

Bar Mitsvah Ceremony marking initiation of a Jewish male, at age thirteen, into the religious community.

Blintz Cheese, groats, or berries rolled into thin sheets of dough, then fried.

Borsht Soup, usually made of beets, cabbage, or sorrel, served hot or cold.

Bris The act and ceremony of circumcision performed on Jewish males on the eighth day of life.

Cantor Trained professional singer who assists in religious services by singing portions of the liturgy. He was subject to scrutiny and comment; his mistakes and gaffes were discussed and enlarged upon.

Challah Loaf of braided bread made of white flour and egg used for Sabbath and holidays.

Channukah Eight-day celebration commencing on the 25th day of Kislev (November-December), commemorating the victory of Judah Maccabee over the Syrian king Antiochus, and subsequent rededication of the Temple. Called the Festival of Lights.

Charoseth Mixture of ground nuts, apples, cinnamon, and wine on the Seder plate symbolizing the mortar used in building the pyramids.

Chelm Name of a real town which folklore has immortalized as the home of amiable simpletons known as the Wise Men of Chelm.

Cholent A hot dish, usually consisting of beans and meat, prepared on Friday and simmered overnight for the noonday Sabbath meal.

Chutspeh Boldness, effrontery, impudence, insolence, nerve, unmitigated gall.

Goy(im) (From the Hebrew, literally *nation*.) Gentile(s), non-Jew(s). Also refers to Jews ignorant of Jewish traditions and observances.

Haggadah	The book of the Passover home service which, through narrative and song, recounts the tale of Jewish slavery in Egypt and the liberation. It is read the first two nights of Passover (one night in Israel).
Haman	An official in the court of the King of Persia and an implacable enemy of the Jews, whom he planned to exterminate. His plans were foiled by Mordechai and Queen Esther, and he was subsequently hanged. The triumph of the Jews over their enemies is celebrated in the holiday of Purim.
Hassid(im)	A follower of an extensive and significant religious movement (Hassidism) founded in the eighteenth century in Eastern Europe, emphasizing religious fervor, mass enthusiasm, close-knit group cohesion, and charismatic leadership. At its height, this movement embraced nearly one half the Jews of Eastern Europe.
Haskalah	A movement for Jewish enlightenment which arose in Germany and Eastern Europe in the 18th and 19th centuries.
Hazzan(im)	Trained professional singer(s) who assist(s) in religious services by singing portions of the liturgy. (same as *cantor*).
Kheyder	An elementary Hebrew school.
Kohen Kohanim	A descendant of the priestly class, holding special status to this day. They are the first to be called to the reading of the Torah in the synagogue, they may not marry divorcees, and they are not allowed onto the cemeteries except for the burial of close kin.
Korakh	A Jew who became Pharaoh's treasurer in Egypt. He amassed so much wealth that 300 mules were required to carry the keys to his treasures. His pride in his wealth brought about his subsequent downfall.
Kosher	Food that is fit for consumption according to Jewish dietary laws; also used to mean someone or something that is proper, suitable, and acceptable.
Latkehs	Potato pancakes, traditionally served at Channukah.
Litvak(s)	Jews from Lithuania, traditionally thought of as being more reserved and scholarly than Jews from other regions. Having a reputation for being dry and humorless.
Mamzer	Literally, *bastard*. Term often used affectionately to describe a clever, ingenious person.
Matzah	Unleavened bread prescribed for all Passover meals to commemorate the bread eaten by the Children of Israel during the Exodus from Egypt.
Mazel-tov	(literally, *good luck*.) Congratulations!
Megillah	Scroll. Chiefly the Book of Esther, read aloud in the synagogue on Purim.
Mezzuzah	A rolled piece of parchment containing biblical quotations, encased in a small box and affixed to the doorposts of Jewish homes and synagogues.
Minyan	Quorum of ten adult males, the minimum requirement for synagogue services.
Mordechai	Consultant to the Queen of Persia. Together with Queen Esther, he was instrumental in averting the extermination of the Jewish people, as planned by Haman.
Musar	Movement for education towards strict ethical behavior within the Jewish tradition which arose in Lithuania in the 19th century among the opponents of Hassidism.
Passover	The eight-day festival commencing the 15th day of Nisan (March-April), which commemorates the deliverance of the Jews from Egyptian bondage.

Purim	Celebrates the Feast of Lots in memory of the triumph over Haman, who had selected the 14th day of Adar (March) for the extermination of the Jewish people. It is a holiday noted for its gaiety, masquerades, and festive meal.
Rabbi	Religious leader of the Jewish community.
Rashi	The great commentator of the Bible and Talmud (1040-1105) whose notes traditionally accompany the text.
Rosh Hashanah	The Jewish New Year, celebrated the first and second days of Tishrei (September-October). Together with Yom Kippur, considered the most solemn days of the Jewish year.
Seder	Home service observed on the first two nights of Passover (one night in Israel), when the Haggadah is recited.
Shabbes	The Sabbath, the weekly day of rest, observed from sunset on Friday until nightfall on Saturday.
Shalom	(Literally, *peace*.) Also, a man's name.
Shevuoth	Feast of Weeks, celebrated on the 6th and 7th days of Sivan (May-June), seven weeks after Passover. Commemorates the giving of the Torah to Moses on Mount Sinai.
Shiveh	Observance of seven days of intense mourning after the death of close kin (parent, spouse, child, sibling).
Shlemiel	An incompetent, inept person; a clumsy bungler.
Shlimazl	A consistently luckless person.
Shofar	Ram's horn, blown several times during the Rosh Hashanah service and once at the conclusion of Yom Kippur.
Sholem aleichem	Peace to you! Greeting to which the response is the reverse: *Aleichem sholem.*
Shtetl	Jewish small-town community of Eastern Europe.
Simkhat Torah	Holiday marking completion and renewal of annual cycle of reading of the Torah in the synagogue. It is marked by singing, dancing and levity. A drink of liquor after reading a portion is usual if not obligatory.
Succah	Wooden hut or booth with thatched roof used for the observance of Succoth.
Succoth	The Feast of Tabernacles: eight-day celebration commencing the 15th day of Tishrei (September-October). It commemorates the Jews living in make-shift dwellings during their wanderings in the desert.
Talmud	The body of written Jewish law and tradition.
Tefillin	Phylacteries. Two leather cases with straps, containing scriptural passages, bound to forehead and left arm during weekday morning prayers. Traditionally worn by male Jews.
Tisheh b'Av	The 9th day of the month of Av. Fast-day commemorating the final destruction of the Temple in the year 70 C.E.
Torah	The five books of Moses, often used as a synonym for the whole complex of Jewish learning.
Treyf(eh)	Forbidden; unfit according to Jewish dietary laws.
Yom Kippur	The Day of Atonement. The holiest, most solemn day of the Jewish year. A fast-day spent in prayer, atonement, and confession of sins by the individual in direct communion with God. Takes place on the 10th day of Tishrei (September-October), eight days after Rosh Hashanah.

Bibliography

YIDDISH

Bal Makhshoves. *Geklibene Shriftn.* Vilna, 1910.

Beilin, Sholem. *Eynige kapitlen un numern fun dem zaml-bukh fun yidishe folks shprikhverter un glaykhvertlekh*, New York: Jewish Theological Seminary of America, Adler Special Manuscript Collection, 1923.

Bernstein, Ignaz. *Yidishe shprikhverter un redensarten.* 2d ed. Warsaw, 1908.

Furman, Israel. *Yidishe shprikhverter un redensarten.* Tel Aviv: Hemenorah Press, 1968.

Katz, Sholem. *Fun folks moyl.* Toronto: Farlag Toronto, 1940.

Miller, Sholem. *Fun yidishn kval.* Winnipeg: Farlag "Dos yidishe vort," 1937.

Olsvanger, Immanuel. *Royte pomerantsen.* New York: Schocken Books, 1965 (transcription).

Shteinberg, Israel. *Khokhme fun yidishn kval.* Tel Aviv, 1970.

Shtutskof, Nokhem. *Der oytser fun der yidisher shprakh.* New York: Yiddish Scientific Institute–YIVO, 1950.

Yehoash-Spivak. *Yidish verterbukh*, New York: Farlag "Veker," 1911.

ENGLISH

Agnon, S. Y. "The Letter." *Twenty One Stories.* New York: Schocken Books, 1973.

Ain, Abraham. "Swislocz—Portrait of a Jewish Community in Eastern Europe." *YIVO Annual of Jewish Social Services*, vol. IV (1939): 86–114.

Alcalay, Reuben. *The Complete Hebrew-English Dictionary.* Tel Aviv: Masada Publishing, 1970.

———. *Words of the Wise: Anthology of Practical Axioms.* Jerusalem: Masada Press, 1973.

Ausubel, Nathan, ed. *A Treasury of Jewish Folklore.* New York: Crown Publishers, 1951.

Ayalti, Hanan J., ed. *Yiddish Proverbs.* New York: Schocken Books, 1963.

Baron, Joseph L. *A Treasury of Jewish Quotations.* New York: Crown Publishers, 1956.

Ben-Sasson, Haim Hillel. "Poland." *Encyclopedia Judaica*, vol. 13. New York: Macmillan, 1972.

Birnbaum, Solomon A. *Yiddish: A Survey and Grammar.* Toronto and Buffalo: University of Toronto Press, 1979.

Davidowicz, Lucy. *The Golden Tradition.* Boston: Beacon Press, 1967.

Dobroszycki, Lucien, and Barbara Kirshenblatt-Gimblet. *Image Before My Eyes.* New York: Schocken Books & YIVO, 1977.

Dubnow, Simon. *History of the Jews in Russia and Poland.* 3 vols. Philadelphia: Jewish Publications Society, 1916–20.

Fein, Richard J. *The Dance of Leah: Discovering Yiddish in America.* Cranbury, N.J.: Fairleigh Dickinson University Press, 1986.

Feinsilver, Lillian Mermin. *The Taste of Yiddish.* New York: A. S. Barnes & Co., 1980.

Geipel, John. *Mame Loshn: The Making of Yiddish.* London and West Nyack: The Journeyman Press, 1982.

Gluckel of Hameln. *Memoirs.* New York: Schocken Books, 1977.

Goldsmith, Emanuel S. *Modern Yiddish Culture: The Story of the Yiddish Language Movement.* New York: Shapolsky Publishers, 1987.

Grade, Chaim. "My Quarrel with Hersh Rasseyner." In *A Treasury of Yiddish Stories,* ed. Irving Howe and Eliezer Greenberg. New York: The Viking Press, 1954. pp. 579–606.

Greenberg, Louis. *The Jews in Russia.* New York: Schocken Books, 1976.

Hapgood, Hutchins. *The Spirit of the Ghetto.* New York: Schocken Books, 1976.

Harshav, Benjamin, and Barbara Harshav, eds. "Introduction." *American Yiddish Poetry: A Bilingual Edition.* Berkeley: University of California Press, 1986.

Heller, Celia. *On the Edge of Destruction.* New York: Schocken Books, 1980.

Heschel, Abraham Joshua. *The Earth Is the Lord's.* New York: Farrar, Straus, Giroux, 1978.

———. "Introduction." In Roman Vishniac, *Polish Jews: A Pictorial Record.* New York: Schocken Books, 1976.

Howe, Irving. *World of Our Fathers.* New York: Harcourt, Brace, Jovanovich, 1976.

Howe, Irving, and Eliezer Greenberg, eds. "Introduction." *A Treasury of Yiddish Stories.* New York: Viking Press, 1954. pp. 1–71.

Howe, Irving, Ruth R. Wisse, and Chone Shmeruk, eds. "Introduction." *The Penguin Book of Modern Yiddish Verse.* New York: Viking Penguin, 1987. pp. 1–50.

Klein, A. M. "The Yiddish Proverb." *Literary Essays and Reviews.* Toronto: University of Toronto Press, Toronto 1987.

Kogos, Fred. *A Dictionary of Yiddish Slang and Idioms.* New York: Castle Books, 1967.

———. *1001 Yiddish Proverbs.* New York: Castle Books, 1970.

Madison, Charles. *Yiddish Literature: Its Scope and Major Writers.* New York: Schocken Books, 1971.

Mendelsohn, Ezra, "Poland." *Encyclopedia Judaica,* vol. 13. New York: Macmillan, 1972.

Metzker, Isaac. *A Bintel Brief.* New York: Doubleday & Co., 1971.

Noy, Dov. "Folklore." *Encyclopedia Judaica,* vol. 6. New York: Macmillan, 1972.

Ozick, Cynthia. "Towards a New Yiddish." *Art and Ardour.* New York: Alfred A. Knopf, 1983.

Peretz, I. L. *My Memoirs.* New York: Citadel Press, 1964.

Poll, Solomon. *The Hassidic Community of Williamsburg.* New York: Schocken Books, 1969.

Pollack, Herman. *Jewish Folkways in Germanic Lands.* Cambridge: MIT Press, 1971.

Roback, A. A. "Sarcasm and Repartee in Yiddish Speech." *Jewish Frontier Anthology.* New York: Jewish Frontier Association, 1967.

Rosenbaum, Samuel. *A Yiddish Word Book.* New York: Van Nostrand Reinhold Co., 1978.

Roskies, David G., and Diane K. Roskies. *The Shtetl Book.* New York: Ktav Publishing House, 1975.

Rosten, Leo. *The Joys of Yiddish*. New York: McGraw Hill, 1968.

———. *Treasury of Yiddish Quotations*. New York: McGraw Hill, 1968.

Rubin, Ruth. *Voices of a People*. New York: Thomas Yoseloff, 1971.

Samuel, Maurice. *In Praise of Yiddish*. New York: Cowles Book Co., 1971.

Schauss, Hayyim. *Lifetime of a Jew*. New York: The Union of American Hebrew Congregations, 1950.

Schoener, Allon, ed. *Portal to America*. Toronto: Holt, Rhinehard & Winston Canada Ltd., 1967.

Schwartz, Leo. *Memoirs of My People*. New York: Schocken Books, 1963.

Shmeruk, Khone. "Yiddish Literature," *Encyclopedia Judaica*, vol. 16. New York: Macmillan, 1972.

Shulman, Abraham, ed. *The New Country*. New York: Charles Scribner's Sons, 1976.

Schwartzbaum, Chaim. *Studies in Jewish and World Folklore*. Berlin: de Gruyter, 1968. Pp. 417–424.

Silverman-Weinreich, Beatrice. "Towards a Structural Analysis of Yiddish Proverbs," *YIVO Annual XVII*. New York: YIVO, 1978. Pp. 1–20

Singer, Isaac Bashevis. *In My Father's Court*. New York: New American Library, 1967.

———. "Nobel Lecture." *The Jewish Almanac*. New York: A Bantam Book, 1980. Pp. 435–436.

Trunk, Isaiah. "Poland." *Encyclopedia Judaica*, vol. 13, New York: Macmillan, 1972.

Vishniac, Roman. *Polish Jews: A Pictorial Record*. New York: Schocken Books, 1947.

Weinreich, Max. *History of the Yiddish Language*. Chicago: University of Chicago Press, 1980.

Weinreich, Uriel. *College Yiddish*. New York: Yiddish Scientific Institute YIVO, 1949.

———. *Modern English-Yiddish, Yiddish-English Dictionary*. New York: YIVO, McGraw Hill Book Company, 1968.

Weltman, Gershon, and Marvin S. Zuckerman. *Yiddish Sayings Mama Never Taught You*. California: Perivale Press, 1975.

Wiesel, Elie. *Souls on Fire*. New York: Vintage Books, 1973.

Wisse, Ruth R. "Two Jews Talking: A View of Modern Yiddish Literature." *Prooftexts* 4, no. 1 (1984): 35–48.

Zborowski, Mark, and Elizabeth Herzog. *Life Is with People*. New York: International Universities Press, 1952.

HEBREW

Even-Shoshan, Avraham. *Hamilon Hekhadash*. Jerusalem: Kiryat Sefer, 1969.

GERMAN

Betteridge, Harold T., ed. *Cassell's German and English Dictionary*. London: Cassell, 1964.

Klatt, E., and G. Golze. *Langenscheidts Deutsch-Englisches Englisch-Deutsches Worterbuch*, New York: Pocket Books, 1961.

Landmann, Salcia. *Judissssche Anekdoten und Shprichworter*. Munich: Deutscher Taschenbuch Verlag, 1965.